Art Therapy with Milita. , ...

Art Therapy with Military Veterans: Trauma and the Image provides a comprehensive framework for understanding and applying art therapy with former and serving armed forces personnel who have Post-Traumatic Stress Disorder (PTSD). This book brings together experienced contributors in one volume to provide the range of information essential to those seeking to understand the complexities of working in this context.

In recent years, art therapy has received increasing attention as a promising treatment for veterans with PTSD. This cutting-edge book provides vital background information on PTSD, military culture and mental health provision, and an effective art therapy working model. The text explores creative partnerships with other disciplines, in different settings, and includes firsthand accounts from veterans about the role art therapy has played in their recovery. This accessible book is a timely response to growing recognition of the value of art therapy with veterans, and it also addresses issues relevant to the wider population of people whose lives have been detrimentally affected by trauma.

With chapters authored by leading clinicians in this field, *Art Therapy with Military Veterans: Trauma and the Image* will be of interest to all art therapists and mental health professionals working with traumatised veterans.

Janice Lobban is Senior Art Psychotherapist at Combat Stress. She has specialised in military trauma for over 16 years, and has lectured on the subject in London, Stockholm, Amsterdam, St Petersburg and New York.

Art Therapy with Military Veterans

Trauma and the Image

Edited by Janice Lobban

Routledge
Taylor & Francis Group

LONDON AND NEW YORK

First published 2018
by Routledge
2 Park Square, Milton Park, Abingdon, Oxon OX14 4RN

and by Routledge
711 Third Avenue, New York, NY 10017

Routledge is an imprint of the Taylor & Francis Group, an informa business

British Library Cataloguing in Publication Data
A catalogue record for this book is available from the British Library

Library of Congress Cataloging in Publication Data
Names: Lobban, Janice, editor.
Title: Art therapy with military veterans : trauma and the image /
edited by Janice Lobban.
Description: 1st edition. | Milton Park, Abingdon, Oxon ; New York, NY :
Routledge, 2018. | Includes index.
Identifiers: LCCN 2017023468 (print) | LCCN 2017024661 (ebook) |
ISBN 9781315564197 (ebook) | ISBN 9781317189787 (ebook) |
ISBN 9781317189770 (ebook) | ISBN 9781317189763 (ebook) |
ISBN 9781138654549 (hbk) | ISBN 9781138654556 (pbk) | ISBN 9781315564197 (ebk)
Subjects: LCSH: Post-traumatic stress disorder–Treatment. | Art therapy. | Veterans.
Classification: LCC RC552.P67 (ebook) | LCC RC552.P67 A78 2018 (print) |
DDC 616.89/1656008697–dc23
LC record available at https://lccn.loc.gov/2017023468

ISBN: 978-1-138-65454-9 (hbk)
ISBN: 978-1-138-65455-6 (pbk)
ISBN: 978-1-315-56419-7 (ebk)

Typeset in Times New Roman
by Out of House Publishing

This book is dedicated to all veterans who have been psychologically wounded through military service. In particular, to those who have sought the help of Combat Stress over its long history, pursuing peace of mind.

Contents

Figures

All unattributed figures and plates were created by veterans as part of art therapy sessions.

Table

Plates

Foreword

In recent years, there has been growing awareness of the devastating impact of Post-Traumatic Stress Disorder (PTSD) on veterans' lives. There is increasing recognition that PTSD affects not only the veterans themselves but also their families and friends, and that providing the right help at the right time can make a profound difference to many lives. Through practice, research and partnership work with veterans, clinicians from a variety of backgrounds are developing a better understanding of which approaches and methods can really help improve the experience of living with PTSD.

It is therefore a great honour to write the foreword to this book as it offers the most moving and comprehensive descriptions of the reality of life with PTSD, and introduces best practice in this area. Since 2004, I have had some involvement with Combat Stress, initially to provide staff support groups and more recently as Jan Lobban's supervisor. I therefore feel a strong connection to its work and mission. Veterans are at the heart of this book as active contributors and this is one of the core strengths of this publication. Another strength is the high quality of experiences that all contributors have shared, and how this reflects a profound dedication and passion for this subject. Chapters introducing historical, cultural and psycho-social issues, and outlining the complex interplay between these issues, add a welcome depth of understanding. Those on research and partnership work illustrate excellent, innovative practice. The contribution of art therapy to improving veterans' lives is particularly poignant: sometimes, finding words to describe internal states is virtually impossible, especially when clients have been so well trained to keep guard over thoughts and feelings.

Importantly, emerging research evidence indicates that trauma and PTSD are often present in the lives of mental health service users who have been given other diagnoses. Therefore, this book addresses issues relevant not only to veterans with PTSD, but to a much larger group of people whose lives have also been affected detrimentally. As such, art therapy is seen to offer hope in the shape of excellent practice, developed from always putting clients at the forefront of its evolution, and steeped in a compassionate understanding of the need to alleviate distress.

Dr Val Huet
CEO of the British Association of Art Therapists

Contributors

Robert Bieber MBE, MA, Visiting Research Fellow in the Department of War Studies at King's College, London and a Vice President of Combat Stress.

Clement Boland, previously a Territorial Army Reservist mobilised into the Regular Army as an infantryman, now an art and design student.

Dr Walter Busuttil, MBChB MPhil MRCGP FRCPsych. Consultant Psychiatrist and Medical Director, Combat Stress.

Liz Ellis, BA(Hons), MA, MA, RMN. Policy Advisor Communities and Diversity at Heritage Lottery Fund, UK where she leads on promoting inclusive practice across the heritage sector. As Curator Community Learning at Tate Modern 2006–2014, Liz led high-quality local, national and international partnerships.

Jon England, artist, exploring traces of history.

Professor Jamie Hacker Hughes, BSc(Hons), DipClinPsychol, MPhil(Cantab), MSc, PsychD, CPsychol, CSci, FBPsS, FRSM, FAcSS, is a clinical psychologist, clinical neuropsychologist, psychotherapist and academic. He is former senior clinical lecturer at King's College London, Head of Defence Clinical Psychology and Defence Consultant Advisor to the Surgeon General. He co-founded the Veterans and Families Institute and Veterans Research Hub at Anglia Ruskin University. He is visiting professor at Anglia Ruskin, Hertfordshire and Northumbria Universities, honorary professor at Lomonosov Moscow State University and is a former President of the British Psychological Society.

Richard Kidgell, IEng, MIET, retired Principal Systems Engineer.

Kathy Kravits, MA, RN, HNB-BC, LPC, NCC, ATR-BC, Senior Research Specialist, City of Hope Comprehensive Cancer Center, Duarte, California, USA.

Janice Lobban, BA(Hons), PG Dip. AT, BAAT, HCPC reg., PG Cert. Research Methods, Cert. Trauma Studies, Cert. Psychotherapy for Dissociation, EMDR Therapist. Senior Art Psychotherapist at Combat Stress, supervisor, lecturer BAAT foundation course and in private practice.

Kirsty Mackay, MSc, BAAT & HCPC reg. artist and Art Psychotherapist at Combat Stress.

Tim Martin, independent artist/curator.

David Murtagh, BSc(Hons), MSc (War and Psychiatry), BAOT. Lead Occupational Therapist formerly with Combat Stress now with HM Prison Service, Barnet, Enfield and Haringey Mental Health NHS Trust.

Sandya Rajagopal, HCPC reg. Art Psychotherapist based at Birmingham and Solihull Mental Health NHS Foundation Trust.

Mark Redgrave, BA(Hons), MSc, BAAT, MBACP & HCPC reg. Art Psychotherapist at Combat Stress and in private practice.

Stuart Rosamond, retired Head of Higher Education Fine Art, Plymouth University.

Alison Smith, BA(Hons), BSc(Hons), MSc, RN (Mental Health), Field Lead Mental Health, School of Health Sciences, University of Surrey.

Christine Sterba, RGN. Retired army trained nurse (C344), Red Cross officer (Hong Kong), former trustee Combat Stress.

Michael Sterba, Professional soldier/medic for 26 years, retired fruit farmer, chairman Staple Branch TRBL, ancient building conservationist.

Acknowledgements

This book has been a cross-disciplinary, multifaceted project and a tremendous privilege to co-ordinate. I thank all the contributors who have shared their inspirational ideas and experiences. Special thanks go to the veteran contributors who have permitted their stories and images to be used to explain the art therapy process, bringing it to life.

My sincere gratitude goes to my daughter Rosemary Lobban, who played a key role in the production of this book. Her expertise has been invaluable. My appreciation also goes to Tom Jenkins for his assistance with imagery editing.

We are all part of wider systems and I acknowledge the influence of my family, past and present, in the motivation and development of this book. First, I have valued the ongoing, sincere encouragement and practical support of my husband Andy Lobban, and the cheering-on received from our sons Tom and Alex. Undoubtedly, my interest in the military context has been influenced by family experiences. Between them, my grandfather, father, uncles and nephews served in the British Army, Royal Navy and RAF Regiment in major campaigns over the last century. I am custodian of some of their medals, tangible symbols of personal stories of those no longer with us. Moreover, I am also indebted to those inextricably connected with the stories, although they did not wear uniforms – the women who held my family together on the home front. Similarly, this text represents the silent stories of many others.

Introduction

Janice Lobban

I rang the doorbell of the large Victorian country house. It was 11 September 2001 and I was at the ex-services mental health charity in Surrey for a job interview. Later that day the world was to change when members of the militant Islamist group al-Qaeda, under the leadership of Osama bin Laden, made suicide attacks in the US that resulted in the death of almost 3,000 people. This included flying hijacked planes into the twin towers of the World Trade Center in New York City. The psychological effects rippled out across the nation and the world to those not directly involved in the event. The US Government responded to the attacks by launching the 'War on Terror'; its eventual consequences significantly impacting the ex-services charity Combat Stress.

The door was opened by a veteran who warmly invited me in. I found myself in a congenial foyer area with five veterans reading newspapers or just sitting. They were interested in why I was there and good humoured banter ensued. This was so familiar as it reminded me of being with my father and uncles, who had all served in the Second World War but never spoke about it. I sat in a comfortable armchair with the friendly and curious men while waiting to be called in for my interview. Little did I know that I would still be working there 16 years later. As it was, I managed to arrive just in time to experience the end of an era. The second Gulf War in Iraq, involving the UK military Operation Telic and UK Operation Herrick in Afghanistan were yet to occur. In due course, I was to discover that three of the five veterans I met in the reception area that day had been Far Eastern prisoners of war during the Second World War, and as such, were held in the highest regard by other veterans. Sometime later I was privileged to be able to explore their experiences with them through their art therapy imagery.

As I was shown around on that day, I noticed old photographs of veterans engaged in recuperative tasks and portraits of the royal patron and benefactors. I was gaining a sense of history not only related to the organisation but of tapping into something much broader and intriguing. A few days later, I was offered and accepted the job. Combat Stress had not employed an art therapist before, so it was new ground for both parties. I read around the subject of Post-Traumatic Stress Disorder (PTSD), as specific art therapy literature was sparse, and I learned much by looking outside of the profession to trauma-focused treatments. The knowledge gained from my previous years of experience as an art therapist was not all directly transferable to this new context. It was also necessary to gain an understanding of military culture. Mostly I recall the encouraging support of colleagues and willingness of the veterans to 'give art therapy a go'.

Veterans who have been physically or psychologically injured through service are the responsibility of the National Health Service (NHS). Currently art therapy is not available routinely through NHS specialist veteran mental health services. So, the art therapy approach offered in this text centres on the model developed at Combat Stress. There has been an increase in the number of combat-related casualties in recent years due to UK involvement in both the Iraq and Afghanistan conflicts. Consequently, it is likely that many NHS and independent therapists will receive veteran referrals over time and will seek literature to inform practice. Consequently, the aim of this book is to collate into a single volume the range of information essential to those seeking to understand the complexities of working with traumatised veterans. Key objectives are to increase awareness of the unique benefits of art therapy with military veterans, and to equip clinicians with an effective working model.

As a profession, art therapy is rooted in the regeneration following the Second World War. In order to set the context, the first section of the book provides an overview of the development and practice of art therapy within military rehabilitation and also provides an explanation of the neuroscience behind PTSD. Possible effects of hearing war stories and the concept of vicarious traumatisation are also explored as part of the discussion around working in this context.

Veterans have played a core part in the book's production. There are two chapters written by veterans about their experiences of PTSD and the part that art therapy has played in their recovery, as well as two chapters written by veterans in collaboration with other contributors. Chapter 2, by veteran Clement Boland, provides an invaluable glimpse into his experience of combat trauma as an Army Reserve soldier. Army Reserves 'come from all walks of life and work part-time as soldiers for the British Army alongside full-time Regular soldiers' ('The Army Reserve', 2016). Recent UK studies suggest that 'after deployment reservists are more likely to suffer from probable PTSD and psychological distress than regular forces' (Hunt, Wessely, Jones, Rona & Greenberg, 2014, p. 10). With current Government plans to reduce the number of regular soldiers and to increase the number of Reservists (Edmunds, Dawes, Higate, Jenkings & Woodward, 2016), it is important for mental health service providers to have an awareness of their particular needs in order to be able to offer appropriate treatment and support when required.

The following chapter, by Kathy Kravits, incorporates the account of veteran Clement Boland's lived experience of stress to explain the underlying biological mechanisms in play, differentiating between PTSD and the adaptive stress response. A recently developed model that integrates the concepts of homeostasis, allostasis and stress is presented, along with current thinking about PTSD. Consideration is given to the part art therapy can play in recovery from PTSD, drawing on ideas from neuroscience and from attachment theory.

Part II of the book is dedicated to providing background information about the British Armed Forces to increase necessary understanding. Professor Jamie Hacker Hughes equips readers with essential knowledge about UK mental health provision within a serving military context. Beginning with an historical perspective, the chapter describes how services have evolved into the current provision. This is followed by a study of 'Military culture effects on mental health and help-seeking' by Dr Walter Busuttil, Medical Director of Combat Stress. This covers a range of influential factors including the uniqueness of the military population, psychological effects of military training, and moral injury. The section closes with the chapter 'Coming home'. Military historian Robert Bieber provides a brief history of the early years of Combat Stress from its establishment in 1919 in response to the plight of traumatised veterans demobilised after the First World War. This is followed by personal accounts written by Falklands War veteran Michael Sterba and his wife Christine Sterba, which allow readers to gain insight into the processes of injury and recovery, and the effects on families.

With the contextual foundation laid, Part III focuses on current approaches to art therapy with veterans using case studies to illustrate the processes in action. It begins with a chapter written by the Combat Stress art therapy team: Janice Lobban, Kirsty Mackay, Mark Redgrave and Sandya Rajagopal, with a detailed description of the adaptive art therapy model used in all the short-stay, inpatient programmes at all three treatment centres across the UK. A phasic, theme-based approach is discussed and an art therapy 'toolbox' of techniques is outlined, suggesting what might be integrated from established evidence-based trauma approaches to assist treatment.

Chapters 8, 9 and 10 explore particular aspects of art therapy with veterans. 'In two minds' examines psychological divisions and disharmony revealed through art therapy imagery. Different frameworks of understanding are considered including the effects of dissociative processes, the way trauma memories are stored and the influence of military culture. Subsequently, veteran Richard Kidgell writes about 'Trauma and dissociation: an insider's view', describing his dissociative experiences and how art therapy is helping to re-integrate the traumatised aspects of his personality back into a complete sense of self. Through first-hand experience, the benefits gained from art therapy are compared with those from talking therapies. Next 'Bypassing the sentinel' discusses an outpatient research pilot designed to investigate how art therapy might help to overcome avoidance and assist therapeutic engagement. A sensitised psychological sentinel, always on guard and driven by threat perception, can present a significant barrier to progress, preventing access to material essential for growth and repair. Results of the study suggest that through symbolic expression participants were able to 'trick' their own defences into exposing the crux of their inner conflict, and to use the insights gained to challenge perceptions and to begin to see their own material from fresh perspectives.

Drawing this section of the book to a close, 'Research and evaluation' by Alison Smith and Janice Lobban underlines the opportunity for creative research partnerships whereby differing theoretical stances might provide enriching collaborative studies. A literature review of published research into art therapy with veterans is provided. Proven benefits of art therapy are highlighted and recommendations are made for further research.

The final section of the book, Part IV, builds on the idea of partnership working and also takes a wider perspective of the therapeutic benefits of art-making and art-viewing. 'Cultural collaborations' written by Janice Lobban and Liz Ellis, looks beyond the art therapy room to working with colleagues from other disciplines and in different settings. Discussing a long-standing collaboration between Combat Stress and Tate Modern, treatment objectives and outcomes are explored and placed within the wider context of art therapists working with museums and galleries. This chapter also includes a discussion of a pilot short-stay art therapy inpatient admission with gallery workshops, and the subject of exhibiting art therapy images in public places based on three exhibitions.

In Chapter 13, Jon England, Tim Martin and Stuart Rosamond discuss the 'Combat Art Project'. In 2013, 500 arts and crafts sets were given to members of 40 Commando Royal Marines when they deployed to Afghanistan for their final tour, with the aim of supporting their emotional well-being through creativity. There was also potential to serve a preventative function whereby expression and processing of experiences as they occurred might positively impact future outcomes. The project provided a new perspective on 'war art', the ultimate aim being to encourage the provision of such resources as 'standard issue' for all forces personnel. The final chapter is written by David Murtagh and Janice Lobban, in collaboration with two veterans who describe the role that art-making has played in their lives as part of recovery from PTSD. The text pays homage to the healing properties of art using a model of post-traumatic growth to explore how creativity through art can help veterans to reclaim life after trauma.

Currently, as I stand in the art therapy room at Tyrwhitt House looking out of the patio doors, I can make out the shape of past ground work just below the surface of the lawn; a kitchen garden that used to provide fresh produce and an area where veterans tended pigs (Figure 6.1). So it is that spaces change in function as requirements develop. During this century, there has been progression away from the enhanced respite care offered to veterans towards providing evidence-based psychological treatment. Combat Stress received a 71 per cent increase in referrals between 2010/2011 and 2015/2016 ('Combat Stress sees 71% increase in referrals', 2016). Necessarily, the organisation has evolved to meet that need. Some of the men and women who come for art therapy now are young enough to be great-grandchildren of those veterans who welcomed me at the outset of my time at Combat Stress, but their stories echo. This book is the product of those stories.

References

The Army Reserve (2016). Retrieved from www.army.mod.uk/reserve/31781.aspx.

Combat Stress sees 71% increase in referrals (2016, 9 September). Retrieved from www.combatstress.org.uk/news/2016/09/combat-stress-sees-71-increase-in-referrals/.

Edmunds, T., Dawes, A., Higate, P., Jenkings, K. N. & Woodward, R. (2016). Reserve forces and the transformation of British military organisation: soldiers, citizens and society. *Defence Studies*, *16*(2), 118–136.

Hunt, E. J. F., Wessely, S., Jones, N., Rona, R. J. & Greenberg, N. (2014). The mental health of the UK Armed Forces: where facts meet fiction. *European Journal of Psychotraumatology*, *5*. Retrieved from www.ncbi.nlm.nih.gov/pmc/articles/PMC4138705/pdf/EJPT-5-23617.pdf.

Part I

Art therapy and Post-Traumatic Stress Disorder

Chapter 1

The development and practice of art therapy with military veterans

Janice Lobban

Introduction

Art therapy is rooted in the regeneration that followed the Second World War. Since then, the profession has thrived, spreading out into a variety of contexts. Beginning at the roots of art therapy in the UK, this chapter follows the branch of its evolution associated with the armed forces up to contemporary practice. Attention is given to the use of art as part of rehabilitation in military hospitals, and connections are made with the growth of art therapy at the UK veterans' mental health charity Combat Stress. Currently, Combat Stress is a key provider of art therapy within specialist veterans' services. Remembrance and ritual are seen to play a part in recovery, and to provide a way for the wider public to acknowledge the sacrifices made through military service. The focus is then turned towards art therapists working within the field of trauma, and the benefits and challenges of working in this context are explored. The possible effects of war stories, the concept of vicarious traumatisation and the likelihood of encountering prejudice towards the military are all examined as part of the complexities of working with this client group.

War art to art therapy

On the bitterly cold morning of 30 December 1917, the 1st Artists Rifles were ordered to push forward at Welsh Ridge, Marcoing towards Cambrai, in response to an attack. Of the 80 men present, 68 were soon killed by a barrage of machine gun fire. One of the 12 survivors was John Nash, who captured the experience in the officially commissioned painting *Over the Top* a few months later (Figure 1.1). The exhausted unit had been recalled from rest at the support line and had to mount the hurried counter-attack upon arrival at the front line, with tragic consequences. The painting is unusual as it captures an actual event (Clark, 2014).

It is the vulnerability of the hunched soldiers going 'over the top' that seems so shocking as they walk forwards exposed to enemy fire. They stand out clearly against the whiteness of the snow with no shields or armour to

Figure 1.1 Over the Top by John Nash (1918)
Source: with kind permission of the Imperial War Museum.

protect them, only 'tin hats'. Their weapons are not raised to fire and one
soldier is carrying his rifle on his shoulder. Already several soldiers have
been shot. One soldier kneels slumped, his helmet on the ground in front of
him, having barely left the trench. His comrades' focus is forwards, with no
attention given to those falling around them. The painting serves as a chill-
ing reminder of the great loss of life experienced by all sides, the sacrifice of
individuals, and the inevitable consequences on families and communities.

What was to become the Artists Rifle Regiment was established in 1860
as part of the Volunteer Corps. Its early headquarters were at the Royal
Academy, Burlington House. Founder members included artists G. F. Watts,
John Everett Millais, William Holman Hunt, Edward Burne-Jones and
William Morris. Frederick Leighton was one of the early commanders and
John Ruskin was an honorary member. The Volunteer Corps was raised in
1859 in response to the threat of French invasion. Initially there seemed to
be more of a social function to the Artists Rifles than military. However, by
1914 the regiment had become an officer training corps and its membership
had broadened to include many other professions. Artists who served in the
regiment during the Great War of 1914–1918 included Paul Nash, sculptor
Frank Dobson, poet Wilfred Owen and playwright R. C. Sherriff. The Artists

Rifles were disbanded in 1945, reformed in 1947 and currently form part of the Special Air Service Reserves (Christiansen, 2014; 'Unit history: 21 Artist Rifles', n.d.).

Both John Nash and his elder brother Paul became commissioned as official war artists. Paul Nash's powerful paintings of devastated battlefield landscapes have become iconic of the era. The British government's War Propaganda Bureau first set up a war artist's scheme in 1916. By 1917, the remit had changed from propaganda to recording and memorialising events. The Imperial War Museum (IWM) was established that year and was tasked by the Department of Information to document the war. The Museum also commissioned its own war artists, the first of whom was Adrian Hill (Smalley, 2016).

Adrian Hill enlisted with the Artists Rifles in November 1914 as it seemed the natural choice, being an art student at the time, but he transferred to the Honourable Artillery Company after encouragement to do so from his brother (Hill, 1975). While serving on the Western Front, he was often sent into 'no man's land', the area between opposing forces, on scouting missions to sketch the enemy position. Later as an official war artist, he created 180 pen and ink drawings of the troops and their environment between 1917 and 1919, which are stored in the IWM, London (Gough, 2010). One of his drawings *Shelling Back Areas* has the subtitle *Where Did That One Go?* referring to a song that was popular at the time (Figure 1.2). It depicts six hunched soldiers looking over a shallow, churned-up ridge of earth in the direction of an explosion. The implied randomness of the shelling and the lack of cover underline the vulnerability of the soldiers, but the subtitle also suggests that humour was used to moderate the sense of threat. This resonates with battlefield humour to this day.

After the war was over, like everyone else, Hill attempted to get on with his life. He had studied art at St John's Wood Art School before the war, from 1912 to 1914, and decided to complete his studies at the Royal College of Art during 1919–20. He then became a practising artist and educator. In 1938, he contracted pulmonary tuberculosis and went to convalesce at King Edward VII Hospital, Midhurst (Hogan, 2001; Waller, 1991).

It is at this point, following the aftermath of the First World War and on the brink of the Second World War, that the concept of art therapy entered the arena. It is Adrian Hill who is attributed as the originator of the term 'art therapy'. Art played a significant part in Hill's recovery from tuberculosis. Through the IWM's invaluable archives, it is possible to listen to Hill's own verbal account of his war-time experiences and the part art played in his recovery from tuberculosis. He refers to himself as an 'unwilling person who had got to rest' and how the enforced rest made him feel as though he was 'shirking' (Hill, 1975, Reel 5). While immobilised in bed, he drew objects around him and seemed to tap into something so valuable that he wanted to share it with others who were in recovery. As an ambulant patient, he turned

Figure 1.2 Shelling Back Areas: Where Did That One Go? by Adrian Hill (1918)
Source: with kind permission of the Imperial War Museum.

his attention towards other patients at the sanatorium and enthusiastically encouraged them to paint. By 1941, King Edward VII Hospital began taking war casualties and Hill was invited to be involved in their care. He did not view art therapy as offering something diversional or recreational but as providing a way to access the source of their difficulties (Hogan, 2001).

Hill became a tireless promoter of art therapy. Benefits could be gained not only from art-making but also art appreciation. He gave lectures on art to patients using prints. These echoed observations by nursing pioneer Florence Nightingale in the previous century. In her *Notes on Nursing* (1860), she wrote about the beneficial effects of colour, form and light towards the healing of body and mind. She promoted the gradual introduction of engravings to be hung near the hospital bed to promote recovery (BJN, 1946; Nightingale, 1860). In 1945, Hill's book *Art verses Illness* was published. It seems to have been well received, as a review in *The British Journal of Nursing* recommended that 'it should be placed in every sanatorium and hospital library' (BJN, 1946, p. 16).

Art therapy is associated with the post-war rehabilitation movement (Waller & Gilroy, 1992). Hill and fellow pioneers such as Edward Adamson played a key role in establishing the foundation of art therapy in Britain. Both Hill and Adamson were involved in the British Red Cross Picture Library, which offered a lending scheme for taking reproductions of artwork into hospitals and providing associated lectures. The benefits of viewing art will be explored further in Chapter 12.

Art activities to art therapy in military hospitals

The Royal Victoria Military Hospital, Netley, Hampshire was founded in 1856 in response to the Crimean War. It was an enormous site, being a town in itself, complete with gasworks, prison and a reservoir (Hoare, 2001). It housed the first military asylum, built in 1870, and half those diagnosed with 'shell shock' during the First World War passed through there. News clips capture the effects of war neurosis on Netley patients and the process of recovery (British Pathé News, 1917–1918). Later, in 1953, radical psychiatrist R. D. Laing, who had worked at Netley when conscripted into the British Army in 1951, wrote that art therapy had been one of the treatments available during his time there, but no details are provided (Beveridge, 2011).

The huge need for hospital and rehabilitation services fuelled by the unprecedented volume of war injured during the First World War of 1914–1918 saw the establishment of more specialist military hospitals. Many stately homes were requisitioned to act as temporary hospitals. Craiglockhart War Hospital, Edinburgh was formerly Craiglockhart Hydropathic Institution, a health spa hotel, before becoming a psychiatric hospital for Army officers from 1916 to 1919. It was there that psychiatrist and psychoanalyst W. H. R. Rivers pioneered the use of talking therapy to treat shell shock and neurasthenia. Perhaps two of the best-known patients were poets Siegfried Sassoon and Wilfred Owen. Shell shock is further considered in Chapters 4 and 5 of this book.

A journal called *The Hydra* was produced by patients at Craiglockhart and featured short stories, articles, advertisements, poems, prints and the occasional sketch. The sketches are usually satirical but the December 1917 edition contains a striking image of *Shell Shock!* (Figure 1.3). It shows someone in bed suddenly sitting up, looking terrified by ghostly monsters and about to be hit by a shell. It has a resonance with work currently produced by veterans as part of art therapy. For instance, Figure 1.4 depicts three shadowy, armed figures standing at the foot of the coffin-like bed of a veteran. The haunting emotions and body sensations of trauma find expression through both images.

In January 1918, a Fine Arts Club was started at Craiglockhart in association with Edinburgh College of Art. In the July 1918 edition of *The Hydra*, Secretary W. G. Shearer draws readers' attention to the arts and crafts classes that were available, which included painting, decorative pottery and wood carving. It seems that pottery painting was the most popular class ('Arts and

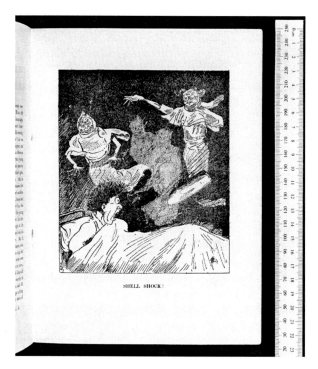

Figure 1.3 The Hydra, December 1917, drawing titled *Shell Shock!*
Source: with kind permission of the Trustees of the Wilfred Owen Estate.

Figure 1.4 Nightmare

crafts', 1918). The arts and crafts approach to rehabilitation was fostered at other hospitals too during the First World War. However, at Hollymoor Hospital, Northfield, Birmingham a new approach to art-making was to emerge during the Second World War.

The 'Northfield Experiments' are acknowledged as having played a crucial role in the development of group psychotherapy and the therapeutic community movement (Harrison & Clarke, 1992). In 1940, Wilfred Bion began to explore the idea of 'using all the relationships and activities of a residential psychiatric centre to aid the therapeutic task' (Bridger, 1990, p. 68). He was given the opportunity to put theory into practice in 1942 at Hollymoor Hospital with troops returning home traumatised by war. This was with a view to enabling them to return to active military service. Bion and John Rickman used group dynamics to promote recovery. However, the First Northfield Experiment, as it became known, was not well received due to the chaos it caused, and it only lasted six weeks. Ideas were developed and revised, leading to the Second Northfield Experiment, led by Sigmund Foulkes, Tom Maine and Harold Bridger. This proved more successful (Harrison & Clarke, 1992).

Sergeant Laurence Bradbury of the Royal Engineers was attached to the Army Education Corps and posted to Northfield in 1944 to set up an art group as part of occupational therapy. In audio recordings made in 1998 and now held at the IWM (Bradbury, 1998), Bradbury shares his opinion that the group he established in the 'Art Hut' had nothing to do with the approach taken by occupational therapy. He states that the art made in the group was 'not deflecting and trying to get people to forget the injury to their mind but rather to face up to it' and he was 'given lease to do it' without any prior experience. He refers to the space as the 'little hut of mayhem' where patients could express themselves rather than let problems fester. There was no rank system in the Art Hut and patients were given freedom of expression, which resulted in a 'form of anarchy' and mess (ibid.). Sometimes there were fights or work was destroyed. Bradbury allowed the tension to build without taking responsibility for addressing the anxieties or mess and eventually the patients would decide to clear up (ibid.; Harrison, 2000).

Bradbury was convinced that it was the process of free expression and allowing people to 'be themselves' that helped (Bradbury, 1998). He painted with the patients and did not take a lead, nor did he require any prior knowledge of the patients. He sensed resentment from some other staff members for allowing the mayhem, with concern that it might spread, and that some considered this approach an indulgence. Dr Foulkes would visit the group once a week and artwork would be spread over a table. Everyone sat quietly until someone broke the silence. Bradbury describes how 'heartrending' it was to witness the grief expressed and that he learned by observation (ibid.). He was not an advocate of interpreting patient's work.

Dr Eric Cunningham Dax, Medical Superintendant of Netherne Psychiatric Hospital, Surrey visited Northfield on several occasions and it seems he was impressed by Bradbury's work to the extent that he decided to introduce a similar approach at Netherne. In 1946, artist Edward Adamson, who visited Netherne as part of his work for the British Red Cross picture-lending scheme, was invited to join the staff and run an art group. He accepted and was employed in a full-time post. His remit was specific as he was not to interpret the work or to have any knowledge of patients' history. Adamson went on to become a key figure in the development of art therapy in the UK (Waller, 1991). Bradbury became an art historian and lectured at Tate Britain.

Another significant development in military rehabilitation occurred in the 1980s when staff at the Royal Hospital Haslar, Hampshire used art-making to help patients express their problems. Haslar was founded in 1753 as a Royal Naval Hospital. It received casualties from many conflicts including the Battle of Trafalgar in 1805. By 1966, the hospital treated patients from the Army and Royal Air Force too. In 1987, Surgeon Captain Morgan O'Connell, Cognitive Behavioural Therapist Jan Beach and their colleagues introduced a four-week Post-Traumatic Stress Disorder (PTSD) treatment programme. It was the first course of its kind in the UK and as such it pioneered new ideas. PTSD had only been classified as a diagnostic condition in 1980 when it was included in the third edition of the American Psychiatric Association *Diagnostic and Statistical Manual of Mental Disorders* (American Psychiatric Association, 1980).

Participants in the non-residential PTSD programme had been traumatised by a range of situations including service in Northern Ireland, the Falklands War and road traffic accidents, and they were from the armed forces and the emergency services. A staff member with a social work background suggested the use of themed image-making to aid recovery. The art-based groups were nurse-led. The five or six group members were required to create individual work to represent them before, during and after the trauma. They could use any medium including newspaper articles, photographs and drawings. The work was rich, varied and innovative. Some used poetry and even Celtic knots to express themselves. Some participants were very reluctant to engage and left it until the end of the programme to complete the task. Each participant was then filmed explaining the finished work to the group and a copy of the video was given to them to show family and friends. This gave them control over what to include and families felt more a part of the recovery process. There was discussion of the work within the group. Feedback was that it had been a powerful experience. People said that they had felt caught out by the process and that they had revealed more than intended but it helped to make sense of their experiences. The courses ran for four years at Haslar (J. Beach, personal communication, 18 January 2016; M. O'Connell, personal communication, 13 January 2016).

One of the most recent purpose-built military hospitals was the Queen Elizabeth Military Hospital, Woolwich, which operated between 1977 and 1995. Initially, it treated soldiers and their families before a tri-service amalgamation. Art therapist Nigel Hilton worked there part-time during the late 1980s until its closure when services were relocation to Catterick. In a personal communication (N. Hilton, personal communication, 15 January 2016), Hilton explained to me how he introduced art therapy to the programme and ran an open studio group, as well as offering one-to-one sessions. It seems that originally the job had been for an occupational therapist but the post could not be filled. In conversations between us, he has described some of the challenges of being a civilian working within a military environment. With a hierarchical structure in place, it was sometimes difficult to know where to fit; for example, which of the dining messes to use. Hilton also experienced ambivalence from staff and patients regarding art therapy.

The art therapy groups were for two-and-a-half hours. Patients did not have to talk about their work but often there was discussion. Participants could choose to display work on the studio walls and this stimulated reflection. Hilton observed the catalytic role of the art-making and how consequential value was given to the experience. Sometimes patients created group paintings on large sheets of paper. The group experience itself was seen as an important component.

The patients were from a range of operational duties including the Falklands War and peacekeeping in Northern Ireland. During Hilton's time at Woolwich, the first Gulf War occurred, and in 1991 casualties were received into the hospital, many of whom had psychological injuries. A percentage of the casualties were subsequently discharged from service through the psychological route. Hilton found that his training in cognitive analytical therapy informed his approach during individual interventions with patients.

The phased closure of dedicated military hospitals was a result of a defence review carried out by the Conservative Government in the 1990s. It concluded that the military hospitals could not provide the same quality of care as the National Health Service (NHS). Since then, the Ministry of Defence has contracted out residential treatment to the NHS. Chapter 4 provides an overview of past and present mental health treatment for serving UK military personnel.

Setting a current context for art therapy with veterans

Art therapy was established at Combat Stress in 2001, as outlined in the introduction to this book. Former Royal Navy Surgeon Captain Morgan O'Connell was Consultant Psychiatrist there at the time. He supported the introduction of art therapy based on his experience of the benefits of expressive art at Haslar. Arts and crafts were already available at Combat Stress, along with activities such as poppy-making and woodwork. The activities room formed the heart of the Surrey treatment centre, where veterans young and old would socialise and keep busy on projects. There was banter and a sense of camaraderie between veterans in that warm and welcoming space.

At the time, there was a respite model in place that was just beginning to be reviewed.

The only room large enough to hold groups at the time was a television lounge. I feared that the sofas and carpet would suffer, but in all seven years that space accommodated the art therapy group, no damage was ever caused. I soon learned that the veterans preferred not to make a mess, and if they did, they would clean it up. I also learned that it is necessary to allow people with anxiety disorders to leave the room when they need to, and in that way, they are more likely to return. However, I did not realise at the beginning of my time there that it is more important to apply brakes than to promote the venting of feelings. Art therapy enables participants to access sensory memories, visual imagery and emotions very quickly. There is a possibility of moving too deeply, too quickly in which case memories are re-experienced rather than processed. A full account of the integrated, adaptive art therapy model that has evolved to ensure safe, gradual exposure will be covered fully in Chapter 7.

Van der Kolk suggests that 'one of the most urgent tasks facing therapists of traumatized individuals is the re-creation of a sense of human interdependence and community' (1987, p. 155). He refers to 'the essential qualities of human existence: belonging, being useful to others and sharing a common culture and past' (ibid., p. 156). It became very clear that something important happened as soon as veterans entered the treatment centres of Combat Stress. The sense of reconnecting with a familiar peer group within a safe environment helped to reduce isolation and improve well-being. I lost count of the number of times that veterans told me 'the best therapy is being with the lads'. The mutual sharing of war stories could be a comfort but also detrimental when it affected sleep and functioning. Veterans showed their support of the organisation by purchasing sweaters, polo shirts and wristbands with the Combat Stress logo, thereby creating an alternative uniform. Some veterans had already met during service years or had friends in common. Service jargon and nicknames were sometimes used, for instance, some former mariners went to the 'galley' for meals and their 'cabin' at bedtime. My two therapist colleagues and I gained our own nickname as the 'stealths'. This related to the stealth bomber that was able to overcome anti-aircraft defences because it was hard to see it coming. Two veterans were overheard discussing that they would not be able to meet later that day because one was going to be 'stealthed' at 15:00; that is he would be having a therapy session at that time (Lobban, 2014).

There was resistance/avoidance of therapy too. Some veterans preferred, and still prefer, to do their 'art therapy' in the activities room. Others who came for individual sessions filled the time with tangential talking and avoided using the art materials. I came to realise that art therapy needed to be paced, and that beginning the sessions with relaxation or emotional regulation techniques could enable veterans to progress on to using the materials.

This method was in tune with the phasic approach in literature on trauma work (Chu, 1998; Herman, 1992). Veterans sometimes referred to an internalised 'Pandora's Box' where trauma memories were stored away under lock and key, but that might break open with disturbing consequences. Trauma affects the ability to trust, so trust might have to be won over time before being ready to open the box and examine the contents. Additional training in a variety of approaches to trauma-focused work proved invaluable for increasing understanding and finding ways of helping veterans to engage. Art therapy is now part of all the programmes at Combat Stress, across all three treatment centres.

Although the vicissitudes of warfare and peacekeeping are frequently at the root of veterans' post-traumatic stress, not all trauma associated with military service is combat-related. Other causes are within the full range of stressor events that are found in the civilian context, such as experiencing or witnessing abuse, accidents or natural disasters. Single incident trauma within this client group is rare, with repeated and prolonged exposure to trauma being a common presentation. There can be pre- and post-service vulnerabilities as well as experiences during military service. A full discussion of these issues will be covered in Chapter 5.

For a number of years, the average age of veterans attending Combat Stress for treatment was 44. This is reducing now due to the increase of referrals from the recent wars in Iraq and Afghanistan. Warfare continues to change too with advances in weapons systems, real-time reporting and the use of the Internet for the recruitment of terrorists (Turitto, 2010). Understanding and defining the psychological effects of trauma has necessarily progressed too. In 2013, the American Psychiatric Association *Diagnostic and Statistic Manual* criteria for PTSD were revised. This included creating four clusters of symptoms instead of three, with negative alterations in cognitions and mood being the additional cluster, alongside avoidance, re-experiencing and hyper-arousal symptoms (American Psychiatric Association, 2013).

Remembrance and ritual

Remembrance through ritual is an important way of honouring the dead. The Royal British Legion poppy has become a national token of remembrance and its purchase provides an opportunity to make a contribution towards the support of veterans and their families. Each year on Remembrance Sunday, a group of veterans and staff from Combat Stress participate in the National Service of Remembrance and March Past at the Cenotaph, Whitehall, London. They join with the nation for two-minute silence when the injured and fallen are held in mind: 'we will remember them' (Binyon, 1914). Small wooden crosses with hand-written messages are placed respectfully in particular regimental areas of the Field of Remembrance at Westminster Abbey until the grass is barely visible. Across the land, poppy wreaths are laid at the foot of war memorials. In 2014, 888,246 ceramic poppies designed by artists Paul Cummins and Tom Piper were placed in the moat at the Tower of London as an installation called 'Blood swept lands and seas of red' to mark the centenary of the outbreak of the First World War. It was a roll of honour to the dead, with each poppy representing a British military fatality ('About the installation', n.d.). Visitors were able to connect with others past and present in this symbol of shared grief.

The grounds of the Combat Stress treatment centres are sometimes used for quiet contemplation when veterans need some space to think. They provide a pleasant and peaceful environment in which to stroll and observe nature. They have also been used for rituals such as symbolically letting go of the past. For instance, items representing trauma have been released into the breeze, the physical action of letting go seeming to fulfil a somatic need. For some veterans, there is a desire to leave something tangible in the grounds to be held in the care of the organisation. This might be a small cairn of stones in the woods or an acorn planted to symbolise hope. Such rituals might be private experiences or involve a small group of veterans with shared memories.

As part of the journey of recovery, some veterans chose to make a pilgrimage back to the place of their trauma, to try to 'lay ghosts to rest', sometimes placing a personal tribute on the spot where a comrade fell. I had the privilege of participating in a pilgrimage to the Falkland Islands with a group of veterans to mark the twenty-fifth anniversary of the 1982 war. It provided an invaluable opportunity to work together at the site of the trauma. Veterans were able to retrace their footsteps, re-evaluate viewpoints and start to work through the traumatic grief of experiences. The wholehearted support and gratitude of the Falkland Islanders undoubtedly helped veterans in the search for personal meaning.

I have heard remarkable accounts of veterans meeting and making peace, for instance with their former prison camp guard or the submarine captain responsible for the sinking of their ship. Veterans and former terrorists have met around a table to find a way of moving on from past hostilities. However, letting go of anger, guilt, shame or suffering can seem an impossible task for some veterans. Remembering the lost might stir survivor guilt or the horror of witnessing suffering and being unable to intervene. Being able to forgive oneself or others for actions of omission or commission might be unacceptable. Self-compassion can be resisted and holding on to pain can be an effective form of self-punishment, reinforcing the view that they do not deserve to enjoy life. One veteran, the sole survivor of an ambush who had been severely injured himself in the attack, explained to me that the pain he continued to experience so many years after the event was not suffering as it served as a reminder that he was alive. When he felt the pain, it kept him close to his lost comrades, thereby maintaining continuing bonds; the identification also seeming to assuage survivor guilt.

Working with traumatised veterans

Veterans can be reluctant to speak about their experiences not only because of the distress it causes them but also due to not wanting to contaminate the listener with knowledge that might have a detrimental effect on them, or affect the way the listener views them. According to contemporary theory, trauma shatters the fundamental assumptions we have about life, namely that the world is benevolent and meaningful, and that the self is worthy (Janoff-Bulman, 1992). Basic trust is lost which causes a profound sense of disconnection, isolation and alienation (Herman, 1992). Hearing stories of suffering or horror, and witnessing it symbolically through the imagery is part of the task of art therapy in assisting the processing of trauma memories. This can make the therapist aware of areas of human experience beyond prior knowledge or understanding. It can stimulate questioning of personal beliefs and assumptions.

Due to the sensory nature of traumatic memories, when veterans reconnect with the trauma in an attempt to express the wordless experience of the event, they might re-experience the original imagery, body sensations and emotions. This can resonate in the counter-transference or empathic attunement of the therapist and might manifest in responses such as nausea, headache or a sense of helplessness. Horrors that cannot be expressed in words might be conveyed in a 'felt' sense. Dissociation might occur whereby the veteran disconnects psychologically from the here and now, and is pulled back in time to a fragmented sense of past trauma, or becomes disorientated and confused. This can be reflected in the therapist's own thought processes affecting concentration and recall of the task in hand. Writing about counter-transference responses to dissociative processes, Pearlman and Saakvitne (1995) note that in such situations, the therapist can feel abandoned and could respond in a number of ways including being relieved, dissociating his or herself and abandoning the client, or becoming angry. It is also suggested that the therapist might not remember material from the previous session, or feel spaced out and unable to think. Without an understanding of dissociation, the therapist might use other concepts such as passive-aggression, psychosis or resistance to explain the situation (ibid.).

It is important to recognise the sensory impact of trauma work on both the client and therapist, and to be prepared to work with this on a practical level. Relaxation, breathing and grounding techniques practised in the early stages of treatment can help to improve affect management and keep therapy within tolerable levels. This subject will be explored in more depth in Chapter 7.

Terms such as 'secondary traumatic stress' (Hudnall Stamm, 1995) and 'vicarious trauma' (Pearlman & Saakvitne, 1995) have been coined to describe a range of symptoms experienced as a consequence of working in the field of trauma. Pearlman and Saakvitne (1995) define vicarious traumatisation (VT) as the 'cumulative transformation in the inner experience of the therapist that comes about as a result of empathic engagement with the client's traumatic material' (p. 31). It is distinguished from 'burnout', which might manifest as apathy, disillusionment, an uncaring attitude or even contempt for clients (Pross, 2006), as it reaches a deeper and more profound level. Symptoms of VT might include increased sensitivity to violence, social withdrawal, cynicism, feeling vulnerable, experiencing intrusive imagery and having no time or energy for oneself (Pearlman & Saakvitne, 1995; Pross, 2006). McCann and Pearlman (1990) suggest that trauma is infectious.

When working in the field of trauma, it is important to be self-aware and to recognise any warning signs of negative effects in order to ensure healthy work practice. Pross (2006) suggests that promoting self-awareness in this way should be an essential part of therapy and job training. He proposes that a flexible and creative work environment that encourages research and development can help to avoid the 'rut of routine' that can lead to burnout (ibid., p. 9). Other factors that help to prevent burnout and VT include having a limited caseload, maintaining professional boundaries and ensuring that an adequate provision for self-care is in place to balance the effects of the work. This might necessitate the seeking out of other pursuits for improving well-being such as physical or creative activity, or introducing times of rest and play. Personal therapy might be considered. Supervision and reflective practice are essential. Pearlman and McKay (2008) also suggest that working through vicarious trauma involves transforming the experience through meaning-making and reconnecting with hope and purpose, as well as challenging personal cynicism.

Over time, I have encountered prejudice against the military from other professionals and trainees. This might be associated with political beliefs and ideals, or life experiences. The armed forces might be viewed as heroes or villains, victors or victims according to circumstances or viewpoint. When speaking at conferences, audience questions have sometimes implied strong views about working with people seen as being professional killers. As with all contexts, art therapists can be drawn towards working with a particular client group or reluctant to work with another. It is important to understand our motives and barriers.

In this context, there can be a sense of tapping into an intrinsic aspect of the human condition. Throughout history, disputes have been settled by setting one army against another. The warrior archetype is cross-cultural and features in the myths and legends of most civilisations. It often embodies qualities such as courage, stoicism, discipline and loyalty. Indeed, the 'Values and standards of the British Army' (2012) expect selfless commitment, integrity and respect, and recruits have to make an oath of allegiance to the monarch. The ultimate personal sacrifice is possible. These are high ideals to reach and maintain. However, post-combat psychological symptoms have long been documented. A recent study suggests that the first account of post-traumatic stress symptoms could be attributed to the Assyrian Dynasty in Mesopotamia, 1300–609 BC (Abdul-Hamid & Hughes, 2014). Between the outbreak of the First World War in August 1914 and the exit of British Forces from Afghanistan in October 2014, the UK was involved continuously in warfare or peacekeeping somewhere in the world (MacAskill & Cobain, 2014), and so it continues.

Alongside the challenges of working with traumatised veterans, there are many benefits. As well as hearing accounts of mankind's cruelty, violence, suffering and despair, I have been privileged to hear remarkable stories of kindness, compassion and resilience, representing the breadth of human experience. I have been amazed by the ability of the human spirit to overcome adversity and to transform a trauma into an opportunity for growth. A Second World War veteran once explained to me how after a mortar attack, he had been trapped for a long time in a tank under the decapitated body of his tank commander. The commander had been his well-respected mentor. For the rest of his life, the veteran suffered from crippling back pain associated with that incident. He described how for him the weight he continued to feel on his back was not a burden, but the presence of his guardian angel, who continued to protect and encourage him through life. Art therapy helped him to express not only the horror of the event but the transformative power of meaning-making and finding peace.

When Pandora's Box is opened, all that is left is hope. Hope plays a vital part in recovery. It is a frequent ingredient of art therapy groups and is nurtured between veterans (Plate 1.1). Newcomers to treatment might have struggled with symptoms for many years before finally asking for help. Although Combat Stress is a civilian organisation, the client group is all ex-military and most veterans say that they feel safe as soon as they come through the gates because they know the other veterans will be looking out for them, and that they no longer feel alone with their problems. They are hopeful that the organisation will be able to meet their needs and guide them along the road to recovery.

References

Abdul-Hamid, W. K. & Hughes, H. J. (2014). Nothing new under the sun: Post-traumatic stress disorders in the ancient world. *Early Science and Medicine, 19*(6), 549–557.

About the installation (n.d.). Retrieved from www.hrp.org.uk/tower-of-london/history-and-stories/tower-of-london-remembers/about-the-installation/.

American Psychiatric Association (1980). *Diagnostic and statistical manual of mental disorders* (3rd edn). Washington, DC: APA.

American Psychiatric Association (2013). *Diagnostic and statistical manual of mental disorders* (5th edn). Washington, DC: APA.

Arts and crafts (1918, July). *The Hydra*. The First World War Poetry Digital Archive. Retrieved from www.oucs.ox.ac.uk/ww1lit/collections/document/3141/2090.

Beveridge, A. (2011). *Portrait of a psychiatrist as a young man: The early writing and work of R. D. Laing, 1927–1960*. Oxford: Oxford University Press.

Binyon, R. L. (1914, 21 September). For the fallen. *The Times*. Retrieved from www.greatwar.co.uk/poems/laurence-binyon-for-the-fallen.htm.

BJN (1946). Art verses illness: A story of art therapy by Adrian Hill. *The British Journal of Nursing*, *94*, 16.

Bradbury, L. (1998). Interview by Blakeway Associates [Tape recording]. The science of war – battle of the mind (interview rushes Part 1 of 4). London: Blakeway Associates, Imperial War Museum Archives. Retrieved from www.iwm.org.uk/collections/item/object/1060035898.

Bridger, H. (1990). The discovery of the therapeutic community: The Northfield experiments. In E. Trist & H. Murray (eds), *The social engagement of social science* (Vol. 1). London: Free Association. Retrieved from www.moderntimesworkplace.com/archives/ericsess/sessvol1/Bridgerp68.opd.pdf.

British Pathé News (1917–1918). Reel 1. Netley Hospital 1917 and Seale Hayne Military Hospital 1918. Retrieved from www.britishpathe.com/video/war-neuroses-version-b-reel-1.

Christiansen, R. (2014, 27 April). When artists fought for Queen and country. *Telegraph*. Retrieved from www.telegraph.co.uk/culture/art/10788905/When-artists-fought-for-Queen-and-country.html.

Chu, J. (1998). *Rebuilding shattered lives: The responsible treatment of complex post-traumatic and dissociative disorders*. New York, NY: Wiley & Sons.

Clark, N. (2014, 22 June). A history of the First World War in 100 Moments: Captured on canvas, the moment when writers and artists went 'over the top'. *Independent*. Retrieved from www.independent.co.uk/news/world/world-history/history-of-the-first-world-war-in-100-moments/a-history-of-the-first-world-war-in-100-moments-captured-on-canvas-the-moment-when-writers-and-9555343.html.

Gough, P. (2010). *A terrible beauty: British artists in the First World War*. Bristol: Sansom & Company.

Harrison, T. (2000). *Bion, Rickman, Foulkes and the Northfield experiments*. London: Jessica Kingsley.

Harrison, T. & Clarke, D. (1992). The Northfield experiments. *British Journal of Psychiatry*, *160*, 698–708.

Herman, J. (1992). *Trauma and recovery: The aftermath of violence – from domestic abuse to political terror*. New York, NY: Basic Books.

Hill, A. (1945). *Art verses illness: A story of art therapy*. Crows Nest: G. Allen & Unwin.

Hill, A. (1975). Interview by J. C. Darracott [Tape recording]. London: Imperial War Museum Archives. Retrieved from www.iwm.org.uk/collections/item/object/80000557.

Hoare, P. (2001). *Spike Island: The memory of a military hospital*. London: Fourth Estate.

Hogan, S. (2001). *Healing arts: The history of art therapy*. London: Jessica Kingsley.

Hudnall Stamm, B. (1995). *Secondary traumatic stress: Self-care issues for clinicians, researchers and educators*. Brooklandville, MD: The Sidran Press.

Janoff-Bulman, R. (1992). *Shattered assumptions: Towards a new psychology of trauma*. New York, NY: Free Press.

Lobban, J. (2014). The invisible wound: Veterans' art therapy. *International Journal of Art Therapy*, *19*(1), 3–18.

MacAskill, E. & Cobain, I. (2014). British forces' century of unbroken warfare set to end with Afghanistan exit. *Guardian*. Retrieved from www.theguardian.com/uk-news/2014/feb/11/british-forces-century-warfare-end.

McCann, L. & Pearlman, L. A. (1990). Vicarious traumatization: A framework for understanding the psychological effects of working with victims. *Journal of Trauma Stress, 3*(1), 131–49.

Nightingale, F. (1860). *Notes on nursing: What it is and what it is not.* New York, NY: D. Appleton & Company. Retrieved from http://digital.library.upenn.edu/women/nightingale/nursing/nursing.html.

Pearlman, L. A. & McKay, L. (2008). Vicarious trauma. Excerpted from *Understanding and addressing vicarious trauma.* Pasadena, CA: Headington Institute. Retrieved from www.headington-institute.org/files/vicarious-trauma-handout_85433.pdf.

Pearlman, L. A. & Saakvitne, K. W. (1995). *Trauma and the therapist: Counter-transference and vicarious traumatization in psychotherapy with incest survivors.* New York, NY. W. W. Norton.

Pross, C. (2006). Burnout, vicarious traumatization and its prevention. *Torture, 16*(1), 1–9. Retrieved from www.irct.org/Files/Filer/TortureJournal/16_1_2006/page_1-9.pdf.

Smalley, U. (2016). How the British Government sponsored the arts in the First World War. Retrieved from www.iwm.org.uk/history/how-the-british-government-sponsored-the-arts-in-the-first-world-war.

Turitto, J. (2010). Understanding warfare in the 21st century. *International Affairs Review, XVIII*(3). Retrieved from www.iar-gwu.org/node/145.

Unit history: 21 Artist Rifles (n.d.). Retrieved from www.forces-war-records.co.uk/units/4375/21-artist-rifles/.

Values and standards of the British Army (2012). Retrieved from http://ethics.iit.edu/ecodes/node/5512.

van der Kolk, B. (ed.) (1987). *Psychological trauma.* Washington, DC: American Psychiatric Press.

Waller, D. (1991). *Becoming a profession: History of art therapy in Britain, 1940–82.* London: Routledge.

Waller, D. & Gilroy, A. (1992). *Art therapy: A handbook.* Buckingham: Open University Press.

Chapter 2

An Army Reservist's story*

Clement Boland

I was a Territorial Army (TA) reservist for three years. I joined the TA in 2004 when I was 19 and studying for an undergraduate degree. My basic training was conducted locally over seven weekends with the regiment, and a two-week course at the Infantry Training Centre. Subsequently, I attended weekly drill nights at the local TA centre, trained roughly every other weekend and attended two-week annual summer camps. This provided me with part-time paid work to help fund my studies, and I enjoyed the adventure and excitement of training in the countryside at the weekends. I was taught basic infantry skills, marksmanship, field craft, physical training, radio procedures and first aid. My local unit was a mortar platoon, so I trained with 81mm mortars on Salisbury plain, and in summer 2005, I attended a two-week camp in Florida where we trained with the National Guard. Some members of my unit were mobilised for an operational tour in Iraq, but some others and I were exempted because we were students. In late summer 2006, I was finishing my exams and watching the Paras on the news fighting their way into a town called Sangin in southern Afghanistan. By spring 2007, I would be patrolling the same streets.

Having finished my degree, I was selected for officer training. Each of the companies in our TA battalion were assigned to different local regular regiments, which were all due to be amalgamated the next year. Around the same time, there was an interest in finding individuals for full-time reserve service with our regular battalions. The military situation seemed to be 'hotting up' and I felt a responsibility to do my bit. I considered that our country and its armed forces were a force for good and stability in the world. I said that I would be willing to go on full-time reserve service and gain practical experience before attempting my commission. My commanding officer was keen on this and willing to hold my place on the officer training programme until my return if I was mobilised.

I received my mobilisation papers informing me that I was to be deployed to Afghanistan. I reported as ordered to the Reserves Mobilisation Centre in

*In this personal account, names have been changed to anonymise identity.

February 2007 with several other members of my TA battalion. Here we were grouped with other mobilised territorials and regular reservists, given medicals and sworn into the regular army for 11.5 months.

Over the next month, we went through our physical fitness and proficiency tests. During this time, we also learned horror stories about where we were going, and I began to be bothered by how haphazard our mobilisation seemed to be. The unit we were to join were already on their pre-deployment training, so we were unable to train with them as a team before we were deployed into the warzone. To me, the training we were given seemed like a collection of tick-box exercises to get us through the process, which felt like a last-minute affair. I felt that we were very much disposable and were about to be massively thrown in at the deep end. However, by this point I had committed to the deployment and felt that I had to see it through. I was now feeling seriously underprepared and fearful of what I had signed myself up for.

In early April, we were sent down to join the regiment and it seemed that we might get time to train and integrate into the unit before we deployed. However, when we arrived, the company was being sent on leave after which they would fly out to Afghanistan. We met our platoon commanders briefly before they left and then we remained at the barracks for further training. At one point, we were shown a beaten up, old WIMIK Land Rover to familiarise us with what we were to deploy in. I had never actually seen one of these vehicles before, and it was in such a state that all I got from the experience was an image of its floor being awash with blood during the total mess we were heading into.

We were due to fly out to Afghanistan a couple of days before my twenty-third birthday. I met my mum in London to say goodbye. We were just getting off the London Eye and I was due back for the flight that evening when I received a telephone call to tell me that our flight had been delayed. So, I visited my housemates before returning for the rearranged flight. Some friends came to see me off at the station. The crowd cheered as I said goodbye to my friends. It all felt very unreal. I was terrified.

Back at barracks, I got into uniform and waited around. I started smoking again after two years without. That night a coach took us to Brize Norton where we were processed for our flight. As we queued with all the other personnel, I was struck by the mismatch between what a momentous time this was for us, being sent off to war for the first time, and how mundane and boring it seemed to be for the RAF staff around us. Everything was so clinical and routine that I was very aware of what a tiny, insignificant piece I was in this great big system.

It was morning when we boarded the Tri-Star. When we reached Afghanistan, the plane flew high over Kandahar airport and then spiralled down so as not to attract enemy fire. All the lights were turned out and the blinds drawn on the window ports, leaving only emergency lighting strips in the aisles. We all had to put on body armour and helmets, and I remember in the gloom seeing a press guy in a dark suit looking like Darth Vader at the front of the rows of fresh, white desert combats.

We landed and disembarked in darkness on the huge airfield at Kandahar. Around us were the shapes of large warplanes, drones and racks of ordnance. We were processed again and taken to a massive hangar full of bunks where we were to stay until our onward flight to Camp Bastion the next day. We smoked outside by the mortar shelter and did not sleep much. In daylight, the base at Kandahar was huge – a sprawling jumble of support areas for all the multinational forces present. There was even a bus service that took us from the hanger to the air head for our next flight. I remember being puzzled in the midst of all this sparse dust, utilitarian concrete and military hardware, by the little, frilly green curtains with a decorative sash in the windows of the bus.

We boarded a C130 Hercules transport plane and flew on to Camp Bastion to join the company and be assigned to our platoons. Bastion was very different from Kandahar. It was a planned military base set out in neat rows of air-conditioned tents. We were taken to our company's line and here I joined the platoon with three other territorials. They were practicing drills on the 50 cal machine gun when I arrived, a weapon I had never even seen 'in the flesh'. The privates were all very young but I remember feeling rather overawed by them as a group – all very 'gobby' and wearing mirror shades as they ran through the drills. I was assigned to one section and shown to a bed space, and we were issued with extra weaponry and equipment. Heavy Osprey body armour, grenades and radio batteries all started to add up. In training, having carried at most six magazines of rifle ammunition plus loose, I now found myself packing 13 filled magazines and a bandolier of loose. Then came the underslung grenade launchers and I realised it was not necessarily just me that felt under-trained. We were asked if anyone had used one before and nobody answered. I said that I had once used the old American version with paint rounds on exercise in Florida, and so I became a rifle grenadier.

After zeroing weapons on the ranges, packing and re-packing kit and going on acclimatisation runs around the perimeter of Camp Bastion, during which we were on standby to fly out as a quick reaction force, we got the news that we would now be deploying to Sangin District Centre (DC). This was the very place I had watched the Paras under siege on the news not eight months before and now widely known as the most dangerous district in Helmand province. 'Sangin? I feel sick!' was one of my section-mate's responses to the news.

We assembled in section lines, and then filed onto the back of one of the Chinooks, crouching under the rotors and gasping in the heat of the engine's back blast. Crammed in and half buried in kit, we took off and flew across Helmand towards the green zone with two Apache gunships escorting. I managed to peer out of one of the window ports as we flew across the desert and could see the lines of dog-legged trenches and knocked-out Soviet era tanks from previous years of conflict and wondered how on earth I had managed to get myself in such a situation.

Our platoon was first assigned to a guard routine at various positions around the perimeter of the compound at Sangin DC. My recollection of time is very hazy during this period because we were overstretched, sleeping on average 20 minutes at a time, 12 times a day over 3 days. Fatigue began to set in and I remember catching people talking to rucksacks and suchlike. During one of the night-time two-hour guard stints in one of the sangars, one of the regular privates and I found ourselves under fire for the first time. It was a strangely anti-climactic event. We had been taking it in turns to catch 40 winks at the back of the sangar while the other watched out. It was my turn to rest and I was flitting in and out of sleep becoming aware of a sort of thumping sound when my companion nudged me awake and said 'I'm not being funny but I think we're being shot at'. I sat up and looked out of the sangar and tracer fire was arching out of the darkness in the distance off to our right and the occasional round was thumping into the Hesco wall near our position. It stopped soon afterwards and we heard on the radio that there had been a firefight involving the Afghan Police nearby.

My first trip outside the compound into Sangin occurred when I was grabbed as part of an ad hoc reaction force in response to a call for assistance. I climbed onto one of the Pinzergauer vehicles as top cover and we rumbled out of the main gate into the town. Much of the town had been completely smashed by airpower when the Paras were under siege and the streets we drove along were under several feet of rubble, which the vehicles bounced over crazily. We got to the scene where one of the Afghan Army units we were working with had been hit by an explosion, with two soldiers injured. An Afghan man who ran after the blast had been shot. We were to retrieve him. I cannot remember all that much about how the situation played out but what I do remember remains vivid to this day.

I was told to help carry him. I think he was in a ditch when I got to him. I was horrified. He had been shot from behind and his intestines were all spilling out from his torn belly. I had never seen a body or anyone so badly hurt before, and I felt so sorry and appalled, I just wanted to help him but did not know how and the first thought that ran through my head was 'Oh my God, he looks like Jesus'. I ended up carrying him to the back of the vehicle by his legs while I think two others were holding him by the arms, though all I can really remember is the image of him in that crucifix-like position. All the periphery of the scene is very vague. His insides were spilling onto my arms and the smell was awful. I remember feeling at the same time how terrible it was how low he had been struck, but also how serene and dignified his face appeared among all the panic and bustle. We put him in the vehicle and I climbed back as top cover, with him at my feet. As we bounced back through the streets of Sangin towards the DC I became aware that the tailgate of the truck was hanging open and that his guts and genitals were hanging out for the locals to see as we drove along. I bent down, pulled up the gate and secured it with the bit of old rope that served as a handle. At some point before or after this, I felt him grab onto the back of my leg. I was told afterwards that he was already dead when we picked him up, but to me he died in the truck with me. I have agonised in dark moments over the meaning of this grab on my leg, whether it was an appeal to close that gate or an acknowledgement of my doing so, and have felt compelled to try and find some meaning in these actions, though really, I know there was no such importance to it. It was probably simple rigamortis or the last desperate reaching out of a pointless, horrible death.

I took from this incident that I never wanted to inflict that kind of terrible hurt on anybody but also that I had another six months left on this tour and that I would probably have to or end up that way myself. I was trapped. I was a fool.

Soon after this, my platoon started on a patrol rotation as well. We started to do a lot of night-time clearance operations out into the surrounding countryside, which was terrifying. We were not allowed to use any light when clearing rooms in compounds and as night-sights only work on amplifying existing moon and starlight, our procedure was simply to walk into the pitch blackness trying to stay straight on so that any shots would be more likely to hit us in the front armour plate. We would wait a few seconds and then declare the room clear if we were not shot at.

An incident occurred during one of these clearances, which although amusing at the time, has stayed with me and became the subject of recurring nightmares for some time. I entered one of these dark rooms ready to wait a few seconds not be shot at and then declare it clear. I could tell on entering that it was somewhat larger than usual with a higher ceiling. Some moonlight was filtering in through a gap in the ceiling and I could vaguely make out shapes in the darkness. Nothing happened, and I was just starting to turn and leave when a cough rang out and I was suddenly aware of something looming towards me. I swung around, brought up my rifle and was beginning to squeeze the trigger. During this split-second I thought 'There's a man in the room; there's a Minotaur. Oh, it's a cow'. I had walked into a room full of cattle in the otherwise unoccupied compound and nearly shot the inquisitive, dark brown cow that came to take a look at me all dressed up like Universal Soldier sneaking round cowsheds in the middle of the night.

While on guard in the sangar at the main gate of Sangin DC, I received a report over the radio that there was word there was going to be a suicide bombing attempt, and that the suspects were expected to be a woman and child. Not 20 minutes later, a woman and child came walking hand in hand up the path towards my position. There was no reason for them to be using this path unless they were coming to the main gate. As I stood there behind a GPMG, I realised that in a few seconds I was going to have to stop them at the designated point and somehow establish what they wanted. What would I do if they did not stop? These checkpoint situations were always very difficult to navigate, with misunderstandings easy when unfamiliar with each other's languages and keeping at a distance. One of my biggest fears was shooting an innocent person accidently or, by hesitating, getting my friends killed. They got closer; they were heading towards the gate. I was terrified. I could not gun down a woman and child, but this was what I was meant to do if they did not stop; neither could I let them run in and blow themselves up, killing my friend who waited down by the gate to search. What would I do? I do not know to this day. At the last possible moment, they left the path and headed back towards the town.

During my time in Sangin, increasingly I came to realise that this deployment was not just about helping a nation complete the removal of the imposed control of a psychotically fundamentalist Taliban regime and establishing peaceful governance. Things were a lot more complicated and I began to question the focus of our involvement.

After about two months in Sangin, we were redeployed to Garmsir, the southernmost town held by British Forces in Helmand. The town and the British base there, FOB Delhi, had effectively been under siege since 2006. We were told that we would be fighting out of trenches down there. I remember having a dream while we were still in Bastion where I was desperately fighting alone in a ditch to hold off attackers. This dream has stuck with me because of how viscerally accurate it turned out to be.

We were flown out again by Chinook to an artillery base in the desert near Garmsir, then moved out by road and established ourselves at the next base. From here we held a strip of ground between the Helmand River and a canal. Our routine consisted of three days of guard/reserve and three days of patrols. We would conduct security and resupply patrols to the checkpoints and raid over the canal, mostly at night, into the Taliban controlled areas to the southeast. We would set ambushes, usually unsuccessful, and then be attacked by the Taliban as we extracted in the morning. Then we would do three days at one of two forward positions that we referred to as 'checkpoints'. Here the fighting became heavy. We would be attacked many times a day in these positions with firefights sometimes lasting several hours. When we started receiving fire, we would all jump onto the firing line and blaze away at the Taliban firing points with every weapon we had. All this was so regular that it began to feel quite routine and even boring. I remember being told off by my Sergeant after one firefight. During the time when you are meant to be looking out for further action, I was absent-mindedly scratching a spot on my arm. 'Enemy, Boland, not spots' he said, and I realised how used to this I had become.

Some of the firefights were extremely close run. During one, the Taliban were pressing forward seemingly determined to storm the base. I was ammo running for two of our machine guns, which were the only things holding them back. I ran into the ammo store to find that we were down to the last box of GPMG rounds. I remember my vision going into tunnel-like focus, like in a horror film. Some Taliban then tried to rush the bridge and claymores were used on them. This was brutal. Black shapes in the dust then bang, nothing.

The bridge clear for a moment, dust, smoke and men smashed down by the blast and sucked away. The rest pulled back, the firefight died down, and the dust settled like nothing had happened.

After a couple of months of this, my time came up for R&R, so I handed over my extra weapons and jumped into a Chinook back to Camp Bastion with two others from the company. Our ride was shot at as we took off, the countermeasure flares were set off and fire shot past the windows. The interpreter riding with us wet himself and no one said anything as the piss ran across the floor.

At Camp Bastion, I washed and shaved, because you had to there, and enjoyed the canteen meals until there was a flight for us. I cleaned and handed in my rifle, ammunition and body armour and we flew to Kandahar where we stuffed ourselves at the American canteen and fast food outlets. We watched some celebrity cheerleading team get mobbed by American and Canadian troops for autographs. We waited in the huge hangar and then boarded the Tri-Star back to the UK and a week of freedom. Would I come back? Another guy had gone AWOL on his leave and many of the other TA guys I knew had been evacuated for one reason or another. Things were really heating up back in Garmsir and although I had grown quite accustomed to fighting from fixed positions, I dreaded the next time we made contact out on the ground, when utter chaos ensued. Just no way was I going to survive the whole tour – it was getting too crazy and I did not have a clue what I was doing. My luck would run out.

We landed at Brize Norton and some of my university mates picked me up. As we drove down the motorway, with me still in my combats and basic body armour from the flight, I could not help but notice how close all the cars were and felt I should be waving them back and pointing a weapon at them. After this I managed to forget about Afghanistan and whether I should return by getting absolutely 'smashed' for the next week, then getting dropped off and bumbling back into the queue for my return flight still in a total daze.

After a couple more weeks, we were told that we were due to leave Garmsir and go back to Camp Bastion to redeploy elsewhere. However, before we left we were to put in a big push with the whole company attempting to clear the Taliban positions in front of our line and push their front back to the south.

I remember smoking cigarette after cigarette while waiting around before heading over to form up with the rest of the company. The whole company was together now and there was a feeling of hysteria among many. I remember some attempt at a dance-off forming in the middle of the area, but many, such as myself, were quieter, busy rechecking kit and hanging around with a rising sense of dread. Many of us privates had to lie down on our rucksacks to get into the straps then be dragged to our feet by another, as the packs were so heavy. I remember noticing an informality, almost friendliness, to the words (now forgotten) used to move us out. For me, that increased the feeling of foreboding that surrounded this operation. I did not know how I would endure those endless hours of nerve-wrecking tedium on top of already aching fatigue. As it turned out I would not have to.

I think we had cleared one compound already, when we began to advance towards the position where we were hit. I had gone about 10 metres from the ditch into the open ground when the night was torn apart by a sudden storm of fire. I hit the ground in an instant and snap fired a few shots at the inferno ahead of me. Raising my head from the dirt I saw the blazing swarm of tracer rounds flying towards and over me, the corkscrew flights of Rocket Propelled Grenades (RPGs) from straight on looking like wheels of fire in the night. All this was tearing towards me from where 2 Section had been only a moment before.

To my left I saw 'Cleon'. His face was in the dirt. I rolled over to him – perhaps five metres – and I remember screaming 'Cleon's hit' as I reached him. He did not respond immediately. 'Ajax' appeared and we grabbed at Cleon, who came to. He got up and ran back to the ditch, I think. Ajax and I scrambled up to do the same and as we did I heard a ripping tearing sound of a round hitting. As I turned I saw him slump and the blood, black in the darkness against the white of his combats, spray out downwards from under his armour. He hit the ground and grabbing onto him I thought I would have to drag him back to the ditch, but as I pulled him he got up to run with me and I pitched forward to the ground. I put a hand down to break the fall and a line of bullet impacts tore across the earth across my outstretched right hand – several hitting just before it and several just after. I recovered my balance and, still grabbing onto Ajax with the other hand, we dashed back into the ditch. I dumped Ajax with the medic. I then turned to fire out from behind the raised bank of the ditch. Others began to arrive into the ditch, scrambling back in dazed and blind from flares or shock.

'Arnold' had been shot in the side of the head but his helmet had stopped the round. He was dazed and delirious – at some point someone had to sit on him to stop him running out of the ditch into fire. I was told to clear down the ditch. I fixed my bayonet and crawled down it. At some point, I fired more rounds down the ditch in the direction of the Taliban. I thought I heard Pashtun voices and movement down the ditch at some point, and have a half-memory of hearing my rounds hit something, making sounds like the one that had hit Ajax. I have a huge block of confusion and blackness when I try to recall exactly what happened down this ditch. Sometimes I feel like I remember more details but my mind recoils. I used 17 rounds in total during this long firefight of three to six hours. Later at Cally Calay, I would expend 11-and-a-half magazines of 30 in about five minutes. So, I think a lot of the time I must have just been frozen, squirming as deep as possible into the ditch as the heavy rounds and blasts of RPGs smashed away the cover.

We could all hear snatches of what was going on elsewhere through our personal radios, which added to the madness. Years later, I have managed, it seems, to lose the recording in my mind of a voice gurgling desperately and fading pleas not to be abandoned, but cannot forget that I did once remember them. Through this same radio, I heard someone say that I was dead.

'Junior' was brought into the ditch at some point and I remember Arnold, dazed and sobbing, trying to push the brains back into the boy's head. At some point, we moved back from that ditch and I remember helping treat 'Dewey's' wounds with 'Cyrus'. Shot in the thigh and then stomach as he was dragged back to the ditch, his eyes were staring and he was pale, but he was calm from the morphine and gave me a thumbs-up as I, having given all my field dressings, hung uselessly to his foot in despair.

Before clearing down the ditch, I had fitted my bayonet and, as I was pulling back from the ditch, I think I remember going to put it back in the webbing on the front of my armour but instead dropping it point first into the ground. I returned without it.

We pulled back to behind some old buildings. The air support dropped 1,000-pound bombs to help us break contact. We had to lie on the ground and open our mouths to take the blast. I remember what must have been a split second as the walls around us were blasted apart, instantly stretching out for what seemed ages as the walls slowly shook themselves apart before my eyes. A chunk fell on Cyrus' head and knocked him out. Then some of the Viking vehicles were able to reach us. We loaded the wounded and extracted on foot. The sun was coming up. I remember being so relieved to be running back towards the safety of those trenches, though two of our friends had been killed and many injured in the firefight.

The morning back in the safety of the base is a blur. Time passed strangely that day, people hid away and there was always someone crying somewhere. I remember lying under a mosquito net weeping by myself for what seemed like hours. Somehow at the same time, kit was taken stock and preparations made to depart that day. I remember waiting in (greatly reduced) section order for the helicopter, feeling so glad to still be alive and so sick with myself for this at the same time.

Returning to Camp Bastion was so strange after this; the petty bullshit of shaving and mess queues. Even before I came home I started to feel odd. We trained on the ranges and I was told off for switching up to auto and blowing away a target. I had not even realised I had done it. Another time, practising drills for a combat flight, my Sergeant noticed me zoning out and almost sent me back to the tents, but I would not let him. He hugged me and became quite emotional – this was strange.

I broke down during a call to my mum from Camp Bastion and later I saw the padre (chaplain). I discussed my disillusionment but he told me he 'didn't feel my change of heart was genuine' and that our mission was moral and valuable. I felt extremely angry at this callous response.

We had an 'inspiring' speech from the senior officer who proceeded to tell our group of 18- and early 20-something-year-olds, who had just had so many of our friends killed and maimed, how important it was for 'us' to 'keep taking the fight to the enemy'. I was so furious with him; he would not be going anywhere near the enemy. There were many other operations after this, as we fought in the Garesh Valley, and increasingly I questioned the morality of warfare and the senseless waste of life.

Eventually our time came to be replaced and we moved out into the desert where a Chinook arrived and off filed Coldstream Guards in brand new, clean desert combats, and on filed us singing 'Merry Christmas', and back to Camp Bastion we went. We went through all the handing in of weapons and packing up of kit, then eventually to the airfield at night and up the steps onto the Tri-Star home.

We didn't go to Cyprus for 'decompression' as we were supposed to but were flown straight back to the UK. There was a quick parade in the morning and off for the weekend. I went to my home town. It was Halloween. The town was full of mini-skirted girls with devil horns, horse's heads and suicide bomber costumes. Someone saw my uniform and asked if I'd killed anyone. The girl I was with shouted at them not to ask me that but I had barely noticed.

Back to barracks on the Monday we hung around, sorting and cleaning kit, did some runs and waited to be released for leave and demobilisation for the remaining TA soldiers. Without really meaning to, I kept to myself and don't remember talking much. My Sergeant mentioned this and I denied it, but already I think I felt quite separate and just wanted to get away. Our mental health care consisted of getting the whole company together in a hangar, telling us that some people have bad reactions after an operational tour, and asking a hall full of young men to put their hands up if they felt they might be having a problem. Incredibly, no hands went up.

Eventually we were released for demobilisation and started the process of form-filling that would turn us back from regular soldiers into civilians and part-time territorials. We went out on the town and I got stupidly drunk. I remember crying at some point in a club and then somehow got in a fight outside a kebab shop. I remember getting handcuffed from behind and bundled into a police car. I woke up the next day in a bare cell and, apparently, a lot of trouble. One officer told me that the other guy was a marine and had been taken to hospital with a broken jaw. I was in a daze and had little memory. I was interviewed, released with a court date and picked up by two corporals. The others had all finished their de-mob and left. I went through the rest of the cursory medical and pay paperwork but was not able to demobilise until after my court appearance.

I was released from the regular army. I had nowhere to live so I returned to my home town. That was the last of my dealings with the army. So, there I was with a criminal record, no job and staying between my mum's and girlfriend's places. Oh well, I had shelter and a bit of money left while I found work. I was very glad to be alive and whole, and felt that at least the Afghanistan part of my life was over and left behind, never to be repeated – except it was not.

Walking at night, I would see snatches of figures lit in night-sight green. A man dying with his guts shot out, a dead dog curled in the shadows; then the dreams of creeping up on Minotaurs, of friends screaming out and not helping them, of being dead and listening in over the radio. I dreamt of running from ambushes – I would wake with aching calves. I kept seeing those who had died in the faces of strangers and I was convinced it was them even though they didn't really look like them.

I felt so bitter about all the horror, injustice and pointlessness of the war I fought in, but also bitter towards those around me who had not been through it, and their what seemed to me petty preoccupations. I felt very alienated from society and those around me. Most of this I kept hidden.

I would get into fights far too often. I felt like I had to react quickly all the time, not show any slowness or weakness. I read aggression into every situation, from cars driving behind me, to passing people on the pavement, and I started taking routes that were actually more dangerous to avoid this fear. I was always so aware of potential for violence in any situation. I was still looking for 'young men of fighting age' as we were told to while on the lookout for Taliban fighters.

My reactions began to scare me and lead me to further withdraw from social situations. But I also had great trouble with being alone. I went from euphoria when I felt that, having survived, I could accomplish anything, to feeling so useless and low in self-esteem that I felt it was a mistake that I survived. I spent all my money without finding work. I tried to make up for it by pushing myself to extremes. I did all kinds of voluntary and traineeships that never came to anything. Then I worked three jobs at once, driving around the county into the night setting up firework displays and never saying 'no' to anything. The strain started to show. I lost jobs. I didn't feel that I fitted anywhere and I found it very hard to trust. I was suspicious and fearful of being used. I was so angry at what I perceived as ill treatment or patronisation. I became unable to cope with pressure, with extreme levels of stress and panic around simple things like paying at a till.

Incidents from Afghanistan would suddenly push themselves into my everyday life without warning, with all the emotional turmoil and physical reactions of the original experience. It did not occur to me at the time but by working with fireworks, I was placing myself among noises and explosions and almost revelling in this because it made me feel normal. Seeing broken down buildings in unexpected places took me back to Helmand. Even a bumblebee would resemble the sound of a Chinook and bring Afghanistan flooding back. A helicopter flying overhead would trigger a sense of dread, and I felt extreme flashes of anger at noises and surprises, which took a long time to calm down from. My neck, shoulders and back ached and my head would explode into pain with no warning. I was tense all the time, my muscles spasmed and hurt. My blood pressure went so high I was fitted with a monitor. I could hear the sounds of battle, bullets ripping flesh. I twitched.

I felt a sense of disconnection. I wasn't sure if the right 'me' had come back to the UK. Was I in a space-time alternative, out of sync with the rest of the world? I had dreams of panic and regressing to things from childhood, possibly to try and hold on to the person that I had previously been. Having been so close to death and around so much hurt and fear, I came to feel somehow as though it had actually happened to me. I had died and some impostor had returned. I doubted the reality of everything, even my most dearly held beliefs and experiences, because the events of Afghanistan had so challenged my assumptions and view of the world.

I was disgusted with society. Rather than a hatred of the 'enemy', I came instead to hate my own society and those who had sent me there. Areas I had fought in were taken over by Americans then abandoned. This reinforced the pointlessness I felt about having been there. There seemed to be no hope of the war somehow working out to make our time there worthwhile. I felt I could not voice my problems, that somehow I did not have a right to them. I felt used and rejected, self-conscious, full of guilt and shame. There was strain on my relationships with family and friends and eventually I broke down on the telephone to my mum in 2012. I had assumed that I was going to die. It is hard to change this.

I ended up living alone and this is when all these things came to a head. I was not sleeping; I was signed off from work; had no food in the house; and was eating old, raw oats out of the bag for meals. I ended up afraid to go out. I would zone out and realise that chunks of time had disappeared. I sat out on the roof of my flat in my unreturned desert smock, not even thinking that it was abnormal. I know now I was entering into the routines that had kept me alive in Afghanistan. I was associating sleep with death and subconsciously did not believe in the future.

The surges of memories, physical reactions and emotions became overwhelming and I recognise now that I was in a very dangerous situation. One night in particular, I came very close to taking flight from it all. Luckily, I had what turned out to be a very good friend who I managed to call. To my surprise, he seemed to know what was going on and drove straight over and sat with me while I blathered on about what a pathetic mess I had become. It was he who suggested contacting Combat Stress and gave me the link to the website.

Strangely, during this time when I was at my lowest, I had also met and was getting to know the woman I love (and who is now my wife). I knew that somewhere underneath all this horror, doubt and turmoil, I still had a life to live that I loved and wanted to reclaim. It was very hard to reconcile these two things. I wanted to be honest and for her to understand what was going on, not to think that my strange behaviour defined me, but also, I did not fully understand it all myself, and was embarrassed and ashamed of my weakness and stupidity. I was afraid that it might all scare her away and that Afghanistan would claim yet another part of my life. She was marvellous, accepting and striving to understand, seeming to know even in our then short acquaintance that the behavioural symptoms were not all of me, but something that could be overcome with the right help. She encouraged and helped me through the process of contacting and getting help from Combat Stress. Moving in together was a good step; our new flat was in a quieter area and I could walk to green space easily and see the sea.

So eventually, after some assessment visits and a two-week diagnostic stay, I found myself, seven years after going to fight in Afghanistan, attending a six-week intensive treatment programme at Combat Stress, Surrey. One very important part of the programme was education on what is a very complicated condition. Through identifying the disparate symptoms and recognising that they are not madnesses unique to you but common reactions to extreme events, it is possible to see that others go through the same thing. It began to break down the layers of denial and shame that exist even after admitting that you need help. I now see the many stages since my return from Afghanistan – ignorance, denial, avoidance, self-medication, breakdown, recognition.

One-to-one cognitive behavioural therapy was central to the course, but I still felt great difficulty in recognising and recounting the incidents that led to the condition and opening up about them. I stalled massively over trying to establish a timeline of events, so jumbled and surging were my memories – 'un date-stamped' as Combat Stress would call it. It is these unprocessed recollections that cause you to relive the traumatic events so intensely that you cannot form them into proper memories but instead become re-traumatised by their repeated recurrences and so block them out again.

It can be very hard to keep in touch with the person you were when in such distress; both in the original trauma and during the times you have relived it. It is necessary to stay in touch with and express those feelings without being overwhelmed by them again. I needed a way to get past this re-experiencing, with all its unpleasant attendant reactions, and to start getting a handle on the backed-up, surging jumble of experiences which clamoured for attention.

It was art therapy that provided me with this. In these sessions, we were given art materials and a theme. Then we were allowed time to draw and paint whatever came to us. When everyone was finished, we were encouraged to show and discuss our work with the rest of the group. In making my first art therapy images, I felt that a dam had broken. In those moments, years of unexpressed anguish found release and value. Art therapy helped me engage with my swirl of emotions and images, and to crystallise these into something lasting that I have then been able to reflect on further. I was able to record a snapshot of the tumult rather than continuously grinding over things to no avail.

Recording an image rapidly and then having the opportunity to step back, take another look and discuss it with others was daunting but incredibly useful. Often important aspects of the image would only become apparent through looking at it again. Sometimes others would notice things or find another way of interpreting the images, which provided great insight and allowed different angles of reflection on the events. This helped to overcome the rumination and make progress. It gave me the chance to express themes directly without the need to 'translate' them; to hint at things I found too horrible to vocalise and to mark stages in my journey. I was then able to use these images to show in my one-to-one cognitive behavioural therapy sessions as a starting point. This improved my engagement and helped to develop further insight.

The art therapy sessions and creative activity in the occupational therapy department gave me an opportunity to engage with trauma through something pleasurable and mindful – to slow down the rush of emotion and sensation, which can be overwhelming when trying to recount in direct therapy or conversation. It also allowed me to re-engage with much that I had felt I had lost through trauma and rediscover strengths of skill, sensitivity and compassion. Also, to realise and be glad of the advantages I have had in seeking recovery. The creative approaches provided a way to harness rediscovered skills that helped to tie down and recognise the traumas that I needed to face.

Minotaur (Figure 2.1) was my first art therapy image. It was drawn from my recurring memory of the incident during night clearances of compounds in Sangin. It helped me to present both the terror of the situation and my fears in beginning treatment at Combat Stress and looking at those memories again. Though based initially on the humorous incident of the Minotaur confusion, it also holds a sense of the dread and blackness I felt around recounting the ambush in Garmsir and finding myself facing those monstrous deeds again.

Figure 2.1 Minotaur by Clement Boland

With this and another picture based on the woman and child approaching Sangin DC (Figure 2.2), I came to realise how much subconscious material comes into these images that you do not realise. In the picture of the two figures approaching the checkpoint, it was not until later when I visited my mum that I realised the shape and postures of the figures, and even their position in the composition was almost exactly that of a painting of me and my mum by our landlady when I was a toddler in the park near our home.

In the case of *Minotaur*, it was a comment made by another veteran in the group that helped me to recognise other perspectives, remarking that the Minotaur looked as though it was shaking with fear, which could be mirroring my feelings, made me notice the third-person view. The way the silhouetted figure is standing could indeed cause fear.

I also made a model and wrote a poem based on the incident in Sangin with the dying man, which had played heavily on my mind. Producing this work helped me process a difficult event both through considering my role and through paying attention to, and treating with respect, someone I was unable to at the time. It is only after producing these that I have been able to recount the incident in plain prose as part of this account.

Clone Trooper (Plate 2.1) helped me express some of my feelings of anger and disillusionment for having been taken for a silly child and used in a terrible and disgusting game. The picture was the result of a session where we had to choose images that appealed to us from a selection of postcards of

Figure 2.2 Woman and Child by Clement Boland

different artwork, and then draw on the themes that the images raised for us. I selected the robot-like bust of Jacob Epstein's *The Rock Drill* (1913–1914) and the exploding shed of Cornelia Parker's *Cold Dark Matter: An Exploded View* (1991). The bust reminded me of a Star Wars battle droid but I was struck by the very human and emotional nature of its pose. The shed full of items of memory by the artist and then blown apart by the British Army made me think both of the physical effect of our actions on the lives of many Afghans and the psychological effect of these events on our own lives.

The themes that arose from looking at these images and creating the associated picture helped me to begin to express some of my very conflicting feelings towards events in Afghanistan and my part in them. I was thinking of *Return of the Jedi* but in the mould of *Platoon*, with the storm trooper as both victim and perpetrator of horror in a confused and inconclusive conflict.

The pastel drawing *Camel Train* (Plate 2.2) was made in response to two session themes of 'movement' and 'patterns'. I drew from my memory of seeing camel trains slowly passing in the distance over the teeth of the Helmand Valley while on guard. I remember the way their shadows were cast so long in the orange of the low, massive sun that they seemed like dinosaurs in their shape and scale. This image held something of my feeling in those calm times between the fear and violence, of the beauty and timelessness of the place; of the inconsequence of our struggles and all the pain involved against the slow cycle of existence. And, since, of how when the urgency of the adventure and importance of the cause you feel as young soldier fade into irrelevance, all you are left with is the personal impact of all the ultimately pointless little individual horrors; a sense of having been used; a strange wistfulness for the time when it all seemed worthwhile; and the feeling that life, though fleeting really, is just a bit too long to remember such things.

As I have moved further with my treatment, this picture has taken on new meaning for me. As memories and feelings have begun to shift, I feel more able to take a wider view of my experiences and appreciate the beauty in my past and future as so much more than a backdrop for fear and pain. This picture has come to represent for me that slow but now determined progression I began with the help of Combat Stress.

Though I still have flashbacks, in the years following my time at Combat Stress they began to shift in focus and perspective. While still disturbing, they began to reflect my processing of those traumas and to lessen in frequency and intensity. In one where I had often seen the man I saw die and felt his grip on the back of my calf, suddenly I was in the place of that man, reaching out to my wife and finding myself relieved to be comforted and at peace.

Through this process, I have rediscovered skills and I am rebuilding a sense of self-worth and engagement with the world around me. I am better able to appreciate all the aspects of my life, which I am so lucky still to have. I have a new family with the birth of our daughter on the 4 July 2015. I have had the opportunity to exhibit work, begun studying design at university and am now making plans and building towards a rewarding and sustaining career. I have come to believe in and look forward to the future rather than living in constant fear of the past coming back to destroy me.

I have now, almost 10 years after the event, been able to build this chronological account of my experiences in Afghanistan; something I was not capable of before my treatment at Combat Stress helped me form the tools to do so. I am really just starting now to come to terms with the impact those events have had on me, but through the insight of art, occupational and talking therapies I feel that, with the aid of continued creative and expressive activity, this reconciliation with my past is achievable.

Glossary

50 cal machine gun: 0.50 calibre heavy machine gun, mounted in fixed positions or on WIMIKs.

AWOL: absent without (official) leave.

Cally Calay: nickname for a big ancient fort we took and occupied in the Geresk area.

Chinook: a heavy, double-rotor helicopter used to transport troops and supplies.

Claymore: an explosive device that acts as a directional mine, spraying hundreds of ball bearings.

Countermeasure flares: flares set off by a Chinook when it comes under fire that confuses heat-seeking missiles by giving another heat source for them to lock onto.

FOB: Forward Operating Base.

GPMG: General Purpose Machine Gun.

Hesco wall: the cages and sack systems, which are filled with earth and used to build defensive positions.

Military structure: the army is divided into: divisions, brigades, regiments, battalions, companies, platoons, sections.

Paras: the Parachute Regiment.

R&R: Rest and Recuperation – brief home leave taken during your tour.

RPG: rocket propelled grenades – a favoured Soviet weapon of the Taliban.

Sangar: protected sentry post, watchtower or bunker used to detect early warning of activity.

Tracer fire: the glowing rounds included every few bullets in automatic fire – used to see where your rounds are hitting at night and to indicate where others should fire.

Tri-Star: RAF passenger aeroplanes.

Universal Soldier: film about futuristic cloned and automated soldiers.

WIMIK: Weapons Mount Installation Kit – open-topped vehicles with heavy weapons on the top mount.

Zeroing weapons: calibrating the weapon's sight.

Chapter 3

The biological basis of Post-Traumatic Stress Disorder and recovery

Kathy Kravits

Introduction

This chapter will focus on the biological basis of Post-Traumatic Stress Disorder (PTSD) and recovery, interweaving insights gained from the lived experience of PTSD as described by the veteran author of Chapter 2, with his use of art therapy as part of treatment. A recently developed model that integrates the concepts of homeostasis, allostasis and stress will be presented as a foundation for understanding the pathophysiology of PTSD. Current thinking about the disorder will be presented and risk factors and vulnerabilities associated with the development of PTSD will be discussed. Consideration will be given to ways in which art therapy might assist recovery from PTSD.

Post-Traumatic Stress Disorder (PTSD)

What is PTSD?

PTSD may be defined as a condition resulting from exposure to actual or threatened violence in which the initial fear response does not resolve (Yehuda & LeDoux, 2007). The symptoms used to diagnose the syndrome include re-experiencing, avoidance, negative cognitions, disturbance of mood, and arousal. These symptoms must reach a level of intensity that results in clinically significant distress; distress that interferes with occupational functioning and/or relationships (American Psychiatric Association, 2013). Growing evidence supports clinical observations of sub-types of PTSD that present with specific symptom clusters and that may occur as a result of specific vulnerabilities associated with the individual, the individual's experience, and the experience of members of the family unit of the sufferer (Breslau, Reboussin, Anthony & Storr, 2005; Breslau, Troost, Bohnert & Luo, 2013; Lanius *et al.*, 2010).

Vulnerabilities

There is mounting evidence that multiple variables contribute to the development of PTSD. These include vulnerabilities within the individual and as the result of environmental conditions to which the individual is exposed. Some of the factors described in the literature that are currently under investigation include those that impair post-trauma recovery (Yehuda & LeDoux, 2007). Current theories about the underlying vulnerabilities supporting the development of PTSD include: pre-existing characteristics of the individual such as genetic predispositions; gender; insecure attachment; foetal and neonatal exposure to maternal stress, trauma and PTSD; childhood and adolescent trauma; decreased hippocampal volume; alterations in amygdala function; dendritic hypertrophy of the medial pre-frontal cortex; lower intelligence (Breslau, 2009; Chavez, McGaugh & Weinberger, 2013; Elzinga, Schmahl, Vermetten, van Dyck & Bremner, 2003; Lanius et al., 2010; Roozendaal, Castello, Vedana, Barsegyan & McGaugh, 2008; Sherin & Nemeroff, 2011; Yehuda & LeDoux, 2007).

Lower plasma cortisol levels are believed to interfere with the restoration of homeostasis (Elzinga et al., 2003). Low levels of cortisol reduce the suppression of corticotropic releasing hormone (CRH) and norepinephrine (NE). CRH/NE are two substances that sustain the stress response. Disinhibition of these substances prolongs the acute stress response and supports the development, over time, of the symptoms associated with PTSD (Sherin & Nemeroff, 2011).

The disorder and the trauma leading to the development of the disorder form a cycle of experience that creates comprehensive vulnerabilities for the development of prolonged and sometimes permanent symptoms that can extend their impact beyond the individual to future generations (Breslau, 2009).

Consequences of PTSD and their implications for treatment

Suffering is an inherent part of the experience of PTSD. By definition, PTSD is associated with impairment of functioning in some of the most significant areas of life; in relationships with the self and others and in successful participation in meaningful work. The veteran author of Chapter 2, Clement Boland, henceforth referred to as Clem, describes this so clearly when he writes,

> I ended up living alone and this is when all these things came to a head. I was not sleeping; I was signed off from work; had no food in the house; and was eating old, raw oats out of the bag for meals. I ended up afraid to go out. I would zone out and realise that chunks of time had disappeared. I sat out on the roof of my flat in my unreturned desert smock, not even thinking that it was abnormal. I know now I was entering into

the routines that had kept me alive in Afghanistan. I was associating sleep with death and subconsciously did not believe in the future.

In addition, for many diagnosed with PTSD there is an overlay of shame. This includes shame associated with the symptoms, shame associated with a faulty belief that the diagnosis is an indication of weakness, and shame associated with the witnessing of and possibly participating in acts that violate deeply held moral beliefs. Treatment of the disorder has legitimately focused on repair and healing of the psychological distress of the individual. Limited strategies have been identified for addressing the moral despair associated with this condition (Litz *et al.*, 2009). It is important that all the domains of experience impacted by a diagnosis of PTSD be addressed as part of the healing.

Visual art-making allows representations of experiences to be externalised and processed outside the self. This allows the client to approach highly charged negative experiences, including those that are associated with shame and guilt, and to acknowledge them in a manner that promotes emotional regulation (Litz *et al.*, 2009). Referring to Plate 2.1, Clem writes, '*Clone Trooper* helped me express some of my feelings of anger and disillusionment for having been taken for a silly child and used in a terrible and disgusting game'.

Given the impact and the presenting symptoms of PTSD, the broad goals of therapy are to: (1) reduce suffering, as evidenced by decreased symptom burden, and (2) reduce functional impairment, as evidenced by pursuit of meaningful occupation and stable relationships. In order to understand the underlying mechanisms in play that affect attainment of these goals, the following sections will outline the body's stress response and the pathophysiology of PTSD.

Biological basis of the stress response

Evolution of the stress response

The stress response in mammals is thought to have evolved to promote survival in the face of threat. According to Heinrichs and Koob (2004), this exposure to threat (internal or external) prompts the organism to respond in a manner that mobilises resources to a degree that is adequate to successfully address the danger. Peripheral and central nervous systems and endocrine processes mediate the stress response. Resolution of danger allows these systems to return to previous levels of functioning. *Homeostasis* describes the baseline level of function most intimately connected to the output of the various physiologic systems involved in the stress response. Many of these systems are maintained through negative feedback loops. Regulation of respiratory rate, for example, is partially managed by the cardiorespiratory centre located in the medulla of the brainstem through the agency of a negative feedback loop. Chemical receptors in the cardiorespiratory centre detect rising and falling levels of carbon dioxide in the blood. Elevations in carbon dioxide are detected by the cardiorespiratory centre and, through the vagus nerve, the diaphragm is stimulated to expand and contract more quickly resulting in an increased respiratory rate. Once the carbon dioxide levels fall below a specific threshold, the information is processed by the cardiorespiratory centre and stimulation of the vagus nerve decreases resulting in a slower respiratory rate. Carbon dioxide levels stabilise and homeostasis is achieved. All of this happens without conscious oversight.

Over time the human brain is believed to have evolved with the capacity not only to respond to a present threat, but to anticipate potential threats (Sterling, 2012). The ability to anticipate and plan a response is centrally mediated by the brain and is often consciously directed. The experience of anxiety in response to perceived threat drives the acquisition of new information and the development of new strategies to promote safety and enhance survival. Satisfaction or pleasure that signals that the strategy was successful results from activation of the rewards system. This is a fluid process and the balance between anxiety and rewards represents the *allostatic state*, a proactive adaptation to the changing needs of the organism (Sterling, 2012).

Homeostasis and allostasis and the mechanisms that maintain them are specific to individuals and species. Until recently, the stress response has been characterised as an attempt to return the organism to homeostasis and allostasis. A new model, the *reactive scope model*, is proposed by Romero, Dickens and Cyr (2009). This model suggests that the physiologic systems that mediate the traditional stress response respond differently in four different ranges: (1) predictive homeostasis; (2) reactive homeostasis; (3) homeostatic overload; (4) homeostatic failure.

Romero *et al.* (2009) explain that usually environmental conditions determine the level of mediators needed in predictive homeostasis. In reactive homeostasis, the mediator required is determined by the need to respond to unpredictable or threatening environmental change. Predictive and reactive homeostasis determine the 'normal' range of response required by an individual. Homeostatic overload occurs when mediators above this normal range are required to maintain the organism. Prolonged periods of time in homeostatic overload are incompatible with health. Homeostatic failure occurs when the mediators are insufficient to meet the needs of the organism. This too is incompatible with health.

Regulatory range and adaptive capacity

According to Romero *et al.* (2009), species and individuals within species operate most effectively within a specific range of circumstances. This range is known as the *regulatory range*. All the processes and systems that mediate challenges are capable of adapting to predicted demands within their usual circumstances or regulatory range. This capability is known as *adaptive capacity*. A *stressor* is that set of circumstances that demands a response that exceeds the adaptive capacity of the individual or species (Koolhaas *et al.*, 2011).

Predictors of regulatory range

Regulatory range can be affected by several developmental, genetic and environmental factors (Belsky, Bakermans-Kranenburg & van Ijzendoorn, 2007). Koolhaas *et al.* (2011) report that prenatal and neonatal maternal environment can impact regulatory range. In one study (Davis, Glynn, Waffarn & Sandman, 2011), prenatal maternal stress in the second and third trimesters was measured using elevated maternal serum cortisol levels as an indicator. Within 35 hours of birth, neonates were subjected to a procedure known as *the heel-stick stressor*. This involves pricking the heel of the infant with a lancet. Prenatal maternal stress was associated with an elevated cortisol response and delayed recovery in infants exposed to the heel-stick stressor. The results of this study suggest that prenatal maternal stress adversely affects the ability of neonates to recover from stress. Suderman *et al.* (2012) conducted a large cross-species study of mice and humans demonstrating long-term changes in behaviour and epigenetic programming of the glucocorticoid receptor gene in the hippocampus, which suggests that there are significant epigenetic regulatory responses in the genome to early life experiences.

Gluckman *et al.* (2009) suggest that the maternal caregiver plays a significant role in creating the regulatory range of the child. If the adult circumstances match this developmentally established regulatory range, then things work well. When there is a mismatch between the anticipated environmental experiences and the actual environmental experiences, there is a regulatory range 'mismatch' (Godfrey, Lillycrop, Burdge, Gluckman & Hanson, 2007).

Circumstances that create demands upon the individual or species that exceed the adaptive capacity of that individual or species lead to either an inadequate response to the threat or an inability to recover from the threat when the threat is no longer present (Koolhaas *et al.*, 2011). This concept is critical to understanding what happens to those individuals who suffer with PTSD. Essentially, extraordinary circumstances invade their lives. These circumstances are outside of their adaptive capacity and they either fail to respond adequately and/or fail to recover from the experience.

Stress response systems

The primary systems that mediate the stress response are the sympathetic adrenomedullary system (SAM), the hypothalamic pituitary adrenocortical axis (HPA), and the polyvagal system (Porges, 2001). Their role is to initiate and sustain the processes that allocate resources necessary to respond to threat (Kravits, 2008).

Clem describes the build-up to an operation conveying a sense of the SAM and HPA preparing for action:

> I remember smoking cigarette after cigarette while waiting around before heading over to form up with the rest of the company. The whole company was together now and there was a feeling of hysteria among many. I remember some attempt at a dance-off forming in the middle of the area.

The sympathetic adrenomedullary (SAM) system

The SAM system consists of the sympathetic nervous system, a component of the autonomic nervous system, which is itself a part of the peripheral nervous system. The sympathetic nerve fibres are widely distributed throughout the body. The neurotransmitter of the sympathetic nervous system is norepinephrine (NE). Norepinephrine belongs to a class of substances called catechol amines. Norepinephrine is released by the sympathetic nerve fibres at the synaptic junction with the end organs (e.g., the smooth muscle of the blood vessels, pupil of the eye and the sinoatrial node of the heart, etc.). The effects of NE include increased respiratory rate, increased heart rate, dilation of the pupils, increased blood flow to voluntary muscles, decreased blood flow to the gastrointestinal tract and stimulation of the liver to release glycogen, a form of stored glucose. The effects of NE prepare the body to respond to threat by increasing available oxygen and glucose, nutrients essential to the functioning of the large muscles, sensory organs and brain. Activation of the SAM system creates the earliest response to threat by preparing the body to fight or flee.

The hypothalamic pituitary adrenocortical (HPA) axis

The HPA consists of the hypothalamus, the pituitary and the adrenal cortex. It is an endocrine system that promotes the release of glucocorticoid. Positioned near the amygdala, hippocampus and prefrontal cortex, it expedites activation of the hypothalamus. The hypothalamus releases a corticotrophin-releasing hormone, which circulates via the blood stream to the pituitary. In response to exposure to the corticotrophin-releasing hormone, the pituitary produces an adrenocorticotropic hormone that circulates via the blood stream to the adrenal gland. The adrenal cortex secretes glucocorticoid in response to exposure to the adrenocorticotropic hormone. Glucocorticoid plays a significant role in metabolising glucose from liver glycogen and releasing the glucose into the blood stream. Glucose is the only substance in the body that the brain can use for nutrition. It is essential that adequate supplies of glucose are available to the brain especially when there are increased demands for performance made of the entire body, most especially the brain.

The polyvagal theory

The *polyvagal theory*, first described by Porges (2001), suggests that the branches of the vagus nerve, a component of the parasympathetic division of the autonomic nervous system, perform unique functions including facilitating heart rate variability in response to changing environmental conditions. Porges further suggests that the myelinated branch of the vagus, the ventral vagal complex (VVC), which services the conductive tissue of the heart, plays a role in social engagement as well as self-regulation. When activated, the myelinated vagus acts as a brake and slows the heart rate through the release of acetylcholine. The slowing of the heart is perceived by the individual as a 'calming' of the system, creating the space for relational interactions to take place (Porges, 2011a).

The unmyelinated branch of the vagus, the dorsal vagal complex (DVC), plays a critical role in promoting survival by conserving resources through behavioural strategies such as immobilisation and avoidance. The DVC mediates extreme responses to overwhelming threat such as freezing and fainting. Actual or perceived loss of oxygen seems to be the primary trigger of this response (Porges, 2011b).

Describing a related physical response Clem writes,

> I was ammo running for two of our machine guns, which were the only things holding them back. I ran into the ammo store to find that we were down to the last box of GPMG rounds. I remember my vision going into tunnel-like focus, like in a horror film.

Activation of the stress response

Activation of the stress response occurs when sensory information is brought to the brain. At least two pathways serve as key mechanisms for relaying sensory data to the limbic system and the prefrontal cortex for processing and action. One path, known as the 'quick' path, carries the sensory input rapidly to the thalamus and from there to the amygdala of the limbic system (LeDoux & Muller, 1997). From the amygdala, the sensory data is routed to the hypothalamus then to the medulla where the sympathetic nerve fibres are stimulated and a SAM response is initiated (ibid.).

The second path, known as the 'slow' path, requires many more neurons to deliver the same sensory information to the prefrontal cortex where it is processed and threat identified, and, if necessary, acted upon. Many stress-management interventions are designed to inhibit the automatic responses in order to allow the slow path to communicate with the prefrontal cortex and to bring it online for information processing and decision-making (Kravits, 2008). An example of one of the strategies used to slow those immediate sympathetic responses is deep breathing. Deep breathing increases the pressure on the stretch receptors within the lungs. This information is communicated to the cardiorespiratory centre in the medulla and the VVC is stimulated resulting in slowed breathing and heart rate. A wonderful aspect of this strategy is that it occurs as the result of a negative feedback loop and conscious control is not required to produce the desired effect.

Art-making as part of art therapy can help with reduction in arousal. A soothing and meditative experience can be created through a thoughtful choice of mediums. With the addition of deep breathing techniques, arousal can be diminished and processed (ibid.).

Pathophysiology of PTSD

Recent research is creating a compelling picture of the pathophysiology of PTSD. Many of the neural correlates supporting the symptomology associated with PTSD have been described (Koolhaas *et al.*, 2011; Sherin & Nemeroff, 2011; Shin, Rauch & Pitman, 2006; Yehuda & Le Doux, 2007). Shin *et al.* (2006) have reported that alterations in the functioning of the amygdala, hippocampus and medial prefrontal cortex are implicated in the development of the symptoms present in PTSD. Alterations in the functioning of neuroendocrine systems such as the HPA axis have been demonstrated as well (Sherin & Nemeroff, 2011).

Amygdala

The amygdala, prefrontal cortex and hippocampus are functionally connected. The hippocampus influences the amygdala in the encoding of emotional memories (Shin *et al.*, 2006). The amygdala is essential to mobilisation of resources in response to threat. In those diagnosed with PTSD, findings suggest that it is hyperresponsive. The result of this change in the functioning of the amygdala is the development of hypervigilance (ibid.).

Hippocampus

In those diagnosed with PTSD, the hippocampus is found to have a smaller volume and function less effectively (Sherin & Nemeroff, 2011). It is suggested in the research that the smaller volume contributes to this decline in expected functioning. There is persuasive evidence that the smaller volume of the hippocampus is not the result of the trauma exposure, but is more likely a pre-existing vulnerability acquired either genetically, or as the result of foetal exposure to maternal trauma (ibid.). Insecure attachment, particularly in the form of disorganised attachment and/or childhood trauma, may also be implicated in hippocampal dysfunction (Yehuda & LeDoux, 2007).

The hippocampus is one of the most plastic structures within the brain. Neural regeneration can be promoted within the hippocampus. Corrective attachment experiences and meditation have been shown to support neural regeneration (Baerentsen *et al.*, 2009; Quirin, Gillath, Pruessner & Eggert, 2009; Tang, Holzel & Posner, 2015). Regeneration of the hippocampus is feasible and may offer an opportunity to re-establish effective functional connectivity with the amygdala and reduce the symptom burden associated with PTSD.

Medial prefrontal cortex

The medial prefrontal cortex is intimately involved in the symptomatology of PTSD (Sherin & Nemeroff, 2011). Like the hippocampus, the medial prefrontal cortex and the anterior cingulate cortex demonstrate reduced volume. In addition, there is decreased medial prefrontal activation (ibid.). It is unclear what the impact of decreased medial prefrontal activation is. However, there is evidence that fear extinction does not occur normally when the medial prefrontal cortex is damaged (Shin *et al.*, 2006). There is significant evidence that the decline in volume of the medial prefrontal cortex and the anterior cingulate cortex contributes to failure of fear extinction and dysregulation of executive functioning (ibid.). These changes contribute to symptoms such as re-experiencing, negative cognitions, disturbance in mood and arousal.

Neurotransmitters

Neurotransmitters are dysregulated in PTSD. Dopamine and norepinephrine levels are increased resulting in disturbed fear conditioning, increased arousal and proneness to being startled. Decreased levels of serotonin are present contributing to a compromised anxiolytic effect (Sherin & Nemeroff, 2011).

Emotional memory

Hamann (2001) proposes that there is a survival and reproductive advantage to remembering emotion-laden experiences, especially as they support anticipation of threat. As a consequence of this, the storage of emotional stimuli in memory is facilitated by specific neural and hormonal mechanisms. Upon exposure to emotional stimuli, the experience is encoded creating the 'first memory'. This initial activity is followed by post-encoding processes, including consolidation resulting in an increased effect of emotion on memory over time.

Clem shares some of his traumatic experiences in this volume. In reading them, we are able to appreciate the immediate impact of trauma. Clem writes,

> I was horrified. He had been shot from behind and his intestines were all spilling out from his torn belly. I had never seen a body or anyone so

badly hurt before, and I felt so sorry and appalled, I just wanted to help him but did not know how.

He goes on to elaborate on his subsequent thought processes,

I took from this incident that I never wanted to inflict that kind of terrible hurt on anybody but also that I had another six months left on this tour and that I would probably have to or end up that way myself. I was trapped.

Back in civilian life in the UK, Clem describes his plight,

I felt like I had to react quickly all the time, not show any slowness or weakness. I read aggression into every situation, from cars driving behind me, to passing people on the pavement, and I started taking routes that were actually more dangerous to avoid this fear. I was always so aware of potential for violence in any situation. I was still looking for 'young men of fighting age' as we were told to while on the lookout for Taliban fighters.

Hamann (2001) explains that the amygdala plays an essential role in assessment of threat, fear conditioning and consolidation of emotional memory by increasing or reducing its own activity as well as that of other structures in the brain involved in memory. The amygdala's ability to assess threat and thereby signal the release of stress hormones amplifies its functional impact on fear conditioning. Consolidation is the primary process impacted by the effects generated by the amygdala especially in the hippocampus.

In summary, there are indications that the amygdala is hyperresponsive during symptomatic states of PTSD and that this hyperresponsivity is associated with symptom severity (Orr *et al.*, 2000; Shin *et al.*, 2006; Yehuda & LeDoux, 2007). The medial prefrontal cortex (anterior cingulate cortex, subcallosal cortex and medial frontal gyrus) is volumetrically smaller and hyporesponsive during symptomatic states (Shin *et al.*, 2006). This is a critical finding as the medial prefrontal cortex is implicated in the process of fear extinction and PTSD is often described as a disorder resulting in delayed recovery from exposure to trauma (Yehuda & LeDoux, 2007). Additional research indicates that the functional integrity of the hippocampus is disrupted in PTSD with decreased volumes and disruption of neuronal integrity (Shin *et al.*, 2006). When the entirety of the research is considered, a compelling pattern emerges. Symptoms of hypervigilance, arousal, reliving, emotional intensity and delay of fear extinction found in PTSD can be associated with the impaired functioning of the amygdala, hippocampus and medial prefrontal cortex.

Biological contributions of art therapy

There is increasing recognition that art therapy can assist the treatment of trauma on a neurobiological level (Avrahami, 2005; Gantt & Tinnin, 2009;

Talwar, 2007; Tripp, 2007). Art therapy accesses non-verbal parts of the brain that communicate in emotions, visual imagery and body sensations, and research suggests it can assist structural recovery (Hass-Cohen, 2008; Lusebrink, 2004). Lusebrink highlights how art therapy is 'uniquely equipped' to benefit from 'alternate paths for accessing and processing visual and motor information and memories' (ibid., p. 133). Initially only associated with early development, neuroplasticity is the brain's ability for structural adaptation (Hass-Cohen, 2008; May and Gaser, 2006). It enables structural and functional change in the brain as it adapts to challenges such as physical injury or psychological difficulties. New neural pathways form as a result of repeated stimulation thereby gradually altering function (Konopka, 2016). This ability to 'rewire' is now seen as a lifelong capacity with significant clinical implications. *Interpersonal neurobiology* (Siegel, 2003) outlines how relationships can not only assist emotional regulation but also affect the brain on a structural level. Furthermore, visual art-making activities have been shown to support vertical and horizontal integration of brain function promoting regulation of neural systems impacted by trauma exposure (Sarid & Huss, 2010).

Bolwerk, Mack-Andrick, Lang, Dorfler and Maihofner (2014) examined the impact of visual art-making versus art evaluation on the functional connectivity of the brain. A non-clinical sample of 28 participants stratified by age and gender and randomised to either a visual art-making group or an art-evaluation group were enrolled in the study. fMRI and psychological assessment data were obtained at baseline and after the intervention. Psychological resilience was measured using an instrument with established reliability and validity. The results demonstrated an improvement in psychological resilience associated with increased functional connectivity of the posterior cingulated cortex to the frontal and parietal cortices in the visual art-making group. These results suggest a promising line of inquiry into the impact of visual art-making on brain functioning and resilience. The limitations of this study include the small sample size, which prevents generalisation to a wider population, and a brief follow-up period after the intervention, which precludes analysis of the durability of the effect. It would also be interesting to investigate clinical populations as well as non-clinical ones. This study was one of a very few visual art-making studies designed as a randomised controlled trial that included measures of brain activity and psychological characteristics.

In the following section, art therapy will be considered in the context of attachment and emotional regulation.

Attachment and emotional regulation

Many argue that the relationship between primary caregiver and child has a significant impact on emotional outcomes later in life, including those relating to PTSD. According to *attachment theory* (Bowlby, 1969), the relationship between caregiver and child is dynamic and bidirectional. Both must pursue attachment to the other and both must respond in an accepting manner to the attachment efforts of the other. It is within this context of consistently experienced attachment efforts and acceptance that secure attachment develops. It is not necessary for every interaction between the dyad to be composed of exactly the 'right' approach and acceptance. There will be missteps and mismatches along the way, but as long as there are enough successes, secure attachment will develop.

Significance of attachment

Attachment is an important part of human experience and a significant factor in the development of the individual and future generations arising from that individual (Stamps & Groothuis, 2010). Failure to achieve a secure attachment results in some form of insecure attachment (Ainsworth & Bell, 1970). Insecure attachment may occur when the attachment efforts of the primary caregiver are insufficient to meet the needs of the child, inappropriately timed for the needs of the child, or offered in a manner that may be frightening to the child. Individuals who have an insecure attachment history frequently struggle with forming satisfying adult relationships and regulating emotion in the face of challenging life experiences (Besser & Neria, 2012; Moutsiana *et al.*, 2014; Warren *et al.*, 2010). Insecure attachment and associated problems with effective emotional regulation are factors that increase the vulnerability of a trauma survivor to the development of PTSD (Breslau *et al.*, 2013).

Attachment theory offers a framework for understanding ways through which art therapy might assist recovery from PTSD by reworking ruptures that prevented attainment of secure attachment, thereby fostering repair.

Elements required for secure attachment

According to Siegel (2003), the attachment experience is a form of intimate communication between two individuals first occurring largely nonverbally and then advancing to more consistently verbal interactions. *Contingent communication* is an essential element of secure attachment. Contingent communication requires that the primary caregiver correctly identifies signals from the child, attaches the correct meaning to those signals, and responds in a timely and effective manner. *Reflective dialogue* is another aspect of secure attachment. It consists of engaging in communication about subjective aspects of human experience including thoughts, feelings, sensations, perceptions, attitudes, beliefs and intentions.

Siegel goes on to explain that 'repair' is required in any relationship and is especially important in forming a secure attachment. Repair is necessary to address the consequences of a rupturing of the attachment. Ruptures often take the form of inappropriate emotions that are projected by the primary caregiver at the child. These emotional outbursts are often internalised by the child as indications that he or she is defective and at fault and should be ashamed. It is the caregiver's responsibility to repair the rupture by taking ownership of his or her behaviour and making an attempt to reconnect. Repeated experiences with a rupture will challenge the child's ability to reconnect leading to an insecure attachment.

Further, Siegel suggests that emotional communication is an essential part of sustaining a secure attachment and laying the foundation for the development of empathy and compassion. Communication of positive and negative emotional content allows the child to build a context for understanding and accept emotion as a natural part of human experience, preparing him or her for managing those experiences effectively.

Finally, the ability to generate a coherent narrative is thought to demonstrate the child's skill in creating meaning from his or her life experiences. Therefore, coherent narratives that economically use language to reflect experience are seen by many as an indicator of secure attachment.

The creation of a coherent narrative is seen as crucial for the purpose of reconsolidation of trauma memories (Collie, Backos, Malchiodi & Spiegel, 2006). Art therapy allows the PTSD sufferer to access non-verbal experience, externalise it, and make it available for verbal processing and integration. This strategy is consistent with the interpersonal neurobiology concept of emotional regulation and integration articulated by Siegel (2003).

Emotional regulation and integration

Emotional regulation is the ability to experience intense emotions and then regulate the experience of them internally (Moutsiana *et al.*, 2014). The ability to regulate emotions effectively is a marker of a secure attachment (Siegel, 2003). Collie and colleagues (2006) identified progressive exposure as a key objective of art therapy with combat-related trauma. This use of art-making to symbolically represent feeling states and/or experiences otherwise avoided could increase distress tolerance by the client and promote emotional integration.

Integration is a concept that describes the incorporation of a wide range of processes and experiences and the synthesis of this information into a new and more complex understanding of the world, self and others (Collie *et al.*, 2006). Successful integration of new information promotes adaptability and flexible self-regulation and is consistent with secure attachment (ibid.). Together, the skills of emotional regulation and integration promote resilience and assist individuals in increasing adaptive capacity, reducing trauma survivors' risk of developing PTSD (Breslau *et al.*, 2013).

The role of art therapy in recovery from PTSD

As discussed previously, exposure to trauma triggers a biological stress response that has a survival advantage for most individuals (Sterling, 2012). In the case of individuals who go on to develop PTSD, the current thinking is that regulation of this response is impeded by low levels of cortisol resulting in a sustained dysregulation (Elzinga *et al.*, 2003). The sustained response is responsible for the persistent symptoms associated with PTSD. Given the impact and the presenting symptoms of PTSD, the broad goals of therapy are to: (1) reduce suffering, as evidenced by decreased symptom burden; (2) reduce functional impairment, as evidenced by pursuit of meaningful occupation and stable relationships.

In Chapter 2, Clem explains the difficulties he faced in treatment and how art therapy helped him to make progress:

> I needed a way to get past this re-experiencing, with all its unpleasant attendant reactions, and to start getting a handle on the backed-up, surging jumble of experiences that clamoured for attention.
>
> It was art therapy that provided me with this … In making my first art therapy images, I felt that a dam had broken. In those moments, years of unexpressed anguish found release and value. Art therapy helped me engage with my swirl of emotions and images, and to crystallise these into something lasting that I have then been able to reflect on further. I was able to record a snapshot of the tumult rather than continuously grinding over things to no avail.

The previous sections of this chapter have included observations of how art therapy might decrease symptom burden. Art therapy can also assist the reactivation of positive emotions (Collie *et al.*, 2006). Creative expression through art-making can stimulate and recover positive emotional memories that confirm that the client has the ability to experience positive emotions (Talwar, 2007). Clem confirms that for him the visual art-making assisted him in reframing his experience in a more positive and life affirming way.

> As I have moved further with my treatment, this picture [Plate 2.2] has taken on new meaning for me. As memories and feelings have begun to shift, I feel more able to take a wider view of my experiences and appreciate the beauty in my past and future as so much more than a backdrop for fear and pain. This picture has come to represent for me that slow but now determined progression I began with the help of Combat Stress.

Key objectives of treatment as identified by Collie *et al.* (2006) are enhancement of emotional self-efficacy and improved self-esteem. Emotional self-efficacy refers to the ability to tolerate and manage emotions. As the client becomes able to tolerate and manage emotions, he or she becomes more self-efficacious and a greater degree of self-esteem will develop as a result. Clem confirms this when he says,

> Through this process, I have rediscovered skills and I am rebuilding a sense of self-worth and engagement with the world around me. I am

better able to appreciate all the aspects of my life I am so lucky still to have … I have come to believe in and look forward to the future rather than living in constant fear of the past coming back to destroy me.

This statement affirms that the broad goals of therapy have been achieved, with art therapy playing a significant role in the journey of recovery.

References

Ainsworth, M. D. S. & Bell, S. M. (1970). Attachment, exploration, and separation: Illustrated by the behavior of one-year-olds in a strange situation. *Child Development, 41,* 49–67.

American Psychiatric Association (2013). Posttraumatic stress disorder. *Diagnostic and statistical manual of mental disorders* (5th edn). Washington, DC: American Psychiatric Association.

Avrahami, D. (2005). Visual art therapy's unique contribution in the treatment of post-traumatic stress disorders. *Journal of Trauma & Dissociation, 6*(4), 5–38.

Baerentsen, K. B., Stodkilde-Jorgensen, H. Sommerlund, B., Hartmann, T. Damsgaard-Madsen, J., Fosnaes, M. & Green, A. C. (2009). An investigation of brain processes supporting meditation. *Cognitive Process, 11,* 57–84.

Belsky, J., Bakermans-Kranenburg, M. J. & van Ijzendoorn, M. H. (2007). For better and for worse. *Current Directions in Psychological Science, 16,* 300–304.

Besser, A. & Neria, Y. (2012). When home isn't a safe haven: Insecure attachment orientations, perceived social support, and PTSD symptoms among Israeli evacuees under missile threat. *Psychological Trauma: Theory, Research, Practice, and Policy, 4*(1), 34–46.

Bolwerk, A., Mack-Andrick, J., Lang, F. R., Dorfler, A. & Maihofner, C. (2014). How art changes your brain: Differential effects of visual art production and cognitive art evaluation on functional brain connectivity. *Plos One, 9*(7), e101035.

Bowlby, J. (1969). *Attachment and loss, Vol. 1: Attachment.* New York, NY: Basic Books.

Breslau, N. (2009). The epidemiology of trauma, PTSD, and other posttrauma disorders. *Trauma, Violence, and Abuse, 10,* 198–210.

Breslau, N., Reboussin, B. A., Anthony, J. C. & Storr, C. L. (2005). The structure of posttraumatic stress disorder. *Archives of General Psychiatry, 62,* 1343–1351.

Breslau, N., Troost, J. P., Bohnert, K. & Luo, Z. (2013). Influence of predispositions on posttraumatic stress disorder: Does it vary by trauma severity? *Psychological Medicine, 43,* 381–390.

Chavez, C. M., McGaugh, J. L. & Weinberger, M. M. (2013). Activation of the basolateral amygdala induces long-term enhancement of specific memory representation in the cerebral cortex. *Neurobiology of Learning and Memory, 101,* 8–18.

Collie, K., Backos, A., Malchiodi, C. & Spiegel, D. (2006). Art therapy for combat-related PTSD: Recommendations for research and practice. *Art Therapy: Journal of the American Art Therapy Association, 23,* 157–164.

Davis, E. P., Glynn, L. M., Waffarn, F. & Sandman, C. A. (2011). Prenatal maternal stress programs infant stress regulation. *Journal of Child Psychology and Psychiatry, 52,* 119–129.

Elzinga, B. M., Schmahl, C. G., Vermetten, E., van Dyck, R. & Bremner, J. B. (2003). Higher cortisol levels following exposure to traumatic reminders in abuse-related PTSD. *Neuropsychopharmacology*, *28*, 1656–65.

Gantt, L. & Tinnin, L. (2009). Support for a neurobiological view of trauma with implications for art therapy. *The Arts in Psychotherapy*, *36*(3), 148–153.

Gluckman, P. D., Hanson, M. A., Bateson, P., Beedle, A. S., Law, C. M., Bhutta, Z. A., Anokhin, K. V., Bougnères, P., Chandak, G. R., Dasqupta, P., Smith, G. D., Ellison, P. T., Forrester, T. E., Gilbert, S. F., Jablonka, E., Kaplan, H., Prentice, A. M., Simpson, S. J., Uauy & West-Eberhard, M. J. (2009). Towards a new developmental synthesis: Adaptive developmental plasticity and human disease. *The Lancet*, *373*, 1654–1657.

Godfrey, K. M., Lillycrop, K. A., Burdge, G. C., Gluckman, P. D. & Hanson, M. A. (2007). Epigenetic mechanisms and the mismatch concept of the developmental origins of health and disease. *Pediatric Research*, *61*, 5R–10R.

Hamann, S. (2001). Cognitive and neural mechanisms of emotional memory. *TRENDS in Cognitive Sciences*, *5*, 394–400.

Hass-Cohen, N. (2008). Partnering of art therapy and clinical neuroscience. In N. Hass-Cohen & R. Carr (eds), *Art therapy and clinical neuroscience* (pp. 21–42). Philadelphia, PA: Jessica Kingsley.

Heinrichs, S. C. & Koob, G. F. (2004). Corticotropin-releasing factor in brain: A role in activation, arousal, and affect regulation. *The Journal of Pharmacology and Experimental Therapeutics*, *311*, 427–440.

Konopka, L. (2016). Neuroscience concepts in clinical practice. In J. L. King (ed.), *Art therapy, trauma, and neuroscience: Theoretical and practical perspectives* (pp. 11–41). New York: Routledge.

Koolhaas, J. M., Bartolomucci, A., Buwalda, B., deBoer, S. F., Flugge, G., Korte, S. M., Meerlo, P., Murison, R., Olivier, B., Palanza, P., Richter-Levin, G., Sgoifo, A., Steimer, T., Stiedl, O., van Dijk, G., Wöhr, M. & Fuchs, E. (2011). Stress revisited: A critical evaluation of the stress concept. *Neuroscience and Biobehavioral Reviews*, *35*, 1291–1301.

Kravits, K. (2008). The stress response and adaptation theory. In N. Hass-Cohen & R. Carr (eds), *Art Therapy and Clinical Neuroscience* (pp. 111–127). London: Jessica Kingsley.

Lanius, R. A., Vermetten, E., Loewenstein, R. J., Brand, B., Schmahl, C., Bremner, J. D. & Spiegel, D. (2010). Emotion modulation in PTSD: Clinical and neurobiological evidence for a dissociative subtype. *American Journal of Psychiatry*, *167*, 640–647.

LeDoux, J. E. & Muller, J. (1997). Emotional memory and psychopathology. *Philosophical Transactions of the Royal Society of London*, *352*, 1719–1726.

Litz, B. T., Stein, N., Delaney, E., Lebowitz, L., Nash, W. P., Silva, C. & Maguen, S. (2009). Moral injury and oral repair in war veterans: A preliminary model and intervention strategy. *Clinical Psychology Review*, *29*, 695–706.

Lusebrink, V. B. (2004). Art therapy and the brain: an attempt to understand the underlying processes of art expression in therapy. *Art Therapy: Journal of the American Art Therapy Association*, *21*(3), 125–135.

May, A. & Gaser, C. (2006). Magnetic resonance-based morphometry: A window into structural plasticity of the brain. *Current Opinion Neurology*, *19*(4), 407–441.

Moutsiana, C., Fearon, P., Murray, L., Cooper, P., Goodyer, I., Johnstone, T. & Halligan, S. (2014). Making an effort to feel positive: Insecure attachment in infancy predicts the neural underpinnings of emotion regulation in adulthood. *Journal of Child Psychology and Psychiatry*, *55*(9), 999–1008.

Orr, S. P., Metzger, L. J., Lasko, N. B., Macklin, M. L., Peri, T. & Pitman, R. K. (2000). De novo conditioning in trauma exposed individuals with and without post-traumatic stress disorder. *Journal of Abnormal Psychology*, *109*, 290–298.

Porges, S. W. (2001). The polyvagal theory: Phylogenetic substrates of a social nervous system. *International Journal of Psychophysiology*, *42*, 123–146.

Porges, S. W. (2011a). The polyvagal theory: New insights into adaptive reactions of the autonomic nervous system. In *The Polyvagal Theory* (pp. 52–59). New York, NY: W. W. Norton & Company.

Porges, S. W. (2011b). Vagal tone: A physiological marker of stress vulnerability. In *The Polyvagal Theory* (pp. 63–74). New York, NY: W. W. Norton & Company.

Quirin, M., Gillath, O., Pruessner, J. C. & Eggert, L. D. (2009). Adult attachment insecurity and hippocampal cell density. *Social Cognitive and Affective Neuroscience Advance Access*, *5*, 39–47.

Romero, L. M., Dickens, M. J. & Cyr, N. E. (2009). The reactive scope model: A new model integrating homeostasis, allostasis, and stress. *Hormones and Behavior*, *5*, 375–389.

Roozendaal, B., Castello, N. A., Vedana, G., Barsegyan, A. & McGaugh, J. L. (2008). Noradrenergic activation of the basolateral amygdala modulates consolidation of object recognition memory. *Neurobiology of Learning and Memory*, *90*, 576–579.

Sarid, O. & Huss, E. (2010). Trauma and acute stress disorder: A comparison between cognitive behavioural intervention and art therapy. *The Arts in Psychotherapy*, *17*, 8–12

Sherin, J. E. & Nemeroff, C. B. (2011). Posttraumatic stress disorder: The neurobiological impact of psychological trauma. *Dialogues in Clinical Neuroscience*, *13*, 263–278.

Shin, L. M., Rauch, S. L. & Pitman, R. K. (2006). Amygdala, medial prefrontal cortex, and hippocampal function in PTSD. *Annals of the New York Academy of Sciences*, *1071*, 67–79.

Siegel, D. J. (2003). An interpersonal neurobiology of psychotherapy: The developing mind and the resolution of trauma. In M. F. Solomon & D. J. Siegel (eds), *Healing trauma: Attachment, mind, body, and brain* (pp. 1–56). New York, NY: W. W. Norton & Company.

Stamps, J. A. & Groothuis, T. G. G. (2010). Developmental perspectives on personality: Implications for ecological and evolutionary studies of individual differences. *Philosophical Transactions of the Royal Society*, *365*, 4029–4041.

Sterling, P. (2012). Allostasis: A model of predictive regulation. *Physiology and Behavior*, *106*, 5–15.

Suderman, M., McGowan, P. O., Sasaki, A., Huang, T. C. T., Hallett, M. T., Meaney, M. J. & Szyf, M. (2012). Conserved epigenetic sensitivity to early life experience in the rat and human hippocampus. *Proceedings of the National Academy of Sciences*, *109*, 17266–17272.

Talwar, S. (2007). Accessing traumatic memory through art-making: An art therapy trauma protocol (ATTP). *The Arts in Psychotherapy*, *34*, 22–35.

Tang, Y., Holzel, B. K. & Posner, M. I. (2015). The neuroscience of mindfulness meditation. *Nature Reviews Neuroscience*, *16*, 213–225.

Tripp, T. (2007). A short-term therapy approach to processing trauma: art therapy and bilateral stimulation. *Art Therapy: Journal of the American Art Therapy Association*, *24*(4), 176–183.

Warren, S. L., Bost, K. K., Roisman, G. I., Silton, R. L., Spielberg, J. M., Engels, A. S. & Heller, W. (2010). Effects of adult attachment and emotional distracters on brain mechanisms of cognitive control. *Psychological Science*, *21*(12), 1818–1826.

Yehuda, R. & LeDoux, J. (2007). Response variation following trauma: A translational neuroscience approach to understanding PTSD. *Neuron*, *56*, 19–32.

Part II

The British Forces

Chapter 4

Mental health treatment for serving UK military personnel

Jamie Hacker Hughes

Introduction

In order to be an effective component of this country's fighting services, psychological fitness is every bit as important as physical fitness. It is for this reason that the UK's military establishment has, as an important part of its composition, mental health services and resources, both uniformed and civilian, whose role it is to maintain the psychological fitness of our armed forces. This chapter will describe those services, beginning with their origins at the start of the last century. It will describe what their roles are in different parts of the system and at different phases of the deployment cycle, including aeromedical evacuation from war zones (sometimes referred to as 'operational theatres'), hospitalisation and rehabilitation.

A brief history of British military mental health services

The story of British military mental health services really begins with World War I, although before that time mental health problems were treated alongside physical health by medical and nursing assets deployed in this country's many overseas campaigns. We know, for example, that although neither of the following were campaigns in which the British participated, there were significant psychological problems recorded both in the One Hundred Years War (Hofer, 1934) and the American Civil War (Freemon, 2001). In the author's personal family history, for instance, there are fairly clear accounts of a relative suffering from post-traumatic stress after his involvement as an infantry soldier in the battle of Waterloo (personal communication).

It was at the beginning of World War I, however, that British military psychological services, and mental health services in general, began to develop. This was largely through the appointment of psychologist and medical doctor Charles Myers as Consultant Psychologist to the British Expeditionary Force in France (Jones, Fear & Wessely, 2007). These developments may also be attributed to the recruitment of, among others, another psychologist and medical doctor, William H. R. Rivers, into the Royal Army Medical Corps to work at the Slateford Military Hospital in Craiglockhart, Edinburgh with officers evacuated from the front in France because of shell shock. Many other civilian hospitals were converted into military psychiatric hospitals including the Maudsley Hospital in London, Maghull (now Ashworth high security hospital), Mill Hill and Northwood. While Myers treated huge numbers of shell shock cases in France, Rivers worked with Wilfred Owen and Siegfried Sassoon, and many others, in Craiglockhart (Barker, 2003).

At the end of World War I, these hospitals largely returned to civilian use and the psychologists, neurologists and psychiatrists who had been brought in were demobbed. Their successors were then called up for the effort in World War II during which pioneering work was carried out by people such as Foulkes, Bion and Rickman at Northfield and by the psychologist John Raven at Mill Hill (Shephard, 2003). Once again, however, at the end of World War II the majority of the mental health staff were released.

Development into the current structure

By the height of the Cold War in the 1960s, the UK had considerable medical assets across the world. There was a British military hospital in Hong Kong, another in Gibraltar, another in Cyprus and some four or five in Germany where the UK had a considerable presence. These included one in Berlin at a time when East Germany (the German Democratic Republic) and West Germany (the Federal Republic of Germany) were separated, and one had to travel through a corridor in order to reach Berlin from the west. In the UK, too, each service, the Royal Navy, Army and Royal Air Force, had several hospitals. But, as the Cold War came to a close and the British strength in Germany was gradually reduced, so these hospitals ultimately closed one after another.

Eventually, the only remaining overseas hospital was in Cyprus, the Princess Marina Hospital Akrotiri, while each Service retained only a few hospitals on mainland UK. These were based largely in the main Royal Naval bases, British Army garrisons and Royal Air Force stations, with a naval hospital at Haslar near Portsmouth; Army hospitals at Catterick, Aldershot and Woolwich; and an RAF hospital at Wroughton. Gradually though, these too were closed, and by the turn of the century all psychiatric services from all three Services were based at the Duchess of Kent's hospital in Catterick, Yorkshire, which, when all the other services moved out and the General Hospital closed, became the Duchess of Kent's Psychiatric Hospital. Up until that time Royal Hospital, Haslar had been the only provider of inpatient mental health services for the Royal Navy; Queen Elizabeth Military Hospital, Woolwich for the Army; and RAF Hospital, Wroughton for the RAF. It was at RAF Wroughton that the three hostages, Brian Keenan, John McCarthy and Terry Waite were all accommodated as they acclimatised following relief from captivity in Beirut (Keenan, 1991).

Defence medical services: the wider picture

Where were psychological and psychiatric services to be located if all the hospitals had closed? The answer is that, in exactly the same way as civilian community mental health teams (CMHTs) developed in parallel with the closure of the large Victorian asylums, the military developed a network of community-based outpatient facilities. These were initially named Departments of Community Psychiatry (DCP) but were soon renamed Departments of Community Mental Health (DCMH) in order to reflect the multi-professional nature of the services provided and the staff providing them.

The three levels of prevention

A very useful way of explaining the role of military mental health services in maintaining the psychological fitness of UK Armed Forces personnel is to use the model of primary, secondary and tertiary prevention (Leavell & Clark, 1979). The role of primary prevention in healthcare generally is to prevent distress, disorder or disease from occurring by promoting a healthy lifestyle. One example of this is the role of promoting exercise in order to prevent cardiac disease or the role of education about smoking as a strategy in preventing lung cancer. Secondary prevention, on the other hand, is about preventing the impact of health problems in situations where they are more likely to occur: vaccination is one example in areas where disease is known to be endemic. Third, tertiary prevention concerns the role of intervention or treatment to prevent a problem that has recently developed and been detected from becoming worse.

Primary prevention

One of the roles of military mental health services, therefore, is in primary mental health prevention. This is carried out in a number of ways including the production of leaflets and other forms of psychoeducation or mental health education, through video on CD or other media, or by mental health promotion activities at unit level, often through unit lectures or by running stands or displays at unit health fairs. Some good examples of this are the numerous videos that have been produced about drinking alcohol (much more of a concern in the military now than cigarette smoking, although that, too, used to be prominent until the 1980s). The *Grim Reaper* video, warning against the hazards of drinking and driving, is a good example of this (IVCA, 2008). There is also an increasing amount of material promoting good psychological and mental health, which is shown and distributed during basic training as well as at other times during the training and deployment cycle.

Mental health services are organised from the 20 or so DCMH that now exist in every major naval base, army garrison, or RAF station throughout the UK, in Cyprus, and, until recently, in Germany.

The majority of members of staff of the DCMH are mental health nurses (RMNs), usually cap badged to the service hosting the DCMH. Thus, for example, they are likely to belong to the Queen Alexandra's Royal Naval Nursing Service (QARNNS) if based in Plymouth, Portsmouth or Faslane; to the Queen Alexandra's Royal Army Nursing Corps (QARANC) if based in the army garrisons of Catterick, Colchester, Aldershot, Tidworth, Leuchars or Donnington; and to the Princess Mary's RAF Nursing Service (PMRAFNS) if on the bases of RAF Kinloss, RAF Marham or RAF Brize Norton. In addition to the basic mental health nursing training that all will have received, the nurses also receive first-level training in cognitive behavioural therapy (CBT) (Alford & Beck, 1997) and eye movement desensitisation and processing (EMDR) (Shapiro & Forrester, 1998) for trauma therapy. Not all of the nurses are uniformed, however; a considerable number are civilian, although many of these have served in military mental health nursing services previously.

In addition to mental health nurses, other members of the team are: social workers from the Defence Mental Health Social Work Service (all of whom are civilian); psychologists (clinical psychologists, counselling psychologists, forensic psychologists and neuropsychologists) from the Defence Healthcare Psychology Service (mostly civilian but with some new, if limited, uniformed capability in the army); psychiatrists (uniformed and civilian with, again, the majority of civilian psychiatrists having served previously).

Secondary prevention

However, not all mental health interventions are carried out by medical, mental health or psychological personnel, by any means. This is in line with the Overarching Review of Operational Stress Management (OROSM, Ministry of Defence, 2005), which places stress management firmly as a responsibility of the chain of command. Thus, a great deal of primary prevention activities are carried out by the single services and at unit level without the involvement of specialist mental health staff.

The same can be said for secondary prevention. Up until about the mid-1990s, if there was a major incident that required mental health intervention, the response would be some form of psychological or critical incident debriefing, almost inevitably conducted by a uniformed mental health nurse or community psychiatric nurse (CPN), which is still the most commonly used term, although the official term is now community mental health nurse (CMHN). However, as a result of a change of policy by the then Surgeon General (Surgeon General's Policy Letter (SGPL), 1995), the preferred and recommended intervention now is TRiM, or Trauma Risk Management (Jones, Roberts & Greenberg, 2003). TRiM is a peer-delivered intervention developed initially by the Royal Marines and Royal Navy in which peers are trained in assessing psychological risk after traumatic incidents and in referring on for treatment if this is necessary. It is now used throughout the British

Armed Forces, and beyond, with many welfare officers and senior non-commissioned officers having been trained to be TRiM assessors.

One of the advantages of the TRiM system is that it reduces the amount of stigma associated with psychological problems (Hacker Hughes & Neville, 2015; Sharp *et al.*, 2015). Traditionally, military personnel are wary of coming forward and discussing their psychological problems publicly because of the fear that the chain of command, friends and others will come to know, and that it will somehow affect their future career prospects. This concern is explored further in Chapter 5. One thing that has not always helped this has been the location of mental health teams in dedicated departments, although of course there are arguments either way. Nevertheless, because TRiM assessors are intended to be people at the same level in the organisation as the recipient (but from a different part of it), and since TRiM is very much seen as a part of standing routines, a lot of the stigma about having to see a mental health professional is eliminated.

Finally, the remaining and, indeed, one of the major secondary prevention tasks carried out by the mental health team involves the consultant psychiatrists who carry out assessments and make recommendations on people's suitability for recruitment or retention.

Tertiary prevention

Tertiary intervention refers to the early intervention that is carried out to prevent problems from worsening. This is the main work of military mental health services. It is estimated that one in four military personnel have some form of psychological problem (Goodwin *et al.*, 2015), and this is exactly the same proportion that is found in the main civilian population. The types of problems seen are very similar too. Thus, depression is often seen, just as it is in the civilian world, as being a common reaction to a number of life stressors. Anxiety problems of all sorts are seen too; panic disorder, general anxiety disorder, fears, phobias, obsessions and compulsions. Individuals can refer themselves for assessment and treatment but more commonly referrals are received via their medical officers.

It is thought that Post-Traumatic Stress Disorder (PTSD) is a common problem in military personnel. However, this is not the case to the extent that is generally imagined; at 7 per cent in combat troops (MacManus *et al.*, 2014) the rate is, in fact, not much higher than that in the civilian population, although the rate increases in reservists and veterans. Serious mental health problems, including so-called personality disorder, bipolar disorder and psychotic disorders are very uncommon indeed and most of these are also incompatible with continuing military service. Again, the majority of these will have been picked up during enlistment procedures.

Most of these problems, together with problems of alcohol misuse, sleeping problems, eating disorders, sexual dysfunction or other difficulties are very amenable to psychological interventions. Thus, most members of the military mental health team will have been trained in CBT and other therapies, together with EMDR for use in treating trauma. Both of these types of treatment are approved by the National Institute for Health and Care Excellence (NICE) for use in treatment of trauma, and the Ministry of Defence adheres closely to NICE guidelines (NICE, 2005).

CBT is a type of treatment whereby individuals learn to spot and correct their own unhelpful patterns of thoughts and behaviour. There are cognitive behavioural protocols for all sorts of psychological problems including the different types of anxiety problem, depression, eating and habit disorders, sleeping difficulties and many other problems.

PTSD may be treated by CBT, or an alternative approach is EMDR. This is a treatment that was developed specifically for trauma. Individuals are encouraged to process traumatic memories and to substitute maladaptive thoughts with more helpful and adaptive ones. Both of these treatments are carried out on an outpatient basis, usually with one or two sessions per week and sometimes accompanied by home-based assignments between sessions. The vast majority of these interventions have a successful outcome.

In the past, if a condition was deemed to be too severe to be treated on an outpatient basis then an admission would be arranged to one of the military hospitals. Gradually, and as described above, the availability of these facilities reduced until, when DKPH Catterick and Royal Hospital Haslar closed in 2003 and 2007 respectively, an alternative solution had to be found.

The Ministry of Defence solved the problem by placing a contract with a private inpatient mental health provider, the Priory Hospital group, such that if anyone needed admitting for inpatient treatment they were admitted to the nearest private inpatient facility closest to the base, with liaison being carried out between the hospital and the base by a military mental health liaison officer who made regular visits to ensure that treatment was going well and that all necessary post-discharge arrangements were being made.

When the contract lapsed, a consortium of NHS trusts put in place a network of NHS facilities around the country to which personnel are now admitted in case of need. This contract has been renewed and reinstated once already.

Operational mental health services

When a substantial force deploys on overseas operations, as has recently been the case in Afghanistan, Iraq and the Balkans, a field mental health team (FMHT) deploys with them. The team is usually composed entirely of mental health nurses during the stabilisation phase of operations, although military psychiatrists also deploy during the war-fighting phase.

When the operation has become stable, the team bases itself at the field hospital and from there conducts outreach clinics to the various outstations, patrol bases, forward operating bases and so on. The team are also involved in giving briefs as part of preparation for deployment, on arrival in theatre and as required. In addition, they maintain a low-level preventive mental health presence in theatre and also administer whatever mental health interventions are required in a variety of locations. These are usually sufficient to maintain people in the theatre. The field mental health teams operate according to the principles of PIE (proximity, immediacy, expectancy), which date back to World War I (Salmon, 1917), whereby if people require help, it is administered as close as possible to the person's base, as swiftly as possible, and with an expectation that the person will make a full recovery. If the person cannot be maintained in theatre then an aeromedical evacuation takes place.

Aeromedical evacuation

Sometimes, despite the best possible provision in theatre at the field hospital and by the FMHT, there is a need to evacuate the person back to the UK, for example in the case of severe mental illness. Military personnel are evacuated on exactly the same basis as those who are being evacuated for physical treatment and are assessed by the local DCMH on arrival back in the UK and, if necessary, are admitted for treatment. They are accompanied on the flight by Aeromed; military mental health nurses specially retrained in aeromedical evacuation.

Hospitalisation

As described above there are no longer any military mental health hospitals in existence in the UK since the last ones closed in 2003 and 2007. The contract for secondary military mental health provision is now with a consortium of NHS trusts that provide inpatient services around the UK with provision in units in Basingstoke, Stafford, Plymouth, Peterborough, Grantham and Aberdeen. NHS staff working on the wards often have a military background and close liaison takes place during the admission between the nearest DCMH and the hospital unit in question. The person is discharged as soon as possible, and, if necessary, outpatient treatment continues in the DCMH.

Operational decompression

In common with a number of other countries, the UK now operates a system of operational decompression (Hacker Hughes *et al.*, 2008) whereby, with the exception of mid-tour rest and recuperation leave (or R&R), people do not directly return to the UK from theatre, but do so via a 36-hour stay in Cyprus. As part of this, military mental health personnel are available to give post-tour briefings and to be on hand if necessary. The 36-hour stay-over follows a fixed pattern of briefings and then a period of rest and relaxation, either within camp or on the nearby beach, before continuing the journey to the UK the following day.

If injured personnel evacuated back to the UK require further surgical or other hospital treatment they are flown to the Royal Centre for Defence Medicine (RCDM), located within the Queen Elizabeth the Second (QE2) Hospital in Birmingham. There is a team of mental health nurses based there to support staff, patients and their families.

Specialist services and rehabilitation

Many of those discharged from the RCDM will go on to the Defence Medical Rehabilitation Centre (DMRC) at Headley Court in Surrey for further rehabilitation. There are numerous military mental health staff based at DMRC to carry out generalised mental health assessments and treatments as above, as well as in specialist roles such as neuropsychology, the treatment of pain and specialised input for those with genital injuries.

Support for reservists

While mobilised, reservists are entitled to treatment on exactly the same basis as regular personnel, whether in theatre or throughout the UK. Thus they might be seen by an FMHT or CMHT, aeromedically evacuated if required, assessed and treated and, if needed, admitted for secondary mental health care and treatment. A centre has also been set up, initially located at the Chilwell near Nottingham but now located at Colchester, so that any reservists who believe that they have psychological problems arising directly as a result of their deployment may be assessed, and if the need is found to exist, may be referred to a DCMH for outpatient treatment, or possibly for a secondary mental health care admission.

Discharge on mental health grounds

Within military regulations there are stipulations that people may, if required, be discharged on mental health grounds. Before this decision is made and before the person goes before a military medical board to ratify this decision they are almost always seen by a service consultant psychiatrist who will make this recommendation.

Transition into the civilian healthcare system

If the person is being discharged from the Services on mental health grounds then they will always be allocated a service social worker who will work with them before, through and after the discharge process in order to make sure that housing and welfare needs are met and so that the transition may be as successful as possible. In all other cases where people are leaving the military routinely, systems are evolving so as to connect them with the civilian healthcare system following their departure from the services so that this aspect of transition is optimally achieved.

Summary and conclusions

Because of the nature of the work of Britain's Armed Forces, a system of occupational mental health care, over and above that which would be provided by the NHS, has evolved. Initially hospital-based, in traditional wards, and with roots back to World War I and beyond, the bulk of provision is now community based so that people may be quickly referred, or self-refer, and be assessed and treated. The response times, as would be expected, compare extremely favourably to those of the civilian health service.

This psychological and mental health care extends through all phases of the deployment cycle, with mental health provision available in theatre, during decompression and throughout aeromedical evacuation. Military mental health staff are also based in the military managed ward at Birmingham and are an important component of provision at Headley Court. Mental health provision is there at all stages of the enlistment and career cycle too, with specialist provision being available for those who have to leave the Services on mental health grounds.

Wherever you are during your uniformed service, military mental health services are not far away in order to ensure that your psychological fitness is maintained in the same way as your physical fitness, because both are vital components of an effective fighting force.

References

Alford, B. A. & Beck, A. (1997). *The integrative power of cognitive therapy*. New York, NY: Guilford.

Barker, P. (2003). *Regeneration*. New York, NY: Plume.

Freemon, F. R. (2001). *Gangrene and glory: Medical care during the American Civil War*. Urbana, IL: University of Illinois Press.

Goodwin, L., Wessely, S., Hotopf, M., Jones, M., Greenberg, N., Rona, R. J. & Fear, N. T. (2015). Are common mental disorders more prevalent in the UK serving military population compared to the general working population? *Psychological Medicine*, *45*, 1881–1891.

Hacker Hughes, J. G. H., Earnshaw, N. M., Greenberg, N., Eldridge, R., Fear, N. T., French, C., Deahl, M. P. & Wessely, S. (2008). The use of psychological decompression in military operational environments. *Military Medicine*, *173*, 534.

Hacker Hughes, J. G. H. & Neville, M. (2015). *Battle against stigma*. London: Wellcome.

Hofer, J. (1934). Medical dissertation on nostalgia. (C. K. Anspach, Trans.). *Bulletin of the History of Medicine*, *2*, 376–391.

IVCA (2008). www.ivca.org/news/2008/winners-announced-at-this-year-s-ivca-awards.htmlb.

Jones, E., Fear, N. & Wessely, S. (2007). Shell shock and mild traumatic brain injury: A historical review. *American Journal of Psychiatry*, *164*, 1641–1645.

Jones, N., Roberts, P. & Greenberg, N. (2003). Peer-group risk assessment: A post-traumatic management strategy for hierarchical organizations. *Occupational Medicine*, *53*, 469–447.

Keenan, B. (1991). *An evil cradling*. London: Vintage.

Leavell, H. R. & Clark, E. G. (1979). *Preventive medicine for the doctor in his community* (3rd edn). Huntington, NY: Robert E. Krieger.

MacManus, D., Jones, N., Wessely, S., Fear, N. T., Jones, E. & Greenberg, N. (2014). The mental health of the UK Armed Forces in the 21st century: Resilience in the face of adversity. *Journal of the Royal Army Medical Corps*, *0*, 1–6.

Ministry of Defence (2005). *Overarching review of operational stress management*. London: Ministry of Defence.

NICE (2005). *Post-traumatic stress disorder: Management*. Retrieved from www.nice.org.uk/guidance/cg26?unlid=29678580220161295178.

Salmon, T. W. (1917). Care and treatment of mental diseases and war neuroses (shell shock) in the British army. *Mental Hygiene*, *1*, 509–547.

Shapiro, F. & Forrester, M. (1998). *EMDR: The breakthrough 'eye movement' therapy for overcoming anxiety, stress and trauma*. New York, NY: Sage.

Sharp, M. L., Fear, N. T., Rona, R. J., Wessely, S., Greenberg, N., Jones, N. & Goodwin, L. (2015). Stigma as a barrier to seeking health care among military personnel with mental health problems. *Epidemiologic Reviews*, *37*, 144–162.

Shephard, B. (2003). *A war of nerves: Soldiers and psychiatrists 1914–1944*. Cambridge, MA: Harvard University Press.

Surgeon General's Policy Letter (SGPL) 07/95 (1995). *The Prevention and Medical Screening of Stress Related Disorders in the Armed Forces*. London: UK Ministry of Defence.

Chapter 5

Military culture effects on mental health and help-seeking

Walter Busuttil

Introduction

The military population is unique. Many of the behaviours determining help-seeking and engagement in mental health treatment in serving personnel and veterans can be understood by virtue of cultural characteristics moulded by military training, experiences surrounding exposure to military operations and combat, and breaking of secure attachments when leaving the military. An understanding of these factors is essential to the clinical management of veterans' mental health.

Military law, culture and hierarchy

The military has a rigid disciplinary system led by hierarchical rank that is deeply ingrained during military training. Respect for the rank as a representative of the Queen is laid down clearly in Queen's Regulations (HMSO, 1975) and all within the military must conform to Military Law and obey orders immediately. Any divergence from this may lead to implementation of the military conduct code and disciplinary system. The disciplinary system is rigid and governed by Queen's Regulations and can result in loss of privileges, punishment or imprisonment in a military prison, accompanied by a dishonourable discharge from the military and loss of pension. These rules are in place in peacetime as well as during combat operations and war. The hierarchy is designed to ensure that during combat, personnel obey instructions without hesitation and carry out orders no matter what they might entail.

This context produces a tension between getting the job done and psychological decompensation. For centuries military organisations have recognised that certain short- and long-term behavioural states could be precipitated by the stress of battle. Terms such as 'shell shock', 'lack of moral fibre' and 'malingering' have been used to describe these behavioural changes seen after combat. Historically, this was thought to be caused by personality deficits, organic brain damage, a damaged heart or simply cowardice (Busuttil, 1995; Moran, 2007). Those at the top of the military hierarchy used disciplinary measures in dealing with individuals so affected. It has only recently been generally accepted by medical practitioners and psychologists that the causes for these observed conditions are primarily psychological (Merskey, 1991). Despite the evidence, people within military hierarchies have had difficulty accepting that (Post-Traumatic) Stress Reactions and Disorders suffered by military personnel are not the result of intrinsic character flaws but rather the direct result of exposure to traumatic insults. Traditionally, as far as the military system was concerned, these individuals were guilty of the ultimate heresy: the betrayal of the unspoken military codes of conduct – honour, glory, loyalty and blind obedience (Moran, 2007).

Joining the military

Attachment theory can explain some of the dynamics relating to joining (and leaving) the military. This psychological model describes the long- and short-term dynamics and the formation of interpersonal relationships and associated behaviours, their strength and security, and the effect on these relationships of threats of separation and actual separation. It was initially described in infants and children regarding their relation to caregivers (Bowlby, 1969) but has been extended to adult interpersonal relationships (Shaver & Hazan, 1988). The model describes predictable patterns of secure and insecure behaviours (which can amount to the development of mental illness in some) relating to separation from caregivers and from 'safe environments' in childhood and adulthood. Resultant psychological behaviours are predetermined by the quality of caregiving and security received in infancy and childhood (ibid.).

The military offers an exciting career, opportunity and a new start. Some are attracted to join to fulfil a childhood dream, a sense of adventure, financial security, trade training and to gain qualifications. Others join out of need: to escape poverty, poor housing, poor work prospects or deprivation. Some join to escape faulty attachments generated by childhood adversity, poor role models and poor caregiving. Others may find the adjustment too great to cope with, and a very small minority may develop brief psychiatric disturbances including time-limited stress-induced psychotic disorders, which lead to an early exit from the military. The majority of recruits join up when they are young (McManners, 1993). For many this will be the first experience of leaving home, employment and work. The lower limiting age for the Royal Air Force (RAF), Army and Royal Navy is 16 years. Joining at a young age is an important issue from a developmental perspective in that personality formation is still ongoing (Roth, Newman, Pelcovitz, van der Kolk & Mandel, 1997; van der Kolk, 1996) and is then shaped by military service and experiences including exposure to psychological trauma.

The majority joining the military 'family' make good attachments and adjust well. Most who join from difficult backgrounds adjust well and take advantage of their opportunities to grow and develop psychologically, and they will have little difficulty readjusting to civilian life when leaving. For the minority, however, their difficulties resurface once they lose the safety of their military family and make their transition back to civilian life; a period of vulnerability as far as their mental health is concerned (Andrews, Brewin, Philpott & Hejdenberg, 2009; Iversen *et al.*, 2005; Novaco, Cook & Sarason, 1983).

Total institution

The military has been described as a 'total institution' (Goffman, 1961). This means everything is done in a certain way and that one needs to conform to fit in. For young recruits, their sergeants become their parents and teach them how to look after themselves and their 'kit' in all terrains and circumstances. Mundane activities such as banking and cooking are sidelined and provided for by the military or simplified by readily available advice. Thus many skills useful in civilian life are unlearnt and are replaced by a whole new set of military skills. Many recruits conform and enter a world that may have a particular slang, humour, traditions, initiation rites and taboos, which are far removed from civilian life and vary between different arms of the military or different regiments. Many of these traditions psychologically protect the individual from the job in hand and can be seen as collective defence mechanisms with, for example, use of black humour and banter commonly seen among combatants during and after engagement with the enemy. This humour can also be active in clinic during assessment and psychological intervention and can be a barrier or confounding factor for the uninitiated mental health worker (McManners, 1993).

The military determines one's life, career prospects, housing, the schooling of children and job prospects of spouses. Families usually move camp and housing every few years and are expected to be flexible and responsive to the needs of the military above all else. Families can be separated from servicemen or women for significant periods of time, and under circumstances where deployment involves a military exercise or even deployment to war.

'Non-conformists' who do not fit in find life in the military difficult. Some may leave voluntarily, others may get into trouble and be discharged on disciplinary grounds, and others might be discharged prematurely from the military under the term 'temperamentally unsuited' – 'a square peg in a round hole' – rather than receive the medical or disciplinary discharge they may need. Leaving the military can also be a difficult time for 'conformists' who have served in the military for years. The transition to civilian life entails the breaking of military bonds and having to relearn how to function in a civilian world that is very different from the military.

Military life is for the vast majority extremely positive. For a small minority, however, it can cause long-term problems relating to the ability to get on the housing ladder, and reduce employability prospects. This may reinforce issues linked to institutionalisation, the development of mental illness through military service and adjustment to leaving the military environment, with the re-ignition of attachment issues stemming from primary (pre-military) families, or a combination of all of these factors. It should also be noted that underlying mental illness can make transition very difficult and, conversely, transition can precipitate mental illness.

Alcohol

The military has a propensity to reflect a *macho* culture. It promotes the use of alcohol to socialise with a widespread 'work hard, play hard' attitude. There is a reliance on social activities revolving around the excessive use of alcohol, especially in the young, and this is commonplace post-deployment, during combat and among peacekeepers (Andrews *et al.*, 2009; Fear *et al.*, 2010; Hooper *et al.*, 2008; Iversen *et al.*, 2007).

A recent epidemiological study conducted on an initial sample of 25,000 participants representing the 180,000 UK personnel who had deployed to Op Telic (Iraq) and Op Herrick (Afghanistan) demonstrated that 19.7 per cent suffered common mental disorders such as phobias and anxiety, with high rates of alcohol misuse at 13 per cent (Fear *et al.*, 2010). This study also identified Post-Traumatic Stress Disorder (PTSD) in 4 per cent of regular service personnel (for deployed personnel overall – this percentage was no greater than comparable non-deployed personnel); 5 per cent in Reservists (compared with non-deployed levels of PTSD at 1 per cent) and 6.9 per cent for front-line combat troops.

Rates of PTSD in British personnel are low compared to findings from US and Australian studies of military personnel deployed to Afghanistan and Iraq, with the latter having PTSD levels of up to 20 per cent among combat veterans in some studies. Longer-term alcohol disorders were thought to be less likely in US personnel compared with British personnel. Reasons cited for these discrepancies include cultural differences, with the UK population thought to be more likely to drink heavily than the US population, and the UK population being less likely to verbalise mental health problems compared to the US population (Fear *et al.*, 2010).

In a study with veteran samples in the UK, Andrews *et al.* (2009) claim that war pensions indicate that ex-services personnel are twice as likely to develop delayed-onset PTSD as civilians. Moreover, 36 per cent of veterans who suffer from delayed-onset PTSD developed it within the first year of leaving the services, suggesting that loss of military support structures and adjustment to civilian life increase vulnerability. Many who had developed delayed-onset PTSD reported major depressive disorders and alcohol abuse prior to PTSD onset, with several reporting that they drank alcohol to excess in order to cope with mental health symptoms while still in the military.

Military mental health services

The role of the military mental health service is twofold: attend to medical needs and fulfil an occupational health role. On appointment every service-man and woman is awarded a coded Medical Employment Standard (MES) incorporating physical and mental health. The MES retains medical confidentiality informing the Executive as to fitness to perform trade and deployability. Physical or mental ill health dictates downgrading of the MES, which might be temporary or permanent. This may lead to loss of the chance of further promotion in the trade, or even medical discharge from the armed forces. Service personnel are well aware of their MES and there seems to be a general reluctance to report sick.

Clinical audits indicate that 4.5 mental health referrals per 1,000 (or 5,000 new referrals) are received annually. Common clinical presentations include alcohol misuse, depression, anxiety and adjustment disorders with low rates of PTSD (4 per cent) in the military population (McMannus, 2009; Rona et al., 2007). Recent epidemiological studies have contradicted the long-held belief that military service reduces mental illness. These studies were conducted comparing the military population with the general population (Iversen et al., 2009). However, when compared with a working civilian population, the rates of common mental illness are about twice as high within the military population (Goodwin et al., 2014). Studies demonstrate that suicide rates in British servicemen and women are similar to civilian rates and are even lower in some age groups with one exception: suicide rates for ex-servicemen under 24 years old are two or three times higher than their civilian counterparts. Reasons for this are unclear, with suggested causes including pre-service vulnerability, trouble re-adjusting to civilian life and exposure to more adverse experiences (Kapur, White, Blatchley, Bray & Harrison, 2009).

Psychological effects of military training

Military training focuses on making individuals work as groups in efficient teams. The emphasis is on missions and objectives rather than individual needs or aims. The linking of small teams is the bedrock of any fighting unit in the British military. Teams that function well are such that all individuals are reliable, dependable and are known not to let the team down. The 'weakest link in the chain' is the individual who does not pull his or her weight. This might be the person one is depending on in a critical situation such as combat. Hence, those who are not perceived as working well as part of a team are likely to be sidelined or fail training, or if this is not the case, ostracised by their peers. The team has no place for those who might let the team down.

Military training shifts locus of control and coping styles, enabling soldiers to function in a more internal locus and problem-solve better (Mikulincer & Solomon, 1988). This enables soldiers to be self-sufficient, resilient and to cope better than otherwise with psychological threat (ibid.). While this works well for the military, it is not necessarily beneficial for individuals who are mentally unwell. This is because these same qualities that make soldiers self-sufficient make them poor at asking for help, especially if the help required is psychological. Soldiers and veterans try to solve their own problems and asking for help is a last resort (Hoge, Auchterlonie & Milliken, 2006). The qualities that make an individual a good soldier may also be the qualities that make that individual a bad patient.

Military operations and combat

Serving personnel are exposed to unique psychological trauma. Deployment to a war zone may be perceived as traumatic for some but not for all. Support personnel may never be exposed to direct danger although some may perceive that they are simply by being deployed to the war zone. Exposing these support personnel to mortaring or bombing (Stouffer, Suchman, DeVinney, Star & Williams, 1949) or potential exposure to Improvised Explosive Devices (IEDs) may prove overwhelming psychologically for some, especially for those who have not been trained for combat itself. Patrolling hostile neighbourhoods, for example as seen during peacekeeping operations in Northern Ireland, can be unnerving and traumatic for some, even when no actual traumatic incident has occurred.

Combat that involves 'eyeball-to-eyeball' killing has a greater potential to cause mental health difficulties, as this is the most intensive risk to life (Figley, 1978; Iversen *et al.*, 2008; Richardson, Frueh & Acierno, 2010). Precision killing at a distance, such as scenarios faced by drone operators or even snipers, can be protective as they involve the perception of being less likely to cause collateral damage to innocent bystanders, given that the mission can be carried out with surgical precision. Peacekeeping will involve the use of rules of engagement, which may sometimes mean that trained combatants become unable to intervene in the face of atrocities. This can cause serious psychological trauma. Body handling and repatriation of bodies also have great potential to cause psychological trauma, as can exposure to ethnic cleansing or the effects of this atrocity, including exhumation of bodies and dealing with victims of concentration camps (Cantor, 2005).

Moral injury

The perceived philosophical meaning related to the impact of trauma exposure was seen by Janoff-Bulman (1985) as an aetiological factor for PTSD. This was described as a 'shattering' of well-held positive values and assumptions about the world, oneself and others.

Incorporated within the diagnostic criteria for PTSD in the *Diagnostic Statistical Manual* (DSM) are concepts such as guilt relating to acts of commission and omission as well as negative cognitive change following trauma exposure (American Psychiatric Association, 2013). The relatively new concept of 'Moral Injury' expands on Janoff-Bulman's concepts and guilt symptoms and was reported by military medical staff and chaplains operating close to combat.

Combat soldiers are exposed to ethical, moral and religious challenges and dilemmas as part of their role, causing violations to deeply held beliefs (Litz *et al.*, 2009). Military operations and training emphasise mission aims with suppression of individual needs and beliefs. Moral Injury usually arises from cumulative events (ibid.). Litz *et al.*'s conceptual model highlights that individuals can become haunted by dissonance and internal conflicts. For example: those who have been engaged in 'carpet bombing', which may cause much collateral damage; trained combatants who may end up as mere bystanders to ongoing atrocities during peacekeeping operations or witness the aftermath of atrocities because rules of engagement do not allow intervention; combatants who find they are powerless when their own leaders and colleagues flaunt the rules of engagement. Perceived organisational or personal betrayal may also cause ethical dilemmas resulting in chronic feelings of guilt, anger and frustration. This does not lead to or amount to diagnosable mental illness, although in some, Moral Injury may form part of a mental illnesses presentation including PTSD. PTSD, it is argued, does not fully capture the effects of these dilemmas. Moral Injury is not a mental illness but is defined as

> perpetrating, failing to prevent, bearing witness to, or learning about acts that transgress deeply held moral beliefs and expectations. Theories of PTSD attempt to explain the long-term phenomenology of individuals harmed by others (and other unpredictable, uncontrollable, and threatening circumstances) and have not considered the potential harm produced by perpetration (and moral transgressions) in traumatic contexts.
>
> (Litz *et al.*, 2009, p. 700)

While it is argued that the diagnostic criteria for PTSD do not fully capture the effects of shattering ethical values, some of the manifestations of Moral Injury have been captured in the latest DSM (DSM-V). These include: shame and guilt; self-defeating behaviours such as self-harm or sabotaging of valued relationships; loss of direction and moral double binds. Litz *et al.* (2009) postulate that Moral Injury can take time to 'sink in' and state that a healthy mind that can empathise is a requirement for its development. They propose a model of intervention that includes generating an understanding of moral codes of conduct and emotions that are linked to this, and to the effect of shame on social behaviour and self-forgiveness. Access to spiritual help, working in conjunction with therapy interventions, is advised. A modified exposure treatment approach is also included.

Military families

Marital relations and family life can be adversely affected by the cycle of peacetime detachments, leading to the 'Intermittent Husband Syndrome' characterised by symptoms of anxiety, depression and sexual difficulties in spouses. This syndrome has been described in wives of oil rig workers, airline pilots and military personnel (Busuttil & Busuttil, 2001). Unhappy wives are a common factor determining premature retirement of husbands from the military (Iversen et al., 2005). More research is required on the impact of absent wives on husbands.

Service personnel deployed to war zones may be exposed to threat of death. Studies have shown that a variety of psychiatric symptoms can develop in spouses as a result of such forms of separation. These include anxiety, low mood, post-traumatic stress symptoms and dysfunctional behaviours such as alcohol misuse and risk-taking behaviours (Bey & Lange, 1974; Quinault, 1992). Separations that are threatened by death of the deployed serviceperson may generate a process of 'anticipatory grief' affecting those left behind (Eliot, 1946; Lindermann, 1944; Meyer, 1981; Teichman, Speigel & Teichman, 1978).

Anticipatory grief was initially described during the Second World War (Lindermann, 1944) as a process whereby a wife goes through all the stages of grief because she fears the loss of the life of her husband who has gone to war. It was also noted that where there are children, their mother's psychiatric symptoms and function will be mirrored in them (Busuttil & Busuttil, 2001). Ultimately, completion of the grieving process before the serviceperson returns home affects reunion and reintegration of the serviceperson within their marriage or partnership such that this might detrimentally affect the quality and longevity of the relationship.

Rates of domestic violence have been reported to increase when servicemen return from combat operations. For example, a study conducted with personnel who had deployed to Afghanistan and Iraq from the UK demonstrated that violent behaviour post-deployment was as high as 12.6 per cent. This was highly associated with pre-enlistment antisocial behaviour, holding a combat role, and being exposed to multiple traumatic events and mental health problems such as PTSD and alcohol misuse (MacManus et al., 2012).

In a further study, violent offending was three times higher in those under 30 years of age, compared to a similar non-military population. Men of lower rank and a history of pre-service violence were seen to be most at risk of violent offending, and being deployed in a combat role and witnessing traumatic events also increased the risk. Direct combat exposure increased the likelihood of committing a violent offence by 53 per cent. Increased frequency of exposure to traumatic events was also a risk factor in increasing the risk of violence. A diagnosis of PTSD, high levels of self-reported aggressive behaviour on return from deployment and alcohol misuse were found to be strong predictors of subsequent violent offending (MacManus et al., 2013).

Living with a serving military member or veteran suffering from PTSD and other mental health illnesses can be difficult on that person's spouse or partner and family members. British studies (e.g., Murphy, Palmer & Busuttil, 2016) demonstrate high levels of anxiety, depression, alcohol misuse disorders and PTSD – developing through a process of emotional contamination – in veterans' spouses and carers, mirroring studies conducted with US veterans (Williams, 1987).

Historically, British service families residing in family marital accommodation (married quarters) received Primary Care medical services through military General Practices. As the drawdown of medical services has progressed and as more service families have opted to live within civilian communities rather than in married quarters, Primary Care delivered by military Primary Care for service families has become increasingly rare. Education of civilian NHS Primary Care health workers relating to the uniqueness of military and veterans' family dynamics and requirements is badly needed.

Leaving the military

In the UK, a veteran is defined as someone who has service of one day in the military. Currently there are some 4.2 million veterans. Psychological symptoms might increase and intensify in some personnel while transitioning out of the military (Andrews *et al.*, 2009; Scheiner, 2008).

During the transition period, long-held attachments with a supportive 'military family' are broken. For some, the civilian setting may feel alien. For some who have families, this will be the first time that they will be afforded more time to be with them after having been freed from the cycle of deployments and exercises (Iversen *et al.*, 2005; van Staden *et al.*, 2007). This might lead to tension and difficulties. Most cope well with transition, which can be a challenging period.

Psychological problems are more likely if the mode of leaving the military is sudden or unplanned, or comes against the wishes of the individual. Some leave because they become subject to the disciplinary system and are ordered to leave under a label of SNLR – services no longer required. Some may be court-martialled and may have to spend time in the military prison based in Colchester before they then are discharged from the military, after having served a sentence, with a label of a 'dishonourable discharge'. Others may have successfully applied for premature voluntary retirement (PvR); perhaps this is because they have been unable to cope with underlying mental health symptoms. Overt alcohol misuse resulting in disciplinary charges may result in a discharge from the military on disciplinary grounds rather than for medical reasons. Redundancy has become more common recently with a reduction of regular forces. Some may suffer psychologically because of redundancy and having to leave the military against their wishes. Others might feel they are missing out on generous payouts, and yet others who remain in the military after the redundancy cycle has run its course are exposed to increased work-load and the potential of amplified occupational stress.

The majority of service leavers do well after leaving and are in full-time employment. Those with poor mental health during service are more likely to leave and have a greater chance of becoming unemployed after leaving (Iversen, *et al.*, 2005; Jones *et al.*, 2014). There is inconclusive evidence that mental illness rates remain static following transition to civilian life; a minority fare badly (Iversen *et al.*, 2005). Other studies demonstrate a deterioration following transition, with PTSD and alcohol disorders becoming more prevalent (Andrews *et al.*, 2009).

Homelessness and the Criminal Justice System

A study conducted at the University of York (Jones *et al.*, 2014) concluded that the number of homeless veterans in the UK is unknown. It is likely that many who are homeless suffer mental health difficulties. Estimates suggest that approximately 9–10 per cent of the homeless UK adult population were veterans in the mid-2000s. Single veterans appeared not to be over-represented in the datasets on housing need. Most of the research studies among single veterans over the last 20 years were unpublished small-scale qualitative studies; no UK peer-reviewed studies among single veterans and no UK evaluations of service provision for homeless veterans exist. Further, no UK national cohort studies of homeless single veterans or longitudinal studies providing insight into pathways into homelessness or long-term outcomes exist.

The reasons for homelessness among veterans have been assessed as being complex with no clear evidence that military service does, or does not, increase the risk of homelessness. Evidence exists that dedicated veteran charities and services provide 'fast-track' access to support and that take-up might be greater if services can provide military 'knowledge' or experience. The York study concluded that there is a lack of research into the discharge and interpretation of local authorities' obligations (under the Armed Forces Act, 2011) and homelessness legislation.

Within the Criminal Justice System, the true number of veterans is uncertain. Figures vary widely between 10 per cent of the prison population, or 8,500 individuals (National Probation Officers Association (NAPO), 2009), and 3 per cent, or 2,500 individuals (Department of Analytical Services and Advice (DASA), 2009). Veterans in prison have been said to represent the largest occupational group among offenders, with a further 12,500 veterans on parole or subject to probation supervision – meaning that in excess of 20,000 veterans are under correctional services control (Veterans in Prison Association (VIPA) 2010, as cited in Busuttil, 2012).

NAPO records that offences are commonly dominated by drug and alcohol misuse and propensity to violence, particularly domestic violence, and that many suffer depression and PTSD. These assertions are supported by academic studies (MacManus *et al.*, 2012, 2013). There is also said to be a higher rate of sex offending, which requires further investigation. The link between offending and mental health is not fully understood within the serving military and veteran population.

Initiatives to reduce the impact of transition from the military

Recently, attention has turned to transition from the military and its accompanying problems. The most significant initiatives are laid down in the Government's paper *Fighting Fit* (Murrison, 2010) and the Military Covenant that is part of the Armed Forces Act 2011. The Armed Forces Act is the legal basis for having an Armed Force. One of the main reasons why this Act was reviewed in 2011 was in order to include the Armed Forces Covenant; Section 2 makes provision for the Defence Secretary to make an annual report on progress towards the 'rebuilding' of the military covenant. The fields of healthcare, education and housing are specifically mentioned.

Fighting Fit, authored by Dr Andrew Murrison, MP (a Reservist and veteran Medical Officer himself), highlighted a cohesive approach to veterans' mental health nationally, including: (i) the setting up of a national helpline for veterans and their families delivered by the charity Combat Stress; (ii) better pre-release mental health screening prior to exiting the military and follow-up health surveillance for those who have left the military, enabling follow-up by Military mental health for six months post-discharge to ensure smooth transition to NHS clinical care; (iii) the provision of clinically supervised web chat rooms through the charity Big White Wall comprising on-line treatments and support. The setting up of NHS/Armed Forces Regional Networks (10 in NHS England and similar networks in the devolved countries of the UK) was aimed at ensuring that veterans are at no disadvantage when receiving healthcare from the NHS. Each network included a mental health sub-group, tasked with carrying out the recommendations of the *Fighting Fit* paper. Unfortunately, the models utilised were not standardised and consequently outcome and efficacy have been difficult to analyse. Some deliver mental health clinical interventions, others provide education and awareness training and signposting to statutory NHS services.

The Armed Forces Covenant sets out the relationship between the nation, the government and the armed forces, recognising that the whole nation has a moral obligation to members of the armed forces and their families, and establishing how they should expect to be treated. This sets down promises to service personnel and veterans that help will be given to those who have risked their lives in the service of freedom and the country, including priority treatment. However, priority on many occasions is not delivered by clinicians and services, as clinical need usually takes preference over veterans' priority. The covenant lays down two main principles. The first is that the armed forces community should not face disadvantages compared to other citizens in the provision of public and commercial services; the second is that special consideration is appropriate in some cases, especially for those who have given most, such as the injured and the bereaved, in relation to treatment they receive for statutory NHS services. The covenant exists to redress the disadvantages that the armed forces community may face in comparison to other citizens, and to recognise sacrifices made.

The Armed Forces Covenant is supported by the Community Covenant and the Corporate Covenant. The Community Covenant encourages local communities to support the armed forces community in their area and promote public understanding and awareness. The Corporate Covenant is a public pledge from businesses and other organisations that wish to demonstrate their support for the armed forces community. The effects of these initiatives need evaluation.

Help-seeking behaviours and Combat Stress

The UK Armed Forces recognise that there are barriers into mental healthcare. Interventions promoting education and help-seeking behaviour are described in Chapter 4 of this book. To date, there appears to be little evidence within the military that these measures have actually made a significant difference in rates of help-seeking among those still serving in the military. There is evidence, however, that these measures may have helped veterans to seek help earlier once they have left the military. Patterns of referral to Combat Stress, the national veterans' mental health charity, over the past 20 years have been the subject of a recent study (Murphy, Weijers, Palmer & Busuttil, 2015b). Over the study period, the time it took for participants to seek help after they left the military reduced by half. Numbers coming for help have accelerated, with an increase of 26 per cent between 2014 and 2015. Reasons for this may include: media coverage surrounding the Afghanistan and Iraq wars, which has highlighted the plight of veterans suffering from mental health disorders; increased education while in the military; better awareness among family members of mental health issues linked to military service; better knowledge and media promotion of the existence of the charity Combat Stress and the clinical and welfare services on offer (van Hoorn et al., 2013).

These findings suggest that there will be increasing numbers of veterans seeking support for mental health difficulties over the coming years (Murphy et al., 2015a). Veterans from the Afghanistan and Iraq wars present earlier compared to veterans from earlier conflicts. Those from Afghanistan and Iraq have presented an average of 2.2 and 4.8 years respectively after leaving the military in contrast to an average of 13.2 years for those veterans involved in all other conflicts and wars (Murphy et al., 2015b; van Hoorn et al., 2013). It must be noted, however, that clinical audits have shown that some 80 per cent of the most unwell group of help-seekers have been known by a mental health or primary care professional to have suffered from mental illness, indicating limited engagement in the NHS statutory services (Busuttil, 2010), although anecdotal evidence exists that if bespoke veteran mental health clinics are set up then veterans will engage and complete treatment (Dent-Brown, 2010).

Conclusion

When working with serving military personnel and military veterans, it is essential to have an understanding of military culture as this is what makes serving personnel and veterans what they are. Ultimately, the culture that moulds civilians into members of the armed forces and helps them achieve their objectives during military operations needs to be understood by those who aim to deliver treatment for mental illness.

These factors govern rates and patterns of help-seeking and engagement into treatment services and treatment completion and outcome. The mental health needs of veterans may not appear to be unique on the surface, however, in reality they are complex and these factors need to be accounted for by those who design clinical services and in their delivery.

References

American Psychiatric Association (2013). *Diagnostic and statistical manual of mental disorders* (5th edn). Washington, DC: APA.

Andrews, B., Brewin, C. R., Philpott, R. & Hejdenberg, J. (2009). Comparison of immediate-onset and delayed-onset posttraumatic stress disorder in military veterans. *Journal of Abnormal Psychology, 118,* 767–777.

Armed Forces Act (2011). Retrieved from www.legislation.gov.uk/ukpga/2011/18/contents.

Bey, D. R. & Lange, J. (1974). Waiting wives: Women under stress. *American Journal of Psychiatry, 131,* 283–286.

Bowlby, J. (1969). *Attachment and loss, Volume 1: Attachment.* New York, NY: Basic Books.

Busuttil, W. (1995) Interventions in postraumatic stress syndromes: Implications for military and emergency service organisations (Unpublished MPhil thesis). University of London, Royal Holloway and Bedford College, Egham.

Busuttil, W. (2010). Veterans' mental health: The role of the third sector charity Combat Stress: Expanding community outreach services and bespoke residential treatment programmes. *British Association for Counselling & Psychotherapy, 68,* 2–9.

Busuttil, W. (2012). Military veterans' mental health – the long-term post trauma support needs. In R. Hughes, A. Kinder & C. L. Cooper (eds) *International Handbook of Workplace Trauma Support* (pp. 458–474). Oxford: Wiley-Blackwell.

Busuttil, W. & Busuttil, A. M. C. (2001). Psychological effects on families subjected to enforced and prolonged separations generated under life-threatening situations. *Sexual and Relationship Therapy, 16,* 207–228.

Cantor, C. (2005). *Evolution and posttraumatic stress: Disorders of vigilance and defence.* London: Routledge.

Dent-Brown, K. (2010). *An evaluation of six community mental health pilots for veterans of the armed forces.* Retrieved from www.dent-brown.co.uk/ComVets%202010.

Department of Analytical Services and Advice (DASA) (2009). Retrieved from http://webarchive.nationalarchives.gov.uk/20140116142443/http:/www.dasa.mod.uk/publications/UK-defence-statistics-compendium/2009/2009.pdf.

Eliot, T. D. (1946). War bereavements and their recovery. *Marriage and Family Living, 8,* 1–8.

Fear, N. T., Jones, M., Murphy, D., Hull, L., Iversen, A. C., Coker, B., Machell, L., Sundin, J., Woodhead, C., Jones, N., Greenburg, N., Landau, S., Dandeker, C., Rona, R. J., Hotopf, M. & Wessely, S. (2010). What are the consequences of deployment to Iraq and Afghanistan on the mental health of the UK Armed Forces? A cohort study. *The Lancet, 375,* 1783–1797.

Figley, C. R. (1978). *Stress disorders among Vietnam veterans: Theory, research and treatment.* New York, NY: Brunner/Mazel.

Goffman, E. (1961). *Asylums: Essays on the social situation of mental patients and other inmates.* Garden City: Anchor Books.

Goodwin, L., Wessely, S., Hotopf, M., Jones, M., Greenberg, N., Rona, R. J. & Fear, N. T. (2014). Are common mental disorders more prevalent in the UK serving military compared to the general working population? *Psychological Medicine, 45,* 1881–1891.

HMSO (1975). *The Queen's regulations for the Army.* Retrieved from www.gov.uk/government/uploads/system/uploads/attachment_data/file/433769/QR_Army.pdf.

Hoge, C. W., Auchterlonie, J. L. & Milliken, C. S. (2006). Mental health problems, use of mental health services, and attrition from military service after returning from deployment to Iraq or Afghanistan. *Journal of the American Medical Association, 295,* 1023–1032.

Hooper, R., Rona, R. J., Jones, M., Fear, N. T., Hull, L. & Wessely, S. (2008). Cigarette and alcohol use in the UK Armed Forces and their association with combat exposures: A prospective study. *Addictive Behaviours, 33,* 1067–1071.

Iversen, A., Dyson, C., Smith, N., Greenberg, N., Walwyn, R., Unwin, C., Hull, L., Hotopf, M., Dandeker, C., Ross, J. & Wessely, S. (2005). 'Goodbye and good luck': The mental health needs and treatment experiences of British ex-service personnel. *British Journal of Psychiatry, 186,* 480–486.

Iversen, A., Fear, N. T., Ehlers, A., Hacker Hughes, J., Hull, L., Earnshaw, M. N., Greenberg, N., Rona, R., Wessely, S. & Hotopf, M. (2008). Risk factors for post-traumatic stress disorder among UK Armed Forces personnel. *Psychological Medicine, 38,* 511–522.

Iversen, A., van Staden, L., Hacker Hughes, J., Browne, T., Hull, L., Hall, J., Greenberg, N., Rona, R. J., Hotopf, S., Wessely, M. & Fear, N. T. (2009). The prevalence of common mental disorders and PTSD in the UK military: using data from a clinical interview-based study. *BMC Psychiatry, 9,* 68.

Iversen, A., Waterdrinker, A., Fear, N. T., Greenberg, N., Barker, C., Hotopf, M., Hull, L. & Wesseley, S. (2007). Factors associated with heavy alcohol consumption in the UK Armed Forces: Data from a health survey of Gulf, Bosnia and era veterans. *Military Medicine, 172,* 956–961.

Janoff-Bulman, R. (1985). The aftermath of victimisation: rebuilding shattered assumptions. In C. R. Figley (ed.), *Trauma and its wake: The study and treatment of post-traumatic stress disorder* (Vol. 1) (pp. 15–35). New York, NY: Brunner Mazel.

Jones, A., Quilgars, D., O'Malley, L., Rhodes, D., Bevan, M. & Pleace, N. (2014). *Meeting the housing and support needs of single veterans in Great Britain*. York: University of York.

Kapur, N., White, D., Blatchley, N., Bray, I. & Harrison, K. (2009). Suicide after leaving the UK Armed Forces a cohort study. *PLoS Medicine*, *6*, 1–09.

Lindermann, E. (1944). Symptomatology and management of acute grief. *American Journal of Psychiatry*, *101*, 141–148.

Litz, B. T., Stein, N., Delaney E., Lebowitz, L., Nash, W. P., Silva. C. & Maguen, S. (2009). Moral injury and moral repair in war veterans: A preliminary model and intervention strategy. *Clinical Psychology Review*, *29*, 695–706.

McManners, H. (1993) *The scars of war*. London: HarperCollins.

MacManus, D., Dean, K., Al Bakir, M., Iversen, A. C., Hull, L., Fahy, T., Wessely, S. & Fear, N. T. (2012). Violent behaviour in UK military personnel returning home after deployment. *Psychological Medicine*, *42*, 1663–73.

MacManus, D., Dean, K., Jones, M., Rona, R. J., Greenberg, N., Hull, L., Fahy, T., Wessely, S. & Fear, N. T. (2013). Violent offending by UK military personnel deployed to Iraq and Afghanistan: A data linkage cohort study. *The Lancet*, *381*, 907–17.

McMannus, F. B. (2009, 2–5 June). *Accessing defence psychiatric services: Clinical pathways to the NHS and other agencies on leaving the military*. Paper presented at Veterans' Mental Health: Annual Meeting of the Royal College of Psychiatrists. Liverpool: BT Convention Centre.

Merskey, H. (1991). Shellshock. In G. E. Berrios & H. Freeman (eds), *150 years of British psychiatry 1841–1991* (pp. 245–267). London: Gaskell.

Meyer, E. J. (1981). Uber das Trauren um Vermisste. Eine blfragung von ehefrauen, knidern und greschwistern [Mourning the missing: A survey of wives, children and brothers and sisters]. *Archives fur Psychiatrie und Nervenkrankheiten*, *230*, 91–101.

Mikulincer, M. & Solomon, Z. (1988). Attributional style and combat-related Post-Traumatic Stress Disorder. *Journal of Abnormal Psychology*, *3*, 308–313.

Moran, (Lord) (2007). *The anatomy of courage: The classic WWI study of the psychological effects of war*. London: Constable & Robinson.

Murphy, D., Hodgman, G., Carson, C., Spencer-Harper, L., Hinton, M., Wessely, S. & Busuttil, W. (2015a). Mental health and functional impairment outcomes following a six-week intensive treatment programme for UK military veterans with Post-Traumatic Stress Disorder (PTSD): A naturalistic study to explore dropout and health outcomes at follow-up. *BMJ Open*, *5*, e007051.

Murphy, D., Palmer, E. & Busuttil, W. (2016). Mental health difficulties and help-seeking beliefs within a sample of female partners of UK veterans diagnosed with Post-Traumatic Stress Disorder. *Journal of Clinical Medicine*, *5*, 68.

Murphy, D., Weijers, B., Palmer, E. & Busuttil, W. (2015b). Exploring patterns in referrals to Combat Stress for UK veterans with mental health difficulties between 1994 and 2014. *International Journal of Emergency Mental Health*, *17*, 652–658.

Murrison, A. (2010). *Fighting fit: A mental health plan for servicemen and veterans*. Retrieved from www.gov.uk/government/uploads/system/uploads/attachment_data/file/27375/20101006_mental_health_Report.pdf.

NAPO (2009). *Armed forces and the Criminal Justice System*. Retrieved from www.revolving-doors.org.uk/documents/napo-report-on-ex-forces-in-criminal-justice-systems/.

Novaco, R., Cook, T. M. & Sarason, I. G. (1983). Military recruit training: An arena for stress-coping skills. In D. Mietchenbaum & M. E. Jaremko (eds), *Stress reduction and prevention* (pp. 377–417). New York, NY: Plenum Press.

Quinault, W. (1992). A study of the incidence of stress and anxiety related health problems among the dependants of RAF personnel during the Gulf War. *Nursing Practice, 5*, 12–23.

Richardson, L. K., Frueh, B. C. & Acierno, R. (2010). Prevalence estimates of combat-related PTSD: A critical review. *Australian and New Zealand Journal of Psychiatry, 44*, 4–19.

Rona, R. J., Fear, N. T., Hull, L., Greenberg, N., Earnshaw, H., Hotopf, M. & Wessely, S. (2007). Mental health consequences of overstretch in the UK Armed Forces: First phase of a cohort study. *British Medical Journal, 335*, 571–572.

Roth. S., Newman, E., Pelcovitz, D., van der Kolk, B. A. & Mandel, F. (1997). Complex PTSD in victims exposed to sexual and physical abuse: Results from the DSM-IV field trial for post-trauamtic stress disorder. *Journal of Traumatic Stress, 10*, 539–556.

Scheiner, N. S. (2008). Not 'at ease': UK veterans' perceptions of the level of understanding of their psychological difficulties shown by the National Health Service (Unpublished doctoral thesis). City University, London.

Shaver, P. R. & Hazan, C. (1988). A biased overview of the study of love. *Journal of Social and Personality Relationships, 5*, 473–501.

Stouffer, S. A., Suchman, E. A., DeVinney, L. C., Star, S. A. & Williams, R. M. (1949). *The American soldier: Adjustment during army life* (Vol. 1). Princeton, NJ: Princeton University Press.

Teichman, Y., Speigel, Y. & Teichman, M. (1978). Crisis intervention with families of servicemen. *American Journal of Community Psychology, 6*, 315–325.

van der Kolk, B. A. (1996). Trauma and memory. In B. A. van der Kolk, A. McFarlane & L. Weisaeth (eds), *Traumatic stress* (pp. 279–302). New York, NY: Guilford.

van Hoorn, L. A., Jones, N., Busuttil, W., Fear, N. T., Wessely, S., Hunt, E. & Greenberg, N. (2013). Iraq and Afghanistan veteran presentations to Combat Stress, since 2003. *Occupational Psychiatry, 63*, 238–241.

van Staden, L., Fear, N. T., Iversen, A., French, C. E., Dandeker, C. & Wessely, S. (2007). Transition back into civilian life: A study of personnel leaving the U.K. armed forces via 'military prison'. *Military Medicine, 172*, 925–930.

Williams, C. M. (1987). *Post-traumatic stress disorders: A handbook for clinicians.* Cincinnati, OH: Disabled American Veterans.

Chapter 6

Coming home

Robert Bieber, Michael Sterba and Christine Sterba

The veterans' mental health charity Combat Stress, as it is now known, was established in 1919 in response to veterans' traumatic experiences during World War I. A brief history of the early years of Combat Stress is described here in order to provide a framework for exploring mental health provision for veterans. In addition, an account from a veteran and his wife provides invaluable insight into the processes of injury and recovery, and the 'ripple effect' that can affect families and communities. As such, one family's history is offered to represent the stories of many others.

Combat Stress: the early years

A consequence of mass demobilisation following the 1918 Armistice was the release into the general population of large numbers of traumatised veterans whose plight could not be ignored. Such had been the nature of World War I that even the smallest hamlet was not exempt from bereavement and the visible presence of the blind and the maimed, both in body and mind. The Lunacy Act 1916 remained the definitive statutory provision under which, in appropriate circumstances, traumatised veterans would be incarcerated in asylums. Furthermore, the Vagrancy Acts for the provision of workhouses were not repealed until 1930, so those unable to provide for themselves, whatever the state of their minds, were at risk of being reduced to beggardom and housed in local workhouses. Many veterans in reduced circumstances and suffering from the emotional wounds of their Crown service found themselves in such institutions.

By the end of the war, there was increasing recognition of many of the problems underlying trauma resulting from military experience. However, because so many of the issues were culturally unacceptable for both the civilian population and military authorities alike, much of what had been learned was filed away in the dusty recesses of the Ministry of War. The Southborough Committee Enquiry into 'Shell Shock' was appointed to investigate how best to avoid an epidemic following World War I. It reported in 1922, but left unanswered the dilemma of how to compensate deserving servicemen without rewarding those for whom psychological breakdown offered an escape from military duty. In an effort to prevent future epidemics, the Committee's report prescribed the elimination of 'shell shock' from official terminology and also that no case of psycho-neurosis or of mental breakdown should be classified as a battle casualty (War Office Committee of Enquiry into 'Shell-Shock', 1922). In so doing, Southborough set the seal on a changing environment whereby the lessons of World War I had to be substantially relearned during the course of World War II.

Confident in the success of the campaign for the female vote, a group of women, some of whom are believed to have been suffragettes, determined to secure help for veterans traumatised by their wartime experiences. They met under the chairmanship of a Mrs Waddingham in London on 1 November 1918. This was no radical, working-class pressure group, but a reformist charity established by a group of middle-class women determined to apply their energies to the relief of traumatised veterans of the Great War. Various well-known persons were invited to be vice presidents; those accepting included Eleanor, Viscountess Gort, and Lady Asquith. The association chose to call itself the 'Fellowship of Reconstruction and Welfare Bureau for Ex-Servicemen of all Ranks and Services, their Wives, Widows and Relatives, including the Merchant Marine'.

Before the end of 1918, the Fellowship was supporting both the concrete block and freshwater fish industries as employers for severely disabled veterans, recognising the importance of securing not only treatment, but training and employment. Within three months of its founding, the Fellowship had resolved to make provision for those cases of acute mental breakdown that would otherwise have been committed to asylums, including those suffering from General Paralysis of the Insane for whom Homes for the Dying were sought. By July 1919, the Fellowship changed its name to the 'Ex-Services Welfare Society', and this it remained for more than 35 years.

The Mental Treatment Amendment Act of 1919 provided that all ex-servicemen confined in mental war hospitals under martial law should be committed, without right of appeal, to asylums operated under the auspices of the Ministry of Pensions. The Society was vehemently opposed to this measure and planned to organise large meetings to protest both against the Act and for the provision of sanatoria other than under lunacy control and administration. At the outset, the campaign achieved a large measure of public sympathy, but this proved to be a double-edged sword when it was seen that, in challenging the Ministry, the Society was in effect accusing Ministers of the Crown of failing in their duty to veterans. As a result of this, the Society had to suffer the humiliation of withdrawal of Royal patronage.

By now, the Society had progressed into the specific realms of care, and it considered establishing a residential home for the treatment of cases of nervous and mental breakdown. A lease of Chartfield, in Putney (a house capable of accommodating 13 patients), was acquired. By this time, the support of the Veterans Association (VA) had been secured to assist in funding, although there was an ulterior motive; it was thought that the prestige of the VA would help especially in fundraising campaigns. The Society benefitted from the support of Earl Haig who, by late 1919, offered the co-operation of the Association of Voluntary Agencies for the benefit of veterans and their dependants. At this moment, the Society, having a substantial waiting list, could only support those with the most acute neurasthenia.

The intention was to introduce, in microcosm, a series of industries suitable to be carried on by those with mental disability. Such employment was regarded as one of the most promising routes by which traumatised veterans could be reintegrated into society. In due course, the Society acquired Thermega Limited; manufacturers of electrically heated textile appliances. Consideration was given to open manufacturing facilities in Manchester and Glasgow, with residential hostels adjoining the factories. The Society acquired additional patents; the principal manufacture being electrically warmed blankets. The venture was a resounding success, employing on average some hundreds of veterans at any one time, each earning £4 a week. Over the life of the employment scheme, nearly 8,000 veterans found employment.

By 1920, despite acute financial stringency, the number of homes run by the Society was growing, as was its co-operation with the Pensions Ministry. As a result, Latchmere Military Hospital was referring patients to Chartfield; notwithstanding that the Ministry's stated preference was for country houses with exclusive fronts, providing gardening, workshops, tennis and other recreational pursuits; a level of facilities that the Society could not hope to match.

The appointment of the first Consultant Psychiatrist was in 1922. Also by this point, the Society was actively supporting the manifesto of the National Council for Lunacy Reform. In due time, the Council was to experience significant funding problems, which the Society attempted to assuage by increasing financial subventions, mixing a charitable objective with overt politico/social campaigning; something that today would be subject to severe questioning by the Charity Commission.

Throughout the interwar years, the Society would financially support families of traumatised veterans and provide Christmas gifts and other support whenever necessary for veterans within the prison system, as well as those incarcerated in lunatic asylums; a scheme of things that rapidly expanded after 1945. Figure 6.1 is taken from the Society's Annual Review 1949 and shows scenes from the 'Curative Centre', Tyrwhitt House. Veterans are engaged in various pursuits: tending pigs, box-making and exercise, which gives a sense of the treatment focus at the time.

By the early years of the new millennium, the Society had cared for more than 100,000 veterans and their families, from all the confrontations in which UK Forces had been engaged, including Northern Ireland, Iraq and Afghanistan. Today, the Society is known as Combat Stress. Treatment has

Scenes from our Curative Centre, Tyrwhitt House

Figure 6.1 Scenes from our Curative Centre, Tyrwhitt House (1949)
Source: with kind permission of Combat Stress.

moved a long way from the respite model of previous years, and includes a range of therapies, including art therapy and occupational therapy.

Of the veterans who have sought the Society's help over the past century, most have found their stories too painful to record. An exception is that of Mike Sterba, a medic and Falklands War veteran. In the story that follows, he offers his experience to support other veterans and raise awareness of the nature and value of work currently being undertaken at Combat Stress.

The veteran's tale

I was a career soldier from 1962 to 1988. It is not necessary to provide a detailed account of my entire career, but I think it is important to give a brief résumé illustrating the training and experience that I had and yet was still left vulnerable to psychological injury.

In 1962, aged 15, I enlisted into the Royal Army Medical Corps (RAMC) as a junior entrant, and underwent further education and military studies. In 1965, when I 'passed out' from the college, I elected to train as an operating theatre technician. Co-incidentally, at that time there was a serious shortage of parachute trained medics, so I volunteered for selection for service with the Airborne Forces.

The Parachute Selection Course is one of the most demanding courses that the Army offers, both physically and psychologically. The attrition rate is very high, the aim of the course being to test you to the limits and beyond. About 10–15 per cent of candidates manage to complete the course. I passed, went to the RAF Parachute Training School, got my wings, red beret and the 25 per cent pay rise that went with the qualification!

I joined 23 Parachute Field Ambulance, which had two six-man surgical teams as part of its formation. These six men jumped with enough kit on their collective backs to perform 10 major surgical cases with the capability of an additional 50 cases when the 'heavy drop' Land Rover arrived.

The next three years were taken up with theatre training and the following 14 years with tours of duty in exotic parts of the world where surgical teams were required in support of the various military commitments of Her Majesty's Government.

In 1966 I met my future wife, Christine, who had just completed her nursing training and was preparing to go off to war-torn Biafra as a civilian nurse. I did all I could to dissuade her from going. Finally, in a moment of madness, I said 'Don't go to the war – marry me instead'. We married in May 1967 and soon started a family.

By 1982 I had served in North Africa, the Middle East, Far East, Europe and, of course, Northern Ireland. I was well acquainted with all types of surgery, both routine and traumatic: gunshot wounds, bomb blast injuries, parachuting accidents, road traffic accidents, even obstetrics and gynaecology. The point is that I was a senior Warrant Officer with 17 years' experience in traumatology. I was extremely physically fit, I had an interesting and fulfilling job and a very happy home life.

In April 1982, the Falkland Islands were invaded by Argentinean forces and a huge Task Force was deployed to the South Atlantic to re-take the islands and return them to British sovereignty. Our surgical and support teams were deployed with the 2nd Battalion, The Parachute Regiment. We embarked on the requisitioned North Sea car ferry MV Norland and put to sea from Portsmouth on 5 April 1982. All that training jumping out of aircraft and then we go to war on a car ferry!

We were at sea for several weeks. We trained hard, made medical plans, refined skills and made modifications to suit the situation. We practised emergency drills and as we sailed further south, watched the Russian planes circling overhead and lived with the threat of submarine attack.

On 21 May (our wedding anniversary), under the cover of darkness, the Task Force entered San Carlos Water, East Falkland and the assault landings took place at Ajax Bay. We secured the only building at Ajax Bay, a disused slaughterhouse, together with a large cold store that we rapidly set about converting into an advanced surgical centre. We also had, co-located with us, the huge stockpile of ammunition and military hardware for the task ahead, so there was no question of marking the building with the Red Cross to indicate that we were a medical unit.

By daylight, we started to come under attack from Argentinean war planes, though they were concentrating mainly on the shipping. This continued relentlessly for three days. There was a constant flow of casualties, mainly bomb blast, shrapnel and burns.

After five days, we came under surprise air attack. Suddenly enemy aircraft appeared from nowhere and dropped four 1,000-pound bombs on to our cold store complex. As it happened, we were working on Argentinean prisoners of war at the time. I had just taken a break to grab a cup of tea and turned aside to pick up some mail that had arrived from UK. The next thing I knew, I was being screwed into the ground, a terrific noise, and I was fighting for breath as my lungs filled up with hot air and gases. I cannot tell how long it was before I regained my senses – seconds/minutes? It was immediately clear that the end of the building where I had been standing only moments before had taken a direct hit, as too, had the ammunition stockpile.

The five lads I had been speaking to only seconds before the blast were reduced to body parts. I briefly helped with the sorting of the wounded and then went back into the cold store, dreading what I might find inside.

Miraculously, the other bombs had failed to detonate. Two were lodged in the wall and roof of the building and the third had passed clean through, over the heads of the casualties awaiting evacuation, and landed on the beach. The surgical teams were shaken but it was business as usual.

Clearly, we now had a serious problem trying to run an advanced surgical centre with two unexploded bombs in situ. We had little alternative but to stay where we were and hope the bombs were not armed with delayed time fuses. The bomb disposal technicians said it was too dangerous to touch so we just had to live with it. I think our training just took over. We cleared our casualties and evacuated as many as possible. Ironically, one of these casualties was the pilot who had dropped the bombs on us and who had been shot down by a missile battery of Royal Marines. He was distraught to witness the havoc that his attack had caused.

Then we had to make ready to support the planned assault on Darwin and Goose Green. This had been delayed 24 hours because of our situation, as casualties were expected. It did prove to be an extremely difficult and hard-won battle, costing the lives of 17 of our very best men, with 35 wounded. Colonel 'H' Jones, our Commanding Officer, was killed and awarded the Victoria Cross posthumously. The wounded were treated and evacuated and our dead were placed in a mass grave at Ajax Bay – a very sad day (Figure 6.2).

The action continued, and a few days later I was deployed forward with one surgical team to Teal Inlet to support the action by 3 Para on Mount Longdon. We were pushed to our limits with casualties arriving in ever-increasing numbers – usually on the trailers of tractors driven by members of the local community. We formed ourselves into two three-man teams so

Figure 6.2 The Paras Bury their Dead (1982)
Source: with kind permission of *Soldier Magazine*.

while our surgeon was dealing with the complex, life-threatening injuries, I
was getting on with the debridement of gunshot and shrapnel wounds. I have
nightmares about it to this day.

We received news that the Royal Fleet Auxiliary Ship, Sir Galahad, on
which the main reinforcement element of our own 16 Field Ambulance,
together with the Welsh Guards, were embarked, had been bombed and was
on fire; also that a dear friend and second in command of the unit, had been
killed along with two of our young Combat Medical Technicians. The battle
moved on and we arrived into Port Stanley. The Argentinean forces surren-
dered. We took over the local hospital for a few days to allow the civilian staff
to get back on their feet and the job was done.

As we were the first 'in', we were the first 'out'. We returned to the UK,
landing at RAF Brize Norton in Oxfordshire to an incredible welcome – quite
unexpected and quite overwhelming really. We just wanted to see our families
and go home. We returned to our various units for a few days to replenish
our equipment, took a week's leave, and life continued much as normal. Or as
normal as life can be in the Airborne Forces.

In early 1984, I started to experience bouts of extreme fatigue, sudden
surges of adrenaline, intense anxiety, loss of concentration and appalling

nightmares, and just felt very unwell. I had been commissioned and took up an appointment as a Company Officer at the very college where my career had begun in 1962. By the summer of 1984 I was still experiencing the symptoms and started to feel very emotional, suddenly crying for no apparent reason. The feeling of total fatigue would overwhelm me. I developed a viral pneumonia and was seriously ill. I made a slow recovery, though the fatigue and tearfulness remained. I sought help from my unit Medical Officer and was referred to the Command Psychiatrist. I was given a short course of medication and made a good recovery. It seemed to me in those days that a visit to the psychiatrist was almost certainly a career stopper. Your Commanding Officer would automatically be informed and when it came to your annual confidential report your 'strengths and weaknesses' were duly noted. Appointments for the 'Shrink' were channelled through the Skin Clinic. I suppose, on reflection, it was done to save embarrassment.

By 1986 I was back with 23 Para Field Ambulance. In the latter part of that year I had a recurrence of the symptoms and felt very depressed. I found problems concentrating on the most routine matters and attending briefings, and was not really taking anything in. Again I saw the Medical Officer and again I was prescribed a course of anti-depressants.

In 1987 I was sent to the Sudan as an advisor/trainer to the Sudanese Medical Services. I found myself in a very difficult situation. I was now involved in a civil war of 20 years' and a famine of five years' duration, and with no clear terms of reference. I was only there for three months but it seemed like a lifetime. I returned feeling terrible and felt that I could no longer continue with service life. I wrote a letter resigning my commission and, a year later, in September 1988, I left the service, much to the surprise of my colleagues and senior officers.

By this time we had a house in Kent and we later bought a small fruit farm with a shop and tea rooms. Together we built up a successful 'pick-your-own' fruit business. My bouts of illness came and went, lasting about six months or so. I would see my GP, who was kind and sympathetic; see a psychiatrist; take whatever medication was prescribed; get better; then relapse again. The bad times were getting longer and the well periods shorter. By Christmas of 1998 I was at rock bottom. I had not slept properly for months. I had total fatigue and felt suicidal. My personal hygiene suffered; complete loss of self-esteem; and my alcohol intake increased as a form of 'self-medication' – a dangerous course to take. There was an occasion on the farm when I first experienced dissociation. I did not know where I was nor have any recall of events that day. It was clear that I could not continue farming and we made the decision to sell the farm and the business.

A close friend and Falklands comrade heard I was unwell and came to visit. He was quick to see the marked change in my health and, after a discussion with my wife, contacted a welfare officer at Combat Stress. The welfare officer made a home visit and within a few days initiated the paperwork to commence my assessment, diagnosis and possible treatment. I was seen by their consultant psychiatrist in June 1999 and made my first visit to Tyrwhitt House, the society's treatment centre in Surrey, for a two-week period of assessment.

At long last I had contact with people who truly understood what I was going through and the opportunity to talk it through. There, too, I had the realisation and relief that others also suffered – I was not alone.

Later that year I went before a Medical Board and was diagnosed with chronic PTSD attributable to my service. I have been going to Tyrwhitt House for treatment since January 2000 and have made steady progress. The treatment programme of individual and group sessions I have undergone means that I am now able to implement coping strategies when symptoms arise. I have good insight into my illness and take full responsibility for it, but it is a comfort to know that Combat Stress is there to help when it threatens to overwhelm me/us again. The tragedy is that it took 18 years for us to find it.

The following text is an account from my wife Christine's perspective.

The wife's tale

The 35th anniversary of the Liberation of the Falkland Islands is fast approaching and, no doubt, the media will re-visit it with relish. For those of us closely involved with the conflict, either directly or indirectly, the story has never gone away. In recent years, books, films and plays, and through them the general public, have shown an increasing awareness of the mind-shattering effect that war has on all who are involved. We watch TV documentaries featuring an old soldier reminiscing. At some point he stops, he cannot go on, he weeps, we weep with him – it is good television. What we do not appreciate is that this is the tip of the iceberg. There are memories, buried underneath, too painful to discuss, to even think about, which visit him with debilitating regularity, and will continue to do so for the rest of his life.

In his groundbreaking book, *The Anatomy of Courage*, Lord Moran – a man with wide experience as a Medical Officer in World War I – maintained that the practice of sending battle-hardened soldiers in to 'stiffen the line' was a myth as, he proposed, each man had a ration of resilience that was finite and so could be used up (Moran, 1945).

My husband was a soldier in the Falklands Conflict, so I can talk with some authority on how the experience affected him and his family and friends. But, in essence, his story is no different from any other soldier's, from any war. We see it still, from the Balkans, from Iraq, from Afghanistan, and we will see it soon from anywhere else that young British servicemen and women are sent by their country in the line of duty.

When he went to the Falklands War, my husband had more than 17 years' experience of trauma and the sight of blown-off limbs and gunshot wounds was not new to him. Mike was Duty Officer when the emergency developed. He was a Warrant Officer in charge of a Field Surgical Team. It was our 15th wedding anniversary when they landed on the beach at Ajax Bay. I am a nurse and was working at Farnham Hospital at the time. I remember bursting into tears, to everyone's consternation, when a bunch of red roses from Mike was delivered. I had not realised how much strain I had been under, sitting at home watching the wall-to-wall coverage on TV. The phrase, 'There's a white flag flying over Stanley', heard first in a news flash announcing the end of the war, can still bring a lump to my throat and tears to my eyes all these years later.

They came home amid much excitement, had a spot of leave and went back to work. What happens after all that adrenaline? Mike got a bit 'scratchy', easily upset with patches of dark brooding. About 18 months after he came home he got 'the flu', went to bed, refused all help, developed viral pneumonia and was quite ill in hospital. With hindsight, the depression and complete lack of energy was the first sign of PTSD. The viral pneumonia had been caused by the bomb blast.

Sudan took another hefty page out of Mike's ration book. His bouts of illness came and went. When he was well, he was his old confident self, full of energy and ideas, adaptable and inventive, fun to be with. Gradually, the well periods became shorter and the periods of illness longer and more intense. At its worst, he is completely debilitated by it – this ghastly thing that happens to my wonderful husband turning him into a stranger who is completely devoid of energy, deeply depressed and suicidal. This man who makes things and can fix almost anything cannot work out how to change a plug or think how to write a letter.

When in its throes, he struggles desperately to appear normal to visitors but does not want to see anybody or do anything. He is completely apathetic, bone tired and suffers crucifying, bed-drenching nightmares. Even with complete insight it is hard to be patient with this for such a long time, never knowing when, or even if, there will be a recovery. Nagging achieves nothing and a flare-up of temper cannot be risked with someone hovering on the verge of suicide. It is a very lonely place to be.

Through the kind offices of an old comrade, Mike was visited by a welfare officer from Combat Stress. He was assessed by their psychiatrist, a Falklands veteran himself, and went for his first visit to their treatment centre. There they have trained staff providing specialised treatment. Most important of all, there are other men and women, of all ages and from all sorts of conflict and at all stages of the illness, who 'know'. This realisation that they are not alone with this problem is a wonderful revelation. They talk to each other, support and laugh with each other and, gradually, that sense of self-worth and self-esteem creeps back. That is the quiet magic of Tyrwhitt House. The formal group sessions are enormously helpful, unlocking long closed doors to give insight and awareness, allowing the informal groups to lift the spirit.

With the benefit of hindsight and long experience, I can spot the effects of PTSD with some degree of efficiency. I read ancient Greek and see it in Homer's descriptions of some of the heroes of the Trojan War (Homer, Fagles & Knox, 1990). I can see that my Grandfather was deeply affected by his service in World War I. He had been a professional soldier, recalled to the colours to go to France with the Expeditionary Force. Wounded and captured on the bitter retreat from Mons in the early months of the war, he was a prisoner in very poor conditions until May 1916, when he was so debilitated that he was one of a number of wounded prisoners sent to Switzerland after an agreement between Britain and Germany. He spoke only of how welcoming the Swiss were and of the wonder of sitting in a glass-bottomed boat on the lake under the Jungfrau. One can only imagine how that must have felt after all that he had been through. He witnessed many atrocities and was physically disabled, weighing only five stone when he arrived in Switzerland.

After the war, he suffered periods of deep withdrawal, sometimes disappearing from the family home. They always knew where to find him. He would be with an old comrade who lived in a town a hundred miles away, but who had fought and been captured with him, was in Switzerland with him, and with whom he need make no pretences and who would make no judgements. There is a particular bond between people who have been in combat together.

My father too, returning from six years in RAF Bomber Command, had his own stress and demons to cope with. With the highest attrition rate, proportionally, of the war, the survivors of Bomber Command mourned more friends lost than most, but he was haunted by the enemy civilian women and children killed, particularly in the firestorm of the Hamburg Raid in which he took part, albeit alongside another 1,000 bombers. He was a popular, gregarious man but tended to drink too much; his coping strategy. He returned from war to find he had no job, despite enlisting from a reserved occupation, and had an eight-year-old son who had been 'brought up by women'. The fact that he had been in a similar position with his own father in 1918 did nothing to ease the difficult relationship they had, my brother resentful of this strange man taking over his mother's attention and father feeling the need to assert his authority. This must have been played out in many households all over the land. As recognised at the establishment of Combat Stress, the effects of war ripple out from individual veterans and can affect whole families.

Having now been close to three generations of servicemen who have suffered the effects of combat, I can see that they all had a deep longing for 'nice' things – nature in all its beauty, poetry, music or art. With depleted reserves of resilience, these resources seem to replenish and restore. Through creativity, veterans seem to be able to tap into pleasure that brings relief. It is a delight to see how many veterans now take up painting for pleasure. This is distinct from art therapy, which unlocks different doors through creativity, which will be explored in subsequent chapters of this book.

Conclusion

It is now almost a century since Combat Stress was founded. During that time, the British Armed Forces have been involved in many major military campaigns and peacekeeping operations across the world. For those who sustained psychological injuries associated with service, there have been gradual advances in understanding and treatment. It is inevitable that there will be psychological as well as physical casualties of war as 'rations of resilience' (Moran, 1945) are expended. Coming home from war is not the end of the battle for some but just the beginning. Consequently, there has also been growing recognition of the effects of trauma on families in recent years.

Combat Stress has provided a place where no pretence is necessary – where comrades old and new have been able to be with others who 'know' and realise that they are not the only one affected by service experiences. Professional treatment and welfare support combined with the benefits of informal peer interaction has helped many veterans over the past century. Clearly the treatment offered at Combat Stress is as vital and relevant today as it ever was.

References

Homer, Fagles, R. (translator) & Knox, B. (introduction and notes) (1990). *The Iliad.* New York, NY: Penguin Books.

Moran, (Lord) (1945). *The anatomy of courage: The classic WWI study of the psychological effects of war.* London: Constable & Robinson.

War Office Committee of Enquiry into 'Shell Shock' (1922). *Southborough Report.* London: HMSO.

Part III

Current approaches to art therapy with veterans in the UK

Chapter 7

An adaptive art therapy model for working with traumatised veterans

Janice Lobban, Kirsty Mackay, Mark Redgrave and Sandya Rajagopal

Introduction

Art therapy does not offer a general purpose fit to suit all situations. Traditionally, art therapy training has been psychodynamically informed, but increasingly art therapists are also looking to alternative frames of reference to provide theoretical models that match the complexities of specific contexts. There seems to be general recognition that art therapy practice exists on a continuum, whereby the approach taken is based on clients' needs and the context (Hogan, 2009; King, 2016). A flexible approach combined with continued learning is enabling the profession to evolve as new discoveries are made, for example, in the field of neuroscience.

This chapter provides a detailed description of the adaptive art therapy model that has evolved at the UK veterans' mental health charity Combat Stress to meet the specific needs of traumatised veterans. Mindful of military culture and shaped by the framework of short-stay admissions, this model is informed by the neurobiological underpinnings of Post-Traumatic Stress Disorder (PTSD) and mechanisms of art therapy.

The biological basis of PTSD and recovery was presented in Chapter 3, linking processes with the lived experiences of the veteran author of Chapter 2. The account reveals how traumatic events produce enduring psychological and physiological changes (Herman, 1992). Furthermore, a key neuro-imaging study using PET scans (Rauch *et al.*, 1996) has revealed how the brain's language centres close down in high arousal states as all energy becomes focused on survival. This study showed that Broca's area of the left brain hemisphere, which translates subjective experiences into speech, decreases in activity during high arousal, whereas there is an increase in right brain activity associated with emotions and visual imagery.

Van der Kolk used the term 'speechless terror' (1994) to describe how trauma is not captured in words. This affects the subsequent ability to create a narrative to process the experience. The brain's danger recognition centre, the amygdala, within the limbic system, becomes sensitised to threat and goes on permanent high alert, so the stress response becomes self-sustaining with each false alarm re-enforcing the cycle (van der Kolk, 1994). The aim of trauma therapy then is to assist the client to move away from the past and to engage in the present. This involves contextualising the experience and processing the material so that it can be stored in the narrative memory system (Tripp, 2016; van der Kolk, 2014).

PTSD can be viewed as a disorder of information processing, storage and retrieval. Traumatic memories follow different neural pathways to normal memories. They are disconnected, unassimilated, non-verbal and inflexible. Dual Representation Theory (Brewin, Dalgleish & Joseph, 1996; Brewin, Gregory, Lipton & Burgess, 2010) offers a useful model for understanding the process, proposing two distinct memory systems. The theory outlines how normal, explicit memories are declarative and part of a verbally accessible memory system (VAM) that manifests as coherent words and stories. These memories are fluid, updateable and linked with other memories in the context of a whole life story. They happened in the past and are usually recalled on purpose. Traumatic memories however, are non-declarative and part of a situationally accessible memory system (SAM) that can be triggered automatically by trauma-related cues. They are primarily non-verbal fragments of sensory information that are frozen in time. Isolated and standalone, trauma memories are re-experienced as happening in the present (Brewin, 2001; Brewin *et al.*, 1996; Lobban, 2014).

Art making engages mind and body, which can enable access of implicitly stored material while simultaneously remaining focused in the present. Art therapy involves communication between brain hemispheres whereby non-verbal right brain sensations are combined with verbal left brain thought processes (Chapman, 2014; Tripp, 2016). In this way, it can help clients to express experiences that are difficult to put into words, thereby assisting the processing and integration of trauma memories (Collie, Backos, Malchiodi & Spiegel, 2006; Klorer, 2005; Nanda, Gaydos, Hathorn & Watkins, 2010). Referring to the work of Lieberman (2007), Hass-Cohen (2008) describes how translating feelings into words enables 'cortical shifts' and emotional regulation, so by talking about images created and 'labelling feelings', clients can 'reduce amygdala activity and increase prefrontal activation' (p. 36). By externalising inner processes in the tangible form of an image, the thinking distance created can be used directly or over time to resolve conflict and find meaning.

According to van der Kolk (2014), the use of imagination is crucial after trauma as it opens up new opportunities and 'the capacity for playfulness and creativity' (p. 205). He emphasises that healing from trauma does not just mean symptom reduction, but a widening of perspective beyond current circumstances whereby other possibilities might be imagined, and adaptive information incorporated. Art therapy provides a way of using focused imagination to explore different ways of being that can help to break fixed, unhelpful patterns of perception and behaviour.

In the US, a number of art therapy trauma treatment approaches have been developed. They include the Expressive Therapies Continuum (Lusebrink

& Hinz, 2016); the art therapy relational neuroscience approach (ATR-N) (Hass-Cohen, 2008); Chapman's (2014) right hemispheric art therapy model; Intensive Trauma Therapy (ITT) (Tinnin & Gantt, 2014); art therapy trauma protocol (ATTP) (Talwar, 2007); and bilateral art therapy (McNamee, 2006; Tripp, 2007, 2016). In the UK, the Children's Accelerated Trauma Treatment (CATT) designed by Carly Raby provides an integrated model for working with children who have experienced trauma. Each model offers an invaluable framework of understanding, often informed by neuroscience, and with specific techniques to guide progress. Overall, there is sense of proactive learning, discovery, structuring and sharing of ideas across the profession. As well as finding new ways of assisting recovery in clients, this movement of ideas is promoting the potential of art therapy as an evolving profession in the field of trauma. We offer an account of the approach we have found useful for traumatised veterans. It is hoped that this text will add to the growing body of knowledge in this area.

Art therapy within a wider treatment programme

Art therapy is part of all the short-stay, inpatient treatment programmes at Combat Stress. Currently the programmes run for two or six weeks according to the focus. The six-week Intensive PTSD Treatment Programme (ITP) has National Specialised Commissioning from the Department of Health. The two-week admissions include Stabilisation and Anger Management programmes. Art therapy is seen as an insight-orientated psychological treatment that combines creative expression with reflective analysis in order to promote change. It provides an alternative approach to the cognitive behavioural therapy (CBT) model that provides the treatment framework at Combat Stress. With different treatment objectives from psycho-educational groups and activities-based rehabilitation, art therapy offers a space for symbolic self-expression and facilitates symbolic thinking. This creates a thinking distance from felt experience that can increase distress tolerance and enable meaning-making. When there are shared treatment objectives with other therapies, such as assisting emotion regulation, art therapy offers a different route.

It can be helpful to consider 'top-down', mind to body cognitive, and 'bottom-up', body to mind somatic, approaches to emotion regulation and information processing (Hass-Cohen, 2008; McRae, Misra, Prasad, Pereira & Gross, 2012). The top-down approach taken by CBT includes strategies like cognitive reappraisal to regulate affect and sensory experience, whereas the involuntary, mainly unconscious bottom-up approach focuses on the visceral 'felt-sense, and the instinctive responses as they are mediated through the brain stem and move upward to impact the limbic and cortical areas of the brain' (Heller & Lapierre, 2012, p. 17). Body sensations and changes in sensorimotor experience 'are used to support self-regulation'; resultantly, 'Meaning and understanding emerge' from these new experiences (Ogden, Minton & Pain, 2006, p. 166).

Through the channels of symbols and sensations, the art therapy process facilitates the emergence of non-verbal, felt experience through image-making. The image can then be deciphered using cognitive evaluation to understand the personal meaning. For veterans who struggle to articulate experiences verbally or find it hard to concentrate for any length of time, or whose thought processes might be disorganised or tangential, art therapy provides a form of self-expression that does not rely on clarity of thought. Once the image is created, it can be left and returned to over time as it acts as a tangible snapshot of internal experience. Its personal interpretation might change as perceptions develop and further insights are gained. In this way, art therapy can combine top-down and bottom-up approaches.

Art therapy can help veterans who might be avoidant to prepare for trauma-focused CBT by beginning to open-up through image-making and increased self-awareness. Gradually, distress tolerance can be increased through image-making while veterans simultaneously gain a sense of control over the material that emerges. For some veterans, art therapy alone is the treatment of choice as it facilitates engagement and helps to access unconscious material that increases understanding.

In the US, brain-imaging data is used in art therapy research. For instance, Belkofer and Konopka (2008) made a study of art activity and brain patterns using an electroencephalograph (EEG). Patterns of electrical brain activity were measured before and after art-making and revealed higher frequencies of brain activity in the temporal lobes after art-making. The temporal lobes play an important role in experiencing a sense of meaning, connections to a higher power and deep feelings of peace (Belkofer & Konopka, 2008). These findings therefore suggest that art therapy holds the potential for accessing a deeper level of self-awareness.

Through an EEG it is possible to see how people experience the world, i.e. some people process visually whereas others are primarily auditory processors, or perhaps a combination of both. Konopka (personal communication, 5 June 2016) suggests that if a visual processor is brought into talking therapy it is a mismatch. He has developed a person-centred model whereby the brain of subjects is mapped out and evaluated using an EEG. Abilities and vulnerabilities can be identified. An understanding of how subjects perceive the world is gained, which can then be followed up by psychological assessment based on the EEG results. This builds a formulation to guide which therapies would be most appropriate for that individual (L. Konopka, personal communication, 5 June 2016; Lobban, 2016).

A phasic model with the use of themes

In her key text on trauma, Herman (1992) outlines three stages of recovery, each with their own task. The first phase focuses on establishing safety; the second concerns remembrance and mourning; and the third phase is about reconnecting with life. Other writers have further broken down and elaborated on the phases (Chu, 1998; Steele, van der Hart & Nijenhuis, 2005). Herman highlights that the process of recovery is not a one-way journey, as progress can oscillate. PTSD can be a chronic, relapsing condition whereby issues re-emerge and need to be re-visited and re-integrated. It is necessary for treatment to match the appropriate phase of recovery. The phasic model is in keeping with the National Institute for Health and Care Excellence (NICE) recommendations, and practice guidelines from the International Society of Traumatic Stress Studies (Foa, Keane, Friedman & Cohen, 2009). In the UK, NICE provides evidence-based treatment guidance and sets standards of care. NICE recommends that non-directive therapy 'should not routinely be offered to people who present with chronic PTSD' (NICE, 2005, 1.9.2.6). Hence a themed, phasic approach to art therapy has been developed at Combat Stress. A non-directive approach presents the risk of clients going too far too soon in therapy, particularly in a short-stay admission when clients might apply self-directed pressure to have made significant change by the end of the stay.

It is often the case that veterans arrive at the first art therapy group in a state of nervous arousal. An open-ended, non-directive invitation to use the art materials may only serve to heighten that anxiety, acting as a trigger to a nervous system already sensitised by trauma. Structure in the form of a theme can be experienced as enabling, offering a secure handle to creatively seize. As one veteran put it using a military term, a theme offers a 'base point' to work from. Veterans are given the freedom of self-expression but boundaries are placed around the sharing of explicit trauma material in the groups. This is a general ground rule in the groups as trauma material could have a detrimental effect on others going through treatment.

The art therapy groups comprise 45 minutes of image-making followed by 30 minutes of reflective discussion. Providing an escape route from the intensity of image-making is an essential component of the initial boundary setting. Making allowance for affect regulation may include permitting such withdrawals as leaving the art room for a break, turning over a picture or having the option of not discussing artwork openly in the group.

Once the therapeutic boundaries have been established, a theme is set by the art therapist, helping veterans to focus their attention. The implementation of other directives, such as creating photomontages with images taken from the Internet, may also have a reduced threat factor, as they place less demand on skill and subsequently are less likely to result in performance anxiety. Creating collages also engages the veteran in a simple, repetitive action integral to that particular task (i.e. cutting out and gluing), itself inducing calm. From a neurological perspective, it has been demonstrated that simple, repetitive art therapy activities can help to reduce situationally accessible memory system intrusions (King-West & Hass-Cohen, 2008).

Overall, veterans seem to find the use of themes helpful and rise to the challenge presented. Some struggle to know where to start and might need further discussion with the facilitators to find a potentially fruitful interpretation to explore. Fear of failure might cause concern for some veterans about responding to the theme in the 'right way', so they might show their artwork to the facilitators prior to the reflective discussion seeking validation. Facilitators are mindful of the challenges involved with making a creative response, and so emphasise that there is no right or wrong way to respond to the theme. The overarching message of the art therapy groups is that perceptions are based on many factors, including our belief system, values and life experiences, so the way we interpret the theme can help with self-understanding. Veterans can be very self-judgemental, setting the bar at perfectionism. This can present a barrier to engagement or lead to frustration. If this can be tolerated and brought to the reflective group discussion, vital material can be explored.

Occasionally, veterans are keen to find out the theme for the next art therapy group, although the majority say that they do not want to know in advance. In general, veterans are encouraged to wait until that session to find out, to enable a spontaneous response. With time to plan, important material might be censored. Prior knowledge of the theme would take away the opportunity of increasing anxiety tolerance. However, there are situations when prior knowledge and preparation might enable highly anxious veterans to participate, so as always, a flexible approach is taken.

Participants might find it difficult to tolerate silence and sometimes request background music during the image-making time. Silence can accentuate awareness of tinnitus or fuel anxiety for some. Gentle music can help to promote calmness and reduce tension. However, musical preference varies and what might be enjoyable and calming for one person might not be for another. Memories can also be strongly associated with pieces of music and might stimulate an emotional connection for some people. The act of listening to music together can help to unite a group, generating conversation and creating a relaxed environment. In general, the option of background music is discussed during the setting of ground rules. Some veterans might choose to listen to their own music through headphones.

Sometimes veterans want to be part of the group but do not want to engage creatively with the theme or the materials. They might say that they are not in the mood or are having a bad day following a difficult session. Although encouraged to engage in some way, for instance by looking through a box of photomontage materials, pressure is not applied to create something. Avoidance symptoms are part of PTSD and are worked with as part of treatment. Despite non-engagement in image-making, veterans might stay for the whole group and witness the process in others. They might respond to their fellow veterans' images, and participate in the group reflections. Viewing images together can be inclusive for those unable or unwilling to create. Frequently they are able to relate to the work of others, which might mirror their own experience. The discussion can provide encouragement and validation through mutual sharing.

Facilitators consider various factors when a selecting a relevant group theme. A theme might be a word, an image, an object or a range of images presented to the group without a clear direction, thereby leaving it open to interpretation. For example, a photograph of Japanese knotweed breaking through tarmac might be seen as an image of resilience and hope for some, or as PTSD symptoms ruining life like a voracious weed by others. Different interpretations can result in thought-provoking, enriching discussions that can challenge perceptions. Themes need to be in tune with the focus of concurrent therapy groups, to enable extension and consolidation of learning. In this way, art therapy groups provide a space for reflection but also somewhere to express and make sense of current feelings. Veterans might need to vent frustrations or anxiety, or express sadness that has been masked by anger. Art therapy can also provide veterans with a space to work with group dynamics and to share how they are managing both collectively and individually.

Phase 1

In the first week of the ITP, anxiety may be running high, so choosing a theme that generates calmness is essential. In trauma approaches, a safe-place visualisation is usually established early on in therapy to assist with the management of the strong feelings and sensations that become stirred while reliving the trauma. The art therapy group provides a way of symbolically capturing this resource and connecting with associated pleasant sensations. This can be a helpful introduction to art therapy for those new to this treatment, and who might have approached the session with apprehension. Veterans may also decide to take these calming images away with them after the first session and use them as a focal point for affect regulation throughout the six-week programme as and when needed.

Themes within themes can be explored. For example, veterans might identify an underlying thread of isolation or avoidance seen in each other's imagery in response to the theme of 'safe place', or a resonance of hypervigilance across the theme of 'perceptions'. A further challenge to matching a relevant theme to a particular group of veterans is the frequent mix of those new to treatment with veterans who might have attended art therapy many times. It is helpful to have a range of ideas to draw from. Table 7.1 illustrates themes commonly used, broken down into categories related to the phasic treatment approach.

Individual art therapy sessions are also paced, even though the veteran might be keen to offload the trauma. Art therapy can access distressing thoughts, feelings and sensations very quickly, which could be destabilising rather than helpful. Sufficient preparation needs to be in place before veterans are ready to process trauma safely. Pacing material fosters a sense of

Table 7.1 A selection of commonly used art therapy themes

Art therapy themes

Phase 1: Stabilisation

Balance	Hope	Inspiration	Calming/safe place
Hidden treasure	Comfort	Simplicity	Strengths
Gardens	Essentials	Rhythms	Energy

Phase 2: Insight-orientation

Puzzles	Patterns	Perceptions	Mind and body
Book cover	Mirror	Eclipse	Inner landscape
Trees	The elements	Ways of seeing	Clouds
Movement	Contrasts	Crossroads	Bridges
Road to recovery	Compass	Jigsaw	Game of life
The mask I wear	Inside/outside	Invisible wound	Identity
My finest hour	Blocks/barriers	Ladders	Hopes, fears,
Reflections	Understanding	Discoveries	expectations
Folklore/symbols	Connections	Letting go	Journeys
Rituals	Respect	Recipe for	A moment in time
Tolerance	Transformation	recovery	Change
Terrain	Seasons	Growth	Mending

Phase 3: Reintegration

Movement	Evolution	Enlightenment	Gateway
Tool box	Achievements	Acceptance	Encouragement
Making it happen	Visualising success	Resources	I can

control, which is essential to recovery (Herman, 1992). It is important to assist clients to stay within a 'window of tolerance' (Siegel, 1999), or optimal level of distress tolerance. If emotional arousal becomes too intense, the client might become overwhelmed by hyper-arousal and intrusive symptoms. Alternatively, the client could dissociate or become hypo-aroused (become numb and shut down). Therapy needs to be within the mid-arousal range in order to be effective (Lanius, Paulsen & Corrigan, 2014). Regaining a sense of control by balancing the effects of post-traumatic stress symptoms with affect management techniques is crucial to the stabilisation treatment phase and can foster hope and optimism. Plate 7.1 represents the theme of 'balance' and uses the ancient symbol of a 'Green Man', which is often associated with renewal, to represent a veteran's psychological transition from death to life.

Phase 2

Within individual art therapy sessions, the second phase of treatment provides the opportunity to target specific traumatic experiences. However, in a group context, themes are provided to draw attention to the secondary features of trauma such as isolation, avoidance, anger, relationship difficulties or grief, with the aim of increasing insight and promoting change. Themes to elicit these issues can be wide-ranging. Some are designed to provide the opportunity for remembrance and mourning so might be 'change' or 'letting go'. In reality, veterans might be in different stages of recovery, so sensitivity is needed on the part of the facilitator to ensure that a broad enough theme is set to encompass all situations. During the introduction on that day, the facilitators might suggest that some participants may prefer to use the session for self-resourcing rather than furthering self-discovery. Sometimes veterans might prefer to 'ground' themselves with the materials at hand, or return to their 'calming place'.

Themes that have proved relevant during the second phase include 'my journey'. A journey might be represented visually as a road, river, timeline or spiral. This theme is aimed at helping veterans contextualize their experiences and explore movement towards change and growth. Figure 7.1 represents one veteran's journey or evolution of recovery, moving away from stigma towards dignity, gradually opening up along the way. An alternative theme might be 'bridge'. A bridge is a powerful symbol to represent movement from one state of being to another. The theme of 'transformation' also provides an opportunity to express what it is like to go through the process of change. Figure 7.2 gives a sense of the remoulding necessary in the reworking of traumatic

Figure 7.1 Evolution of Recovery

Figure 7.2 Transformation

Figure 7.3 Broken Links

memories, here using the symbols of 'swords into ploughshares', transforming weapons of conflict into tools for growth.

Sometimes a list of titles of novels or poems is handed out to the group with the invitation to free-associate. The titles offered are from both classic and contemporary work and might include well-known work such as *Robinson Crusoe, Macbeth, One Hundred Years of Solitude* or *Ode to a Nightingale*. Both the titles and implicit content of such literary works can provoke interesting, explorative responses.

The theme of 'relationships' might be suggested midway through the programme in line with other groups that focus on the subject at that time. It provides an opportunity to explore possible connections or fractures creatively (Figure 7.3). The utilisation of artistic metaphor is particularly well suited as a therapeutic intervention for combat veterans, furnishing them with an indirect, less confrontative way of appropriating powerful emotion, lessening the risk of re-traumatisation. A safe distance is created, allowing for exploration and gradual exposure. Wise and Nash (2013), writing of the merits of using metaphor in creative arts therapies for veterans, point out that 'the simultaneous capacity for metaphor to create safe distancing, whilst transforming traumatic material, provide dual influences for containment and restructuring of the suffering' (p. 103).

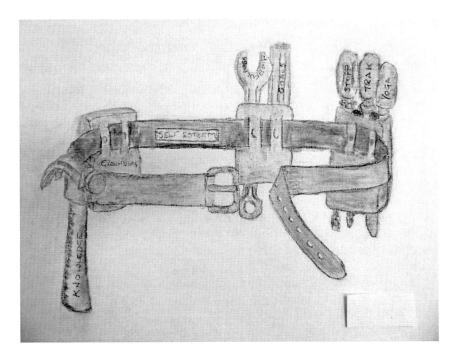

Figure 7.4 Tool Belt

Phase 3

During the final phase of therapy, including the last two weeks of the six-week programme, the focus shifts towards setting and achieving manageable life goals, as the veterans prepare for discharge. Goals might be geared towards seeking employment or repairing relationships. Themes for art therapy groups at this point reflect this change from introspection towards reconnecting with society. The theme of 'toolbox' provides the opportunity to reflect on what participants have gained from the treatment programme and how these skills or personal qualities might be applied in everyday life. For example, Figure 7.4, made in response to this theme, shows a hammer of knowledge firmly attached to a belt of self-esteem. Alternatively, the theme 'making it happen' is an encouragement to rehearse achieving a particular goal. Veterans are invited to imagine what it will look and feel like when a personal goal is achieved. Studies into the use of positive prospective imagery to foster optimism and assist change have yielded promising implications in a range of treatment approaches, including CBT (Holmes, Lang, Moulds & Steele, 2008); Eye Movement Desensitisation and Reprocessing (EMDR) with the use of a future template (Shapiro, 2001); and positive psychology, connecting with a sense of purpose (Wilkinson & Chilton, 2013).

In the following section, we offer a case study to demonstrate progression through a programme of art therapy groups.

Mike: a participant in an inpatient art therapy group

Mike served with the British military in most of the major war zones in the decades around the turn of the twenty-first century. As a consequence of some aspects of service, he had experienced numerous traumatic incidents. His experiences affected him deeply, although he continued to be a high-functioning individual. His regular nightmares, rumination and difficulties with anger and avoidant behaviour were all typical symptom presentation for PTSD. After a short-stay admission, he was assessed as suitable for the six-week ITP and was keen to engage with the one-to-one CBT sessions. Mike had not participated in any art therapy sessions before the ITP commenced and initially presented as dubious about how it might benefit him. Despite his trauma experiences, Mike's military identity had remained strongly intact since leaving the services, and early on in the art therapy groups it was clear that he was extremely proud of many aspects of his military career and keen to discuss it among his cohort group of six fellow veterans. Military life was where his expertise lay. Being in an art therapy group did not obviously play to his strengths and may have been an anxiety-provoking environment, even though in the introduction to the group, clear boundaries are established and the rationale of the sessions discussed.

Figure 7.5 Safe Place by Mike

In the initial art therapy group, participants were invited to make a creative response to the theme of a 'safe place'. Veterans were encouraged to create as full an image as they could, engaging memory or imaginative capacities and drawing on the sensory qualities of their subject matter. Mike responded to the theme by creating an image of sightlines as viewed through a gun's viewfinder (Figure 7.5). He was the last member to share his imagery in the group discussion and spoke briefly to say that being behind a gun gave him a feeling of safety, before moving on to more familiar territory of detailing the specifications of different guns. Some veterans do use military environments as a setting for their safe place, which may at first seem contradictory to the idea of safety, but for veterans it may represent a feeling of being in control, competent, fulfilling an important role, being able to achieve clear aims and being 'in it together' with the people they served with; all of which are factors that can feel less tangible for veterans in civilian life. Over time it may be more helpful for veterans to establish safe-place imagery that is not connected to military experiences so that there is a clear distinction between trauma flashbacks and the safe-place resource. At this time for Mike, being behind the sights of a gun represented being in a well-defended position where his training allowed him to concentrate and focus.

In the second session, Mike again used imagery to speak about his military expertise. A wide selection of postcards of artwork and photography covering

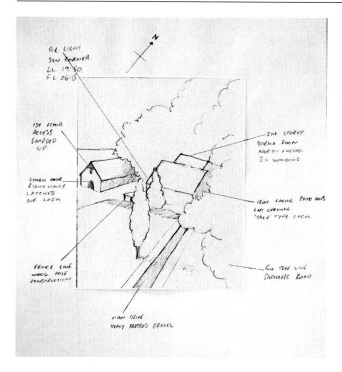

Figure 7.6 Perceptions by Mike reproduced by Kirsty Mackay

a range of subjects and locations was offered to the group and they were simply asked to select a couple of images that they found interesting, and to make
a creative response to them. In the art therapy room, there is access to colour
printing and copies of the postcard imagery are made so that veterans can
alter, annotate, cut up and collage with the imagery they have selected. Mike
chose an image of a rural landscape painted from a bird's-eye perspective
(*Backyard*; Tuymans, 2002), which Mike had annotated as if it was a location he had been tasked with surveying (Figure 7.6). He had noted down all
the areas of potential risk such as access points and land cover. He spoke to
the group about this skill for reconnaissance, which others in the group were
familiar with. Another veteran responded by describing how he still does this
scoping behaviour in his civilian life, such as at the supermarket, even though
he knows realistically there is no threat there, something others in the group
could identify with. Hyper-vigilant behaviours are a common symptom of
PTSD, where the threat systems are on alert and this type of military training
feeds this threat response.

By the third week, veterans are heading towards the mid-point of the
ITP and will have begun to fully engage with their one-to-one CBT sessions
two or three times a week, in which they begin to safely revisit their trauma

experience using reliving techniques, and engaging in exposure activities to challenge avoidant behaviours and ways of thinking. In the third art therapy session, 'patterns' was introduced as a theme to offer a space for self-reflection and to encourage insight into their own patterns of behaviour that they may be bringing into awareness in CBT sessions. It is important in the art therapy groups to be mindful that each veteran in the group may be coping better or worse on any given group as a result of their one-to-one trauma-focused therapy and to facilitate a creative space and theme that is responsive to this. The theme of 'patterns' is broad enough to embrace the processing responses to some of the challenging work they may be dealing with from one-to-one CBT sessions, or to offer an opportunity for veterans to engage in the intrinsic sensory and soothing aspects of the art materials, finding focus in the here and now through what they are creating with patterns of colour, texture and form.

In this third session, Mike found a piece of roughly sawn wood and began sanding the surface with the intention of revealing the pattern of rings in the wood. After maintaining his focus on the repetitive sanding process for all of the 45 minutes of art-making time, Mike returned to the group and passed the piece of wood around the group table for others to see and feel. He spoke about the patterns in this natural material and others in the group expressed an interest in the effect of 'good' or 'bad' years in the tree's life on the space between the growth rings. One veteran noticed that the piece of wood looked roughly heart shaped and joked that Mike was letting go of his tough guy image. Mike responded with good humour to this and also used his artwork to speak about the rough surface of the wood having been sanded to reveal the quality of the wood underneath. It is possible he was finding himself undertaking a symbolic parallel process on the ITP and, as the other group member suggested, allowing another aspect of himself to be seen by the veterans in this session. The importance of this artwork for Mike developed over the remainder of the ITP. Instead of leaving the piece with the art therapist for safekeeping until the following week, he asked to take it at the end of the session. He continued to work on sanding it down in his own time and shaping the edges of the cut-off so that it brought out the heart shape more strongly and began to engrave into the wood.

Mike used his time in the military as a subject for the fourth art therapy group where 'inside/outside' was the theme, but the focus moved away from his military aptitude to connection with others in his regiment, and a shared joke they had all enjoyed. In retelling the story behind the incident, Mike presented himself as someone who could enjoy a laugh with others and didn't always take himself too seriously. Mike was observed to be taking more interest in group discussion and listening to what others in the group were contributing with increasing sensitivity. In the following art therapy sessions, Mike was able to respond to the theme of 'balance' by connecting more with his emotional self rather than his military identity. He reflected on a desire to find more balance in his own emotions. He used a picture of a snarling black

Figure 7.7 *Balance* by Mike reproduced by Kirsty Mackay

dog to represent his anger and depression, but also allowed a more compassionate self-image of a 'noble stag' to intersect this image (Figure 7.7). He shared with the group that in one-to-one CBT sessions his negative self-image had been explored and new ways of viewing himself thought about. Mike used the art therapy session to visualise this alternative aspect of himself to which he could attribute positive qualities. Through sharing the meaning of his imagery with the group, Mike received affirmation that the positive qualities the stag symbolised were evident in his personality.

Mike collaborated with the construction of this case study and commented that the image of the stag and dog is something he intends to return to at some point. He recalled that one of the group members had rated it and that while he had cut corners to create it in the time available during the session, it serves as a good reminder of his aspirations.

In the final art therapy group, Mike brought his finished wooden heart back into the session. Plates 7.2 and 7.3 show both sides of the completed wooden heart with an image on one side and a poem on the reverse. Mike also made a new artwork in response to the theme of 'resources' that was offered to the group. Coming at the end of the six weeks, this theme aims to provide an opportunity for veterans to reflect on what resources they have to enable them to continue to manage and improve their PTSD symptoms and their overall well-being. Mike made an image of a golden heart (Figure 7.8) mirroring the sanded piece of

Figure 7.8 Resources/Heart of Gold by Mike

wood he had now completed and engraved. On both he had depicted the silhou-etted figure of a soldier with his gun and a woman with children alongside her. He explained that he had intended to leave the wooden piece at Combat Stress so it could inspire others in the future. However, after he had shared a photograph of it with his partner, she had responded very strongly to what it symbolised for them as a family and asked if he would bring it home. His new image on paper included a golden-coloured background as he described that he had been able to allow a warmer view of himself to emerge. Mike could tell the group with pride that he was able to see that he 'had a heart of gold'.

Integrating approaches to create an art therapy toolbox

It can be helpful to look beyond core art therapy training to consider what might be learned from evidence-based psychological approaches to trauma. This might be learning from colleagues from other disciplines through in-service lectures, or by taking trauma-specific courses. In their thematic analysis of information from US art therapists working with veterans with combat-related PTSD, which offers guidelines for best practice, Collie *et al.* (2006) recommend 'specialized training in trauma intervention and PTSD the-ory' (p. 157). The following section provides an overview of some techniques gained from sister therapies such as CBT, EMDR and Compassion Focused Therapy (CFT) that have been integrated into art therapy practice at Combat Stress, thereby offering a range of tools for use in therapy.

The early treatment phase places an emphasis on establishing safety, building affect management skills, psycho-education and history-taking. Although there are programmed groups on stabilisation techniques at Combat Stress, it has proved useful to consolidate this work during individual art therapy sessions so that both veteran and therapist know how to respond should a dissociative episode occur during a session. Familiarity with breathing, grounding and simple relaxation techniques can prove invaluable, and might be used to end sessions as part of a wind-down. The availability of grounding materials like drinking water, stress balls, polished stones and other sensory materials such as essential oils for olfactory stimulus can help veterans remain connected with the 'here and now', and resist becoming pulled back into past experiences. Simple techniques such as asking the dissociating veteran to identify and describe three things in the room that are blue, or to count backwards in fours from 100 can help to focus attention on the current environment, distinguish it from the intruding past and stimulate verbal and cognitive parts of the brain to engage, creating a balance to the sensory, nonverbal material emerging. Such techniques help to lay a foundation of safety and gradual pacing towards more in-depth work.

The environment might be enhanced by offering veterans familiar talking points. These might be objects associated with the military that help to make a connection in an unfamiliar space. For instance, there is a model of a ship in the corner of one Combat Stress art therapy room. It regularly gets attention from naval veterans new to the space who are able to recognise its identity, and speak about it as experts. Using picture postcards or paintings as anchoring points can help veterans 'stay in the room' if on the verge of dissociation, or highly anxious. They can provide a shared point of contact for grounding.

Resource-building, as used in the early stages of EMDR, can help veterans to access self-selected personal qualities to assist subsequent in-depth trauma work (Mollon, 2005). This might involve creating a picture of a time when they felt confident, thereby retrieving associated imagery and physical sensations, and reminding their depleted system what it feels like to be confident. It could involve reawakening a sense of achievement, regaining hope or accessing encouragement. There might also be a need to develop self-compassion, as shame might hamper recovery, in which case a CFT approach can help.

Evidence-based research done in the field of CFT has provided a model for understanding the effects of self-attacking thoughts and other triggers that stimulate a threat response (Gilbert 2009; Lee & James, 2012). Shame is socially constructed and involves self-criticism associated with a fear of judgement. Exposure of shame-based trauma can lead to an exacerbation of shame and self-attacking thoughts so it is important for clients to learn to self-soothe before beginning trauma-focused work (Lee & James, 2012).

CFT theory is based on the interactions between our three affect regulation systems – the *incentive system* that focuses on doing and achieving; the *affiliative system* that focuses on feeling safe and contented; and the threat-focused *self-protection system*. Building self-soothing techniques that promote a sense of safety can help to moderate the threat system and reduce stress (Gilbert, 2009). Self-soothing can trigger memories of feeling loved and valued, but this can only be accessed if previously experienced, otherwise the capacity to self-sooth has to be learned (Lee & James, 2012).

Self-compassion can be experienced as an alien concept to veterans who are often highly self-critical. Developing a soothing image of a supportive inner helper can help veterans to access their internal calming system and tackle self-criticism associated with shame (Lee & James, 2012). Through this 'compassionate image', different perceptions might be gained (Gilbert, 2009). If unable to think kindly of oneself, a third-party perspective might open up other ways of evaluating situations. Veterans might draw on the memory of a past role model, an animal, a landscape or an imaginary figure, associated with wisdom, strength, warmth and non-judgement (Compassionate Mind Foundation, 2017). Situations can then be seen from that viewpoint. Accessing a compassionate image can prove crucial later on during trauma-focused work. For instance, one veteran imagined his current worldly wise, compassionate self in a trauma memory alongside his younger suffering self, providing the warmth, understanding and encouragement that he did not receive at the time. This enabled emotional expression and the challenging of long-held negative cognitions related to self-worth.

History-taking might take the form of creating a visual timeline through the use of art materials, which can help to contextualise experiences. Different sizes, textures, colours and symbols facilitate rich expression that can be explored over time. As meaning is explored, attention can be paid to emerging core beliefs about how the world, self and others are viewed. Experiences and beliefs can then be gathered together to create a formulation of how presenting difficulties came about. A simple CBT formulation framework (Ehlers & Clark, 2000) can provide a helpful visual construct, devised collaboratively with the veteran that gathers together key components such as precipitating and maintaining factors related to PTSD. Further broken down into interlinking thoughts, emotions, behaviour and body sensations can help to make sense of experience and establish a firm base of understanding to work from. For instance, one veteran was able to recognise a sense of inadequacy in childhood that became amplified during subsequent trauma and became a blocking belief. This insight assisted later work.

Recent research in trauma-focused CBT with veterans has explored adapting the approach for a subset of clients with 'high levels of dissociation and avoidance' that 'places a stronger emphasis on grounding and allocentric processing' (Kaur, Murphy & Smith, 2016, p. 1). It is suggested that viewpoint-independent allocentric processing of trauma imagery can assist the contextualisation of the trauma memories that is disrupted in PTSD (Brewin *et al.*, 2010; Kaur *et al.*, 2016). In essence, the trauma viewpoint is manipulated during imaginal reliving to enable different perspectives to be examined and to facilitate cognitive reappraisal (Brewin *et al.*, 2010; Kaur *et al.*, 2016). This approach has a strong resonance with imagery manipulation possible through art therapy.

Manipulation of mental imagery is a crucial part of approaches such as EMDR (Shapiro, 2001). To reduce the intensity of trauma imagery, clients might be encouraged to imagine, for example, that the trauma scene is fading, diminishing in size or changing from colour to black and white. Creative ideas are developed during the process to help transform the traumatic experience into something more manageable. This might involve considering what is really needed by the client in the traumatic memory that is being reworked, for instance a compassionate figure, and to introduce that element into the imaginal experience. This approach is transferable to art therapy whereby images created can be changed as part of the dynamic interactive process. Clients might be encouraged to make changes of their choice by adding, removing or reworking symbols used and re-evaluating meaning (Hass-Cohen, Findlay, Carr & Vanderlan, 2014). When working with a recurrent nightmare of a traumatic experience, one Combat Stress veteran added an escape route and supportive elements into his art therapy image, which helped to regain a sense of control. Combined with an exploration of personal meaning, this resulted in the cessation of the nightmare.

As part of the exploration of traumatic events, veterans sometimes draw the situation from an aerial perspective, which provides an opportunity to examine the scene from a distance and to observe the different elements in play. This can lead to alternative viewpoints whereby the veteran might realise, perhaps for the first time, that a previous assumption could not have been possible, for example, related to the physical position of those involved, or the timeframe in question. This adaptive information can help to contextualise the experience and assist memory integration.

Laying a foundation of coping skills and visual prompts in this way and taking a proactive stance in imagery manipulation might constitute unfamiliar approaches for some art therapists. However, these strategies can enhance practice and provide the necessary safe base to enable deeper exploration at a manageable pace, whereby veterans feel more in control and empowered. The toolbox also helps to establish a common language between professional disciplines through which we can work alongside each other towards shared goals.

Summary

In this chapter, an overview of the adaptive art therapy model for traumatised veterans in use at Combat Stress has been presented. Although offering an integrated, phasic, theme-based framework, flexibility within that structure is recognised as crucial. In this context, art therapists require an awareness of post-traumatic stress symptom presentation and management, and some understanding of military culture. Veteran feedback through group evaluation questionnaires is used to inform service development as part of a collaborative process. Art therapy is part of wider treatment programmes and has been tailored to fit current outcome objectives by offering an alternative to the CBT and activities-based rehabilitation models that are also provided. It is hoped that the ideas and methods shared in this text will be transferable to other contexts where traumatised veterans are seeking treatment.

In the following three chapters, individual work with veterans will be discussed with particular attention to the therapeutic benefits of art therapy for veterans with high levels of dissociation and avoidance. Recent research suggests that 'higher levels of baseline anxiety and dissociation are associated with worse post-treatment PTSD outcomes' (Murphy & Busuttil, 2015, p. 441), which underlines the significance of addressing these barriers to recovery in the formative stages of treatment.

References

Belkofer, C. M. & Konopka, L. M. (2008). Conducting art therapy research using quantitative EEG measures. *Art Therapy: Journal of the American Art Therapy Association, 25*(2), 56–63.

Brewin, C. (2001). A cognitive neuroscience account of posttraumatic stress disorder and its treatment. *Behaviour Research and Therapy, 39*, 373–393.

Brewin, C., Dalgleish, T. & Joseph, S. (1996). A duel representation theory of post-traumatic stress disorder. *Psychological Review, 103*(4), 670–686.

Brewin, C. R., Gregory, J. D., Lipton, M. & Burgess, N. (2010). Intrusive images in psychological disorders: Characteristics, neural mechanisms, and treatment implications. *Psychological Review, 117*, 210–232.

Chapman, L. (2014). *Neurobiologically informed trauma therapy with children and adolescents: Understanding mechanisms of change.* New York, NY: W. W. Norton.

Chu, J. (1998). *Rebuilding shattered lives: The responsible treatment of post-traumatic dissociative disorders.* New York, NY: John Wiley.

Collie, C. A., Backos, A., Malchiodi, C. & Spiegel, D. (2006). Art therapy for combat-related PTSD: Recommendations for research and practice. *Art Therapy: Journal of the American Art Therapy Association, 23*(4), 157–164.

Compassionate Mind Foundation (2017). Retrieved from https://compassionatemind. co.uk/uploads/files/building-a-compassionate-image.pdf.

Ehlers, A. & Clark, D. M. (2000). A cognitive model of posttraumatic stress disorder. *Behaviour Research and Therapy, 38*, 319–345.

Foa, E. B., Keane, T. M., Friedman, M. J. & Cohen, J. A. (eds) (2009). *Effective treatments for PTSD: Practice guidelines from the International Society for Traumatic Stress Studies* (2nd edn). New York, NY: Guilford Press.

Gilbert, P. (2009). *The compassionate mind.* London: Constable & Robinson.

Hass-Cohen, N. (2008). Partnering of art therapy and clinical neuroscience. In N. Hass-Cohen & R. Carr (eds), *Art therapy and clinical neuroscience* (pp. 21–42). Philadelphia, PA: Jessica Kingsley.

Hass-Cohen, N., Findlay, J. C., Carr, R. & Vanderlan, J. (2014). Check, change what you need to change and/or keep what you want: An art therapy neurobiological-based trauma protocol. *Art Therapy: Journal of the American Art Therapy Association, 31*(2), 69–78.

Heller, L. & Lapierre, A. (2012). *Healing developmental trauma: How early trauma affects self-regulation, self-image, and the capacity for relationship.* Berkeley, CA: North Atlantic Books.

Herman, J. (1992). *Trauma and recovery: The aftermath of violence from domestic abuse to political terror.* New York, NY: Basic Books.

Hogan, S. (2009). The art therapy continuum: A useful tool for envisaging the diversity of practice in British art therapy. *International Journal of Art Therapy, 14*(1), 29–37.

Holmes, E. A., Lang, T. J., Moulds, M. L. & Steele, A. M. (2008). Prospective and positive mental imagery deficits in dysphoria. *Behaviour Research & Therapy, 46*, 8.

Kaur, M., Murphy, D. & Smith, K. V. (2016). An adapted imaginal exposure approach to traditional methods used within trauma-focused cognitive behavioural therapy, trialled with a veteran population. *The Cognitive Behavioural Therapist, 9*(10), 1–11.

King, J. L. (ed.). (2016). *Art therapy, trauma, and neuroscience: Theoretical and practical perspectives.* New York, NY: Routledge.

King-West, E. & Hass-Cohen, N. (2008). Art therapy, neuroscience and complex PTSD. In N. Hass-Cohen & R. Carr (eds), *Art therapy and clinical neuroscience* (pp. 223–253). Philadelphia, PA: Jessica Kingsley.

Klorer, P. (2005). Expressive therapy with severely maltreated children: Neuroscience contributions. *Art Therapy: Journal of the American Art Therapy Association, 22*(4), 213–220.

Lanius, U. F., Paulsen, S. L. & Corrigan, F. M. (2014). *Neurobiology and treatment of traumatic dissociation: Towards an embodied self.* New York, NY: Springer Publishing Company.

Lee, D. & James, S. (2012). *The compassionate mind approach to recovering from trauma.* London: Constable & Robinson.

Lieberman, M. (2007). Social cognitive neuroscience: A review of core processes. *Annual reviews of Psychology, 58*, 259–289.

Lobban, J. (2014). The invisible wound: Veterans' art therapy. *International Journal of Art Therapy, 19*(1), 1–14.

Lobban, J. (2016). *Art therapy for military veterans with PTSD: A transatlantic study.* Retrieved from www.wcmt.org.uk/fellows/reports/art-therapy-military-veterans-ptsd-transatlantic-study#downloads.

Lusebrink, V. J. & Hinz, L. D. (2016). The expressive therapies continuum as a framework in the treatment of trauma. In J. L. King (ed.), *Art therapy, trauma, and neuroscience: Theoretical and practical perspectives* (pp. 42–66). New York, NY: Routledge.

McNamee, C. M. (2006). Experiences with bilateral art: A retrospective study. *Art Therapy: Journal of the American Art Therapy Association, 23*(1), 7–13.

McRae, K., Misra, S., Prasad, A. K., Pereira, S. C. & Gross, J. J. (2012). Bottom-up and top-down emotion generation: Implications for emotion regulation. *Social Cognitive and Affective Neuroscience, 7*(3), 253–262.

Mollon, P. (2005). *EMDR and the energy therapies: Psychoanalytic perspectives.* London: Karnac.

Murphy, D. & Busuttil, W. (2015). Exploring outcome predictors in UK veterans treated for PTSD. *Psychology Research, 5*(8), 441–451.

Murphy, S. E., Drazich, E. H., Blackwell S. E., Nobre, C. A. & Holmes, E. A. (2015). Imagining a brighter future: The effect of positive imagery training on mood, prospective mental imagery and emotional bias in older adults. *Psychiatry Research*, 230(1), 36–43.

Nanda, U. H., Gaydos, L. B., Hathorn, K. & Watkins, N. (2010). Art and posttraumatic stress: A review of the empirical literature on the therapeutic implications of artwork for war veterans with posttraumatic stress disorder. *Environment and Behavior*, 42(3), 376–390.

NICE. (2005). *Post-Traumatic Stress Disorder: Management*. Retrieved from www. nice.org.uk/guidance/cg26/chapter/1-Guidance.

Ogden, P., Minton, K. & Pain, C. (2006). *Trauma and the body: A sensorimotor approach to psychotherapy*. New York, NY: W. W. Norton & Co.

Rauch, S. L., van der Kolk, B. A., Fisler, R. E., Alpert, N. M., Orr, S. P., Savage, C. R., Fischman, A. J., Jenike, M. A. & Pitman, R. K. (1996). A symptom provocation study of posttraumatic stress disorder using positron emission tomography and script-driven imagery. *Archives of General Psychiatry*, 53, 380–387.

Shapiro, F. (2001). *Eye movement desensitization and reprocessing: Basic principles, protocols, and procedures* (2nd edn). New York, NY: Guilford Press.

Siegel, D. (1999). *The developing mind: Toward a neurobiology of interpersonal experience*. New York, NY: Guilford Press.

Steele, K., van der Hart, O. & Nijenhuis, E. R. (2005). Phase-oriented treatment of structural dissociation in complex traumatization: Overcoming trauma-related phobias. *Journal of Trauma & Dissociation*, 6(3), 11–53.

Talwar, S. (2007). Accessing traumatic memory through art-making: An art therapy trauma protocol (ATTP). *The Arts in Psychotherapy*, 34, 22–35.

Tinnin, L. & Gantt, L. (2014). *The instinctual trauma response and dual-brain dynamics: A guide for trauma therapy*. Morgantown, WV: Gargoyle Press.

Tripp, T. (2007). A short-term therapy approach to processing trauma: Art therapy and bilateral stimulation. *Art Therapy: Journal of the American Art Therapy Association*, 24(4), 176–183.

Tripp, T. (2016). A body-based bilateral art protocol for reprocessing trauma. In J. L. King (ed.), *Art therapy, trauma, and neuroscience: Theoretical and practical perspectives* (pp. 173–194). New York, NY: Routledge.

Tuymans, L. (2002). *Backyard* [painting]. Los Angeles, CA: Museum of Contemporary Art.

van der Kolk, B. (1994). The body keeps the score: Memory and the evolving psychobiology of posttraumatic stress. *Harvard Review of Psychiatry*, 1, 253–265.

van der Kolk, B. (2014). *The body keeps the score: Brain, mind and body in the healing of trauma*. New York, NY: Viking Penguin.

Wilkinson, R. A. & Chilton, G. (2013). Positive art therapy: Linking positive psychology to art therapy theory, practice, and research. *Art Therapy: Journal of the American Art Therapy Association*, 30, 4–11.

Wise, S. & Nash, E. (2013). Metaphor as heroic mediator: Imagination, creative arts therapy, and group process as agents of healing with veterans. In R. M. Scurfield & K. T. Platoni (eds), *Healing war trauma: A handbook of creative approaches* (pp. 99–114). New York, NY: Routledge.

Plate 1.1 Hope

Plate 2.1 Clone Trooper by Clement Boland

Plate 2.2 Camel Train by Clement Boland

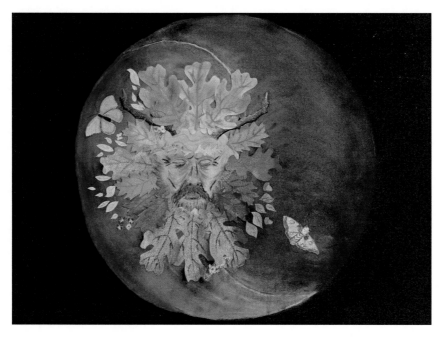

Plate 7.1 Balance/Green Man

Plate 7.2 *Patterns/Wooden Heart Image* by Mike

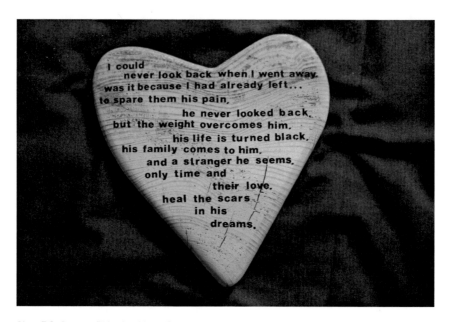

Plate 7.3 *Patterns/Wooden Heart Poem* by Mike

Plate 8.1 Past and Present by Simon

Plate 8.2 In Two Minds by Vic

Plate 8.3 Looking on From a Distance by Richard

Plate 9.1 Taffy the Friendly Dragon by Richard Kidgell

Plate 10.1 Mask 2 by Steve

Plate 10.2 Joint Image by Ian and Janice Lobban

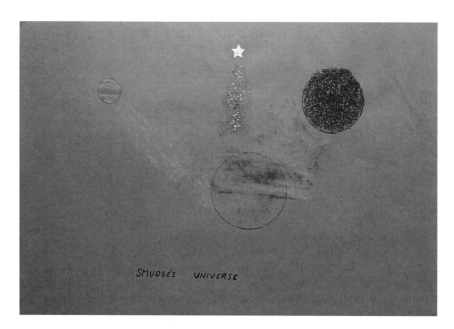

Plate 12.1 Smudge's Universe

Plate 13.1 Land Rover Silhouetted Against a Sunset by Captain Morgan (left) and Marine Lowry (right)

Plate 14.1 Swans by Spike

Plate 14.2 A City Garden by Ron

Chapter 8

In two minds

Janice Lobban

Imagine that every time you hear a loud, unexpected bang you dive for cover because you re-experience being under attack. Imagine being overwhelmed by fear in an instant. Your heart is pounding, your breath is shallow, and you are sweating and cannot think straight. Your throat is dry and you cannot get words out. You hear the sound of heavy artillery and smell and taste cordite. It is happening all over again with the same intensity of emotion and sensation. Then gradually you begin to realise that you are not in Afghanistan anymore and feel burning shame as you notice people are staring at you in this public place, some are laughing, and all you want to do is get away and never go there again. This hyper-arousal state will linger for hours afterwards. You 'beat yourself up' continuously for reacting in that way and ruminate on your self-assessed inadequacies, concluding that you are a 'waste of space'. The experience sets you back as you determine not to risk letting yourself be exposed to that kind of situation again. So you go back to isolating yourself in your flat with the curtains drawn.

The title of this chapter is taken from a recurring theme in veterans' art therapy imagery of experiencing 'two minds'. This is not just referring to indecision that we might all struggle with from time to time, although loss of self-confidence and the consequence of past choices might negatively impact decision-making. 'Two minds' underlines a pervading sense of division, inner conflict and disharmony. The division can be approached using different frameworks of understanding, some of which are explored in the following text. Namely, the neurobiology of Post-Traumatic Stress Disorder (PTSD) and how the human brain responds to threat and stores trauma memories; the different 'realities' associated with left and right brain hemisphere function (McGilchrist, 2010); the theory of trauma-related structural dissociation of the personality (Nijenhuis, van der Hart & Steele, 2004; Steele, van der Hart & Nijenhuis, 2005; van der Hart, Nijenhuis & Soloman, 2010); and psychodynamic theory of unconscious thought processes and defence mechanisms (Freud, 1920; Garland, 1998). Division might also be associated with the trained military way of thinking and behaving in contrast with civilian perceptions and approaches.

Veterans often refer to the two minds as being an angel and a devil in battle within, in constant argument and often resulting in harsh, self-directed hostility. This suggests a moral element in play. Another commonly used analogy for the division is being both 'Jekyll and Hyde', with the latter state damaging relationships, affecting social integration and negatively impacting on a sense of self-control. One of the four clusters of symptoms that make up the diagnostic criteria for PTSD, along with avoidance, intrusion and hyper-arousal, is negative alterations in cognitions and mood. This includes 'Persistent, distorted cognitions about the cause or consequences of the traumatic event(s) that lead the individual to blame himself/herself or others' (American Psychiatric Association, 2013, p. 272). In practice, this can present as self-sabotaging thoughts that undermine progress in therapy. Steps forward might stimulate guilt or self-judgement within the veteran that he/she does not deserve to feel better, thereby presenting a barrier to recovery.

Divisions

The influence of neurobiology and brain structure

As outlined in previous chapters, there is a firm biological basis for PTSD. According to Dr Steven Southwick, Deputy Director of the Clinical Neurosciences Division of the National Center for PTSD, USA, people with PTSD tend to have a more responsive Sympathetic Nervous System (SNS). The SNS stimulates fight-flight survival responses. Research has shown that areas of the brain become damaged by stress. For instance the amygdala, involved in danger recognition, becomes sensitised to threat. The hippocampus, which is related to new learning and memory consolidation, creates an internal map that helps to inform the contexts in which we should be afraid. Consequently, threat perception can become more generalised if the hippocampus is damaged (Lobban, 2016; S. Southwick, personal communication, 16 June 2016). With PTSD, traumatic memories do not fade naturally over time.

Understanding of brain hemisphere specialisation and asymmetry has been revised as a result of advances in neuro-imaging. Nevertheless, it is accepted that language comprehension is associated with the left brain hemisphere, whereas the right hemisphere is associated with perception and the integration of non-verbal information (Konopka, 2016). Traumatic memories are believed to be held mainly in the right hemisphere (Schore, 2012) without 'narrative organization and cognitive perspective' (Tripp, 2016, p. 173). During a trauma, the hippocampus encodes everything present such as sights, sounds and smells, and the traumatic experiences become stored as raw, unprocessed sensory information that is frozen in time. Traumatic memories are isolated from normal memories and can become re-experienced in the here and now when sub-cortically or unconsciously triggered by a trauma-related cue, such as a similar sight, sound or smell (Brewin, Dalgleish & Joseph, 1996; S. Southwick, personal communication, 16 June 2016). This can stimulate fear even though there is no danger present, as demonstrated in the opening paragraph of this text. The traumatic memories are experienced as having 'a life of their own' (Herman, 1992, p. 34), thereby creating a sense of having 'two minds'.

In his work on the asymmetrical nature of brain function, McGilchrist (2010) argues that human beings have 'two fundamentally opposed realities' (p. 13). Further, 'Both brain hemispheres are involved in almost all mental processes' but they have distinct ways of understanding experiences (p. 10). Although they need to work in co-operation, McGilchrist suggests that they are in conflict. Concerning hemispheric differences in function and approach, McGilchrist outlines how the right hemisphere is non-verbal but can 'understand metaphor' and the non-literal aspects of language (p. 51); it can see the 'bigger picture' and activates shared mental states (p. 43); it connects with the world, with attention on 'betweeness' (p. 72); and is involved in 'unconscious emotional processing' (p. 62). The verbal left brain hemisphere takes a 'sequential, linear approach' (p. 228), tends to stick with the familiar and is 'unconcerned about others' (p. 58). It is disembodied and isolated, with attention to context and the 'short-term view' (p. 431). It depends on language, can confabulate in order to be right, draw false conclusions, and has 'relative inflexibility' (p. 45).

McGilchrist (2010) suggests that the dissociative experiences of depersonalisation and derealisation involve right hemisphere disconnection and left hemisphere functional dominance. During the process of depersonalisation there is a sense of detachment from self, and with derealisation the world around does not seem real. He notes that people with right hemisphere damage have reported an acquired feeling of 'foreignness' and disconnection, as though not 'belonging in the world', and suggests that dissociation in 'normal subjects' involves 'an interhemispheric imbalance in favour of the left' (p. 236).

Dissociation

Dissociation is a term used to describe the disconnection 'between things usually associated with each other', which can be the 'usually integrated functions of consciousness, memory, identity, or perception' (ISSTD, 2016). Dissociation has been conceptualised as being on a continuum from normative day-dreaming, or absorption in reading a book or watching a film, to the more extreme, clinical end of the continuum whereby people might have out of body experiences, have gaps in memory, or experience derealisation or depersonalisation (Carlson & Putnam, 1993). Generally, it is now accepted that although normal dissociation is on a continuum, there is a discontinuous, subset of symptoms associated with pathological dissociation. Evidence-based psychometric measures such as the Dissociative Experiences Scale II (DESII) are able to distinguish between the phenomena, with a taxon of eight symptoms identifying pathological dissociation (Putnam, 1989; Spitzer, Barnow, Freyberger & Grabe, 2006; Waller, Putnam & Carlson, 1996).

In certain circumstances, dissociation acts an evolutionary survival mechanism. Trauma can cause a fragmentation of our normally integrated system of self-preservation (Herman, 1992). When the other survival mechanisms of flight, fight, freeze or flop are futile and escape is not possible, the mind detaches from the traumatic experience in order to reduce its intensity. This causes a break in conscious awareness and disrupts the sense of self (ISSTD, 2016). The memory of the experience remains detached and disintegrated but might be triggered into awareness at a later date. Dissociation in this context can be seen as an adaptive process that enables the person to maintain functioning. It provides analgesia to manage the psychic and/or physical pain being experienced (Putnam, 1989).

The three areas that distinguish pathological dissociation from the normal range are an alteration in sense of identity, memory disturbance and trauma (Nemiah, 1981; Putnam, 1989). Putnam outlines how in a dissociative flashback, a person can 'experience an alteration in sense of self along dimensions such as age or body image' (1989, p. 119). So in the flashback, the person might re-experience being a teenager and running, whereas in current day he/she might be elderly and wheelchair dependent. Memory disturbance might mean no recall of the traumatic event or a detached, distorted recall from a third-person stance.

Once used for survival, dissociation can affect subsequent emotional functioning, fostering detachment and numbing (ISSTD, 2016). Veterans sometimes report that they felt nothing at the death of a loved one and judge themselves harshly because of this. Or they describe how emotions overwhelm them suddenly without warning, completely unsynchronised with the current context. They might use symbols like a roulette wheel to express the seemingly random way their emotions present. This amplifies the sense of not being in control.

In Chapter 9, veteran Richard Kidgell presents his experience of dissociation from a personal perspective, which provides an invaluable glimpse into the processes in action.

Structural dissociation of the personality

The theory of structural dissociation of the personality suggests that complex trauma causes psychological division, whereby one or more motivational-driven, 'apparently normal parts' (ANPs) of the personality continue to engage in everyday life, attempting to avoid reminders of the trauma. Simultaneously, one or more threat-orientated, 'emotional parts' (EPs) of the personality become fixated in traumatic experiences and are stuck in trauma time (Steele *et al.*, 2005). The parts are dissociated and un-integrated. Primary structural dissociation, as seen in PTSD, involves a single ANP and a single EP. The divisions become more complicated according to early life trauma, prolonged exposure or chronicity. Secondary structural dissociation is associated with complex PTSD and trauma-related Borderline Personality Disorder, and tertiary structural dissociation applies to people with Dissociative Identity Disorder, where there can be more than one ANP and multiple EPs in operation (van der Hart *et al.*, 2010). The aim of treatment is synthesis and integration. A systems approach is taken by negotiating with the different parts to get them all working together.

The theory of structural dissociation developed from the work of Pierre Janet (1859–1947) who used the term 'dissociation' to describe alteration in consciousness as a result of psychological trauma, during his work on hysteria (Herman, 1992; Janet, 1898). He developed a phase-orientated model for working with trauma, with each phase targeting a trauma-related phobia preventing progress. Janet proposed that the core phobia is 'an avoidance of full realisation of the trauma and its effects on one's life' (Steele *et al.*, 2005, p. 14). Janet proposed that in a flashback, traumatised individuals attempt to complete unfinished actions from the event leading to 'everlasting recommencements' (Janet, 1919; van der Hart *et al.*, 2010).

First World War psychologist Charles Myers also influenced the theory of structural dissociation. He first used the terms 'apparently normal part' and 'emotional part' of the personality when describing the presentation of traumatised soldiers with shell shock. The ANP presented as being 'phobically avoidant of the trauma', which manifested in 'degrees of detachment, numbing, depersonalisation' or even 'complete amnesia' (Myers, 1940, as cited in Steele *et al.*, 2005, p. 15).

In a lecture on structural dissociation, leading authority Otto van der Hart gave examples of First World War soldiers affected by shell shock to illustrate how somatic and hysterical conversion disorder diagnoses given at the time validated the presence of dissociation. Through viewing British Pathé news clips of soldiers in hospital recovering from the effects of battle at that time, it is possible to witness the physical manifestations of psychological trauma. One soldier presents as 'apparently normal' but certain triggers caused an 'emotional part' to manifest with trembling legs. Other soldiers experience dissociative contractures, with physical pain seeming to be more bearable than psychological pain (British Pathé News, 2016; van der Hart, 2011).

The ANP enables functioning to continue from the basic level of taking sustenance to raising a family and earning a living. Life goes on and people can demonstrate the most amazing resilience while having unresolved traumatic experiences just below the surface. Whether traumatised by conflict, natural disaster, abuse, or witnessing suffering, people demonstrate the capacity to endure. However, the EP(s) remains fixed in trauma time and progress involves reintegration.

Psychological defence mechanisms and military culture

During the development of psychoanalytic theory, Freud (1900) proposed different levels of consciousness. To describe this, an analogy is sometimes made with an iceberg. At the top is the conscious mind with moment-by-moment awareness. Below that is the preconscious mind where thoughts and feelings are just below the surface but can come into conscious awareness straightforwardly, for example, when recalling a date or a name. The deepest level is the unconscious mind, which is out of conscious awareness but affects emotions and behaviour. Instincts and urges are based at this level. Psychological defence mechanisms might be used to avoid having to deal with 'aspects of the self, which, if consciously experienced, might give rise to unbearable anxiety or psychic pain' (Brown & Pedder, 1991, p. 24).

In psychodynamic theory, it is the concept of *repression* rather than dissociation that might be used to understand mechanisms in operation when difficult material is out of conscious awareness. Freud developed the concept of repression in his work with Breuer on hysteria (Breuer & Freud, 1895). Theory suggests that the defence mechanism of repression is a response to anxiety-provoking internal stimuli whereas dissociation is a response to trauma/external stimuli. However, dissociation can be measured clinically by using evidence-based psychometrics such as DESII, whereas repression is a concept (Singer, 1990). They have 'different theoretical underpinnings' (Bremner & Marmar, 1998, p. 117).

Other psychodynamic defence mechanisms relevant to the current discussion include *projection* with the associated use of *splitting*. With projection, unacceptable feelings are externalised, disowned and attributed to others. In splitting, there is a 'separation between good and bad aspects of the self and others' that can manifest as the polar opposites of idealisation and contempt (Brown & Pedder, 1991, p. 26). This can be seen in veteran admonishment of civilian attitudes and approaches. A ground rule of the majority of therapy groups at Combat Stress is 'no civvie bashing'. This means no generalised criticism of non-military approaches in society, as this can create a sense of 'us and them', although this attitude is rarely targeted towards clinical staff. The military way can be seen as being well structured with everyone knowing what is of expected of them, and rising to the challenge. A sense of personal responsibility is recognised as crucial to this process, whereas civilians can be perceived as slack and self-centred, doing as little as they can get away with. Clearly this offers important material for consideration as these perceptions/defences can hamper social reintegration. Although providing a sense of connection and belonging to a societal sub-group, this form of splitting creates a division from society as a whole.

Splitting can also be turned on the self, with the past military-self viewed as competent and able and by contrast the veteran-civilian deemed unworthy and incompetent. Admirable values and beliefs can be held safely in the past self, whereas self-attacking admonishments of weakness and blame can hamper recovery in the present.

Identification can be a defence mechanism after trauma and can occur with either with the victim or the aggressor. Identification with the victim or lost object can be a way of avoiding guilt for having survived the trauma, which could be amplified by feeling responsible (Garland, 1998). Identifying with lost comrades keeps their memory alive but maintains suffering. Survivor guilt can present a considerable barrier to recovery often encountered with veterans. It might be related to acts of omission or commission, for instance not being able to rescue someone or escaping from a situation when others did not. It is not unusual for veterans to be haunted by the lost, who are experienced as demanding retribution.

Through *sublimation*, veterans might channel aggression into sport or working out in the gym. This allows for the venting of impulses in a manner more acceptable in society. An ulterior motive might be to stay in shape in order to be prepared to meet anticipated threat. Exercise can become obsessive and turn into self-punishment. Adrenaline rushes from risk-taking in extreme sports, and the endorphin release associated with exercise can fulfil a need.

Phobic avoidance defence mechanisms include agoraphobia. Although associated with the fear of open spaces, with veterans who have PTSD this often manifests as remaining indoors and avoiding public places for fear of what might be encountered and how they might react, as demonstrated in the introduction to this chapter.

Denial can provide a means of delaying acknowledgement of a painful reality. However, trauma overrides the possibility of temporary denial when the system is overwhelmed by the raw reality of the experience (Garland, 1998). Horowitz (1999) describes denial, emotional numbing and avoidance as 'post-traumatic omissions' (p. 4) that are often linked with unconscious defence processes, which serve to restore equilibrium and to prevent becoming overwhelmed by emotions. However, such defences are breached by intrusive post-traumatic symptoms. Garland (1998) observes the effects of trauma on the 'machinery of the mind' (as described by Freud, 1924), but also stresses the significance of the 'collapse of meaning' associated with trauma that affects the personality (p. 11).

Although conceptual understanding, terminology and therapeutic approach might differ, there is agreement between schools of thought that traumatic experiences need to be brought into conscious awareness, enabling understanding, meaning-making and integration in order to assist recovery from trauma (Ehlers & Clark, 2000; Garland, 1998; Herman, 1992).

Working with division through art therapy

In the following section, examples of work with individual veterans are used to discuss ways in which art therapy might assist reintegration of the 'two minds'.

Past and present

Sometimes traumatic experiences can lead people to leave military service long before expected. Serving personnel might aspire to rise up through the ranks and develop a full career over 22 years. A premature ending can leave veterans bereft. Unable or unwilling to adjust to civilian life, some veterans struggle to rediscover a sense of identity and regain self-worth after leaving the armed forces.

Simon, the veteran who created Plate 8.1, was expressing his conflict of self-perception in relation to his past and present circumstances. On the left-hand side of the image, he stands upright and able as a serving soldier. Shoulders back and meeting the gaze of the viewer, the fresh-faced, clean-shaven soldier self with a half-smile is dressed in uniform with regimental cap badge in place. The surrounding environment is bright and flourishing, reflecting his inner state of well-being. By contrast, the right-hand side of the image is dark and desolate. The trees are broken and the frowning, half-figure is disheveled and scarred. The figure looks as though he has been caught up in the devastation that has damaged the whole landscape. The whole world has changed. The image enabled Simon to express his profound sense of loss and current experience of being in a wilderness. The past, able self is holding qualities inaccessible to the veteran at that point, such as hope, optimism, competence and a sense of belonging.

Remembrance and mourning are part of the process of working through loss. Sometimes there can be obstacles to overcome along the way. Defence mechanisms such as splitting, whereby a military mindset is seen as all good and civilian approaches as all bad, can make acceptance of the change of circumstances undesirable. Veterans might cling onto military identity and the associated value system. Even when a veteran is feeling rejected and abandoned by the military, the attachment can remain self-defining. Through the expression of loss and inner conflict, the journey of reevaluation and rebuilding can begin.

In two minds: stuck in time

Art therapy at Combat Stress is usually offered as group or individual sessions within an inpatient setting. This was the case with Vic, who attended both options during admissions to the Surrey treatment centre. However, a further dimension entered the work when he began painting at home between admissions. He brought the paintings into our sessions in order to explore their meaning.

Vic attended a number of short-stay inpatient admissions of two weeks, with up to a year between stays. This meant that progress was slow and paced to enable change, while at the same time not opening up material that could not be processed safely within the time constraints. Vic travelled a long way to be at the treatment centre, and the journey itself caused discomfort and stress that took a few days to overcome after arrival. He experienced a high level of physical pain associated with a restrictive and debilitating condition, as well as having a diagnosis of PTSD.

It took a while to establish a degree of trust between us due to his heightened hyper-arousal symptoms. Individual sessions were short at 20 minutes, as that was the limit of toleration at first. The high doses of painkillers required to manage his physical problems, combined with anxiety and hyper-arousal, affected his ability to concentrate and retain information from sessions. Consequently, ground was revisited in art therapy sessions at the beginning of each admission. The stabilisation techniques we worked on during sessions seemed to be forgotten after he returned home, so were not put into practice. Vic has an extremely supportive wife. After he returned home, to try to consolidate learning, she would go through all the handouts with him that he had collected from his attendance at therapy groups during admissions.

Problems with peripheral vision meant that Vic had the sense that there was an ominous presence lurking to his left. His hyper-vigilance was high and he always chose to sit at one particular table in the art therapy room, with his back to the wall, where he could see all approaches as well as what was going on outside through the window.

Our work together entailed exploring his life history to get a sense of his core beliefs and perceptions, as well as charting the ups and downs of his journey. Life had presented challenges right from his early days, but moderating factors were his hard-work ethic and resourcefulness. These helped him to overcome adversity. He had always wanted to join the army, and when his dream was realised, he rose to the challenges presented in training. This provided a career pathway that took him away from his situation at home. His service led to him working in many locations within the UK and overseas. He took pride in his achievements and enjoyed being part of a team working towards shared goals.

Vic was not able to get anywhere near speaking about his traumatic experiences without dissociating. He would take on a 'thousand-yard stare', whereby he was transported back in time to the trauma, and lose connection with the present. After some grounding back into the here and now, he usually chose to end the session at that point. Consequently, the life history we were working on had significant gaps in it. He was highly motivated to attend art therapy sessions but seemed to struggle with the psycho-educational groups that took a cognitive behavioural approach.

His sleep pattern was poor due to physical pain, nightmares and night terrors, so he tended to be constantly fatigued. Vic began painting at home. When disturbed by a nightmare he found that he could distance himself from the emotions aroused by painting the nightmare. He said that he felt nothing while painting, yet the images were full of references to pain and horror and coded symbols relevant to his experiences. He was happy for other people to see his work, so he began bringing the paintings with him to the admissions at Combat Stress. One by one, we began looking at the work together in art therapy individual sessions. By viewing them together in this way, he was able to start to reconnect with associated emotions, to disclose elements of his trauma and to begin to make meaning of his experiences.

Plate 8.2 represents a nightmare but also graphically illustrates the struggle with dysfunctionally stored trauma memories that intrude into the present. There is also a sense of the strong link with the past identity as a soldier. The two figures are looking in different directions but have three points of dynamic connection. Words are added to stress and clarify meaning, such as 'stuck in time'. Bosch-like grotesques add to the surreal and nightmarish quality of the work.

Usually in psychodynamically informed art therapy sessions, the focus is on artwork created in that session within the triangular relationship of client, therapist and image. Transference and counter-transference responses might be used to inform understanding of interactions, and the past becomes understood in the light of the present. Bringing into a session an image from home that was created without the therapist's presence introduces further considerations. It echoes the fragmentation of dissociation. Visual imagery, sensations and emotions associated with trauma surfaced in a nightmare, bypassing psychic defences and causing distress. These responses were contained by projecting them into an image and detaching from them. Sometime later, when it was deemed safe enough to reconnect with the content, meaning could be made of the image and distress tolerance gradually increased.

Sometimes veterans are encouraged to use a sketchpad to put marks on paper when awaking from a nightmare. The image-making can help to vent the residue of the nightmare; assist grounding back into the here and now; and can be brought into an art therapy session for further reflection. A small study by Morgan and Johnson (1995) found that a drawing task was more effective than a writing task in the treatment of nightmares in veterans with PTSD. Nightmare work offers a promising symbolic route to explore the effects of trauma that is less confrontational than expressing trauma memories directly.

Looking on from a distance

Art therapy can offer a way to make inroads into traumatic memories, while simultaneously maintaining contact with a calming place. This is consistent with the findings of a study of 15 programmes for veterans with severe PTSD symptoms where art therapy was found to be the most effective because 'it combined pleasurable distraction with exposure to difficult content' (Johnson, Lubin, James & Hale, 1997, as cited in Nanda, Gaydos, Hathorn & Watkins, 2010, p. 382).

Plate 8.3 was created by Richard, a veteran who found it difficult to approach trauma-focused work without becoming overwhelmed by sensory intrusions and dissociating. He was invited to divide the paper into two sections and to begin by creating an image or design with pleasant, calming associations in one, unspecified section. Then, when any connections he might like to explore began to come into mind, it was suggested that he could make some marks to represent them on the other side of the paper. Inspired by the bright colours of a new box of pastels, he decided to draw a bonfire night scene on the right-hand section of the paper.

After a while, he made an association and so began drawing an image on the left-hand side of the paper. It was suggested that if he should experience any level of distress, he should return to the pleasant image on the right-hand side and add more marks to it, and tune back into the calming associations. Following this process of mark-making on alternative sides of the sheet, images emerged that we were able to explore, looking alternately at the calming and distressing material. We looked over the shoulder of his past self and present self in the different scenarios, from a step away. When distress began to mount through witnessing and reconnecting with the image of trauma, he was able to divert attention back to a comforting place and ground himself through the sensory qualities of the art materials.

Enjoying the memory of being at a bonfire and watching the firework display, Richard then made a sensory association with serving in the army during the Falklands War and witnessing the battle of Mount Longdon. An assault had been mounted under cover of darkness and there were many casualties. The sensory aspects of the memory, such as the noise, flashes of colour and felt impact of explosions, were conveyed through the image and verbal reflection. A sense of powerlessness in the trauma scenario was identified and felt, but balanced by taking action and reconnecting with the pleasant place. In this way, he was able to verbalise the experience and tolerate the sensory memories.

Reflecting on the session together in the preparation of this text, Richard confirmed the benefits of developing

> a psychic safety area, almost as if the art working created a barrier between my past and present selves, so that I could see and feel – seemingly at second hand – what the person I had been was seeing and feeling and, when it all got a little fraught, I could retreat to the bonfire party and the fold of my family who were with me there until the crisis passed, then to venture out again.

US art therapists McNamee (2006) and Tripp (2007, 2016) have written about art therapy and bilateral stimulation in relation to *neuroplasticity* – the brain's ability to generate new neural pathways. Bilateral stimulation that purposely involves both brain hemispheres is used in Eye Movement Desensitization and Reprocessing (EMDR) (Shapiro, 2001), an evidence-based intervention that is recommended for the treatment of PTSD. It is proposed that bilateral art-making 'purposefully engages both left and right hemispheres of the brain, as well as multiple sensory systems in responding to client-identified conflicted elements of experience' with the aim of creating balance and integration by changing 'maladaptive neural organization' (McNamee, 2006, pp. 7–8). Tripp has used of a modified version of EMDR combined with art therapy and describes how distressing memories can become 'transformed with new associations to adaptive and positive information' (Tripp, 2007, p. 178), rather than remaining frozen in time.

In the case of Plate 8.3, bilateral stimulation enabled Richard to link emotions and sensations with cognitive evaluation. He was able to gain distance from the trauma material by stepping out of the experience. Simultaneously witnessing a 30-year-old memory alongside a recent experience underlined the separation in time. The art-making provided a way of accessing sensory triggers that opened a gateway to the past but also supplied ways of managing and transforming the material.

Finding equilibrium through art therapy

Art therapy provides a channel for non-verbal, sensory material to unfold and to be thought about. Emerging symbols are decoded into words, thereby creating a narrative shift. In this way, communication between brain hemispheres is improved, which assists meaning-making and the processing of trauma material. Dissociated parts of the whole self can be revealed and reintegration can begin. Art therapy provides a means through which communication between conflicting aspects of the 'two minds' can take place, with the aim of restoring equilibrium following imbalance caused by trauma.

Art therapy can help to focus attention in the present while expressing difficult material from the past. Essentially, the tactile, sensory qualities of the materials, the pleasure of art-making and movement made during art engagement can assist self-regulation while expressing unprocessed, disturbing memories. The art materials provide a tangible connection that anchors one in the present while enabling access to creativity and imagination, which in turn open up new possibilities.

References

American Psychiatric Association (2013). *Diagnostic and statistical manual of mental disorders* (5th edn). Washington, DC: APA.

Bremner, J. D. & Marmar, C. R. (eds) (1998). *Trauma, memory and dissociation.* Washington, DC: American Psychiatric Press.

Breuer, J. & Freud, S. (1895). Studies on hysteria. In J. Strachey (ed. & trans.), *The standard edition of the complete works of Sigmund Freud*, Vol. 2. London: The Hogarth Press.

Brewin, C., Dalgleish, T. & Joseph, S. (1996). A duel representation theory of post-traumatic stress disorder. *Psychological Review, 103*(4), 670–686.

British Pathé News (2016). Reel 1. Netley Hospital 1917 and Seale Hayne Military Hospital 1918. Retrieved from www.britishPathé.com/video/war-neuroses-version-b-reel-1.

Brown. D. & Pedder, J. (1991). *Introduction to psychotherapy: An outline of psychodynamic principles and practice* (2nd edn). London: Routledge.

Carlson, E. B. & Putnam, F. W. (1993). An update on the dissociative experiences scale. *Dissociation, 6*, 16–27.

Ehlers, A. & Clark, D. M. (2000). A cognitive model of posttraumatic stress disorder. *Behaviour Research and Therapy, 38*, 319–345.

Freud, S. (1900). The interpretation of dreams In J. Strachey (ed. & trans.), *The standard edition of the complete works of Sigmund Freud*, Vol. 4. London: The Hogarth Press.

Freud, S. (1920). Beyond the pleasure principle. In J. Strachey (ed. & trans.), *The standard edition of the complete works of Sigmund Freud*, Vol. 18. London: The Hogarth Press.

Freud, S. (1924). The loss of reality in neurosis and psychosis. In J. Strachey (ed. & trans.), *The standard edition of the complete works of Sigmund Freud*, Vol. 19. London: The Hogarth Press.

Garland, C. (1998) (ed.). *Understanding trauma: A psychoanalytical approach.* London: Karnac.

Herman, J. (1992). *Trauma and recovery: The aftermath of violence from domestic abuse to political terror.* New York, NY: Basic Books.

Horowitz, M. J. (1999). (ed.) *Essential papers on Post-Traumatic Stress Disorder.* New York, NY: New York University Press.

ISSTD (2016). *International Society for the Study of Trauma and Dissociation.* Retrieved from www.isst-d.org/?contentID=76.

Janet, P. (1898). *Névroses et idées fixes*, Vol. 1. Paris: Felix Alcan.

Janet, P. (1919). *Les medications psychologiques* (3 volumes). English edition: *Psychological healing* (2 volumes), New York, NY: Macmillan. Reprint: New York, NY: Arno Press, 1976.

Johnson, D. R., Lubin, H., James, M. & Hale, K. (1997). Single session effects of treatment components within a specialized inpatient posttraumatic stress disorder program. *Journal of Traumatic Stress, 10*, 377–390.

Konopka, L. (2016). Neuroscience concepts in clinical practice. In J. L. King (ed.), *Art therapy, trauma, and neuroscience: Theoretical and practical perspectives* (pp. 11–41). New York, NY: Routledge.

Lobban, J. (2016). Art therapy for military veterans with PTSD: A transatlantic study. Retrieved from www.wcmt.org.uk/fellows/reports/art-therapy-military-veterans-ptsd-transatlantic-study#downloads.

McGilchrist, I. (2010). *The master and his emissary: The divided brain and the making of the western world.* London: Yale University Press.

McNamee, C. M. (2006). Experiences with bilateral art: A retrospective study. *Art Therapy: Journal of the American Art Therapy Association, 23*(1), 7–13.

Morgan, C. A. & Johnson, D. R. (1995). Use of a drawing task in the treatment of nightmares in combat-related Post-Traumatic Stress Disorders. *Art Therapy: Journal of the American Art Therapy Association, 12*(4), 244–47.

Myers, C. S. (1940). *Shell shock in France.* Cambridge: Cambridge University Press.

Nanda, U. H., Gaydos, L. B., Hathorn, K. & Watkins, N. (2010). Art and posttraumatic stress: A review of the empirical literature on the therapeutic implications of artwork for war veterans with posttraumatic stress disorder. *Environment and Behavior, 42*(3), 376–390.

Nemiah, J. (1981). Dissociative disorders. In A. M. Freeman & H. I. Kaplan (eds), *Comprehensive textbook of psychiatry* (3rd edn) (pp. 1554–1561). Baltimore, MD: Williams & Wilkins.

Nijenhuis, E. R. S., van der Hart, O. & Steele, K. (2004). Trauma-related structural dissociation of the personality. Trauma Information Pages website, January 2004. Retrieved from www.trauma-pages.com/a/nijenhuis-2004.php.

Putnam, F. W. (1989). *Diagnosis and treatment of multiple personality disorder.* New York, NY: Guilford Press.

Schore, A. N. (2012). *The science of the art of psychotherapy.* New York, NY: W. W. Norton.

Shapiro, F. (2001). *EMDR: Eye Movement Desensitisation and Reprocessing: Basic principles, protocols and procedures* (2nd edn). New York, NY: Guilford Press.

Singer, J. L. (ed.). (1990). *Repression and dissociation: Implications for personality theory, psychopathology, and health.* Chicago, IL: University of Chicago Press.

Spitzer, C., Barnow, S., Freyberger, H. J. & Grabe, H. J. (2006). Recent developments in the theory of dissociation. *World Psychiatry, 5*(2), 82–86.

Steele, K., van der Hart, O. & Nijenhuis, E. R. S. (2005). Phase-orientated treatment for structural dissociation in complex traumatisation: overcoming trauma-related phobias. *Journal of Trauma & Dissociation, 6*(3), 11–53.

Tripp, T. (2007). A short-term therapy approach to processing trauma: art therapy and bilateral stimulation. *Art Therapy: Journal of the American Art Therapy Association, 24*(4), 176–183.

Tripp, T. (2016). A body-based bilateral art protocol for reprocessing trauma. In J. L. King (ed.), *Art therapy, trauma, and neuroscience: Theoretical and practical perspectives* (pp. 173–194). New York, NY: Routledge.

van der Hart, O. (2011). *Dissociation and the personality: The key to understanding chronic traumatisation and a guide to EMDR treatment.* Presented at the EMDR Association UK & Ireland 9th Annual Conference, Bristol, UK.

van der Hart, O., Nijenhuis, E. R. S. & Soloman, R. (2010). Dissociation of the personality in complex trauma-related disorders and EMDR: Theoretical considerations. *Journal of EMDR Practice & Research, 4*(2), 76–92.

Waller, N. G., Putnam, F. W. & Carlson, E. B. (1996). Types of dissociation and dissociative types: A taxonmetric analysis of dissociative experiences. *Psychological Methods, 1*, 300–321.

Chapter 9

Trauma and dissociation

An insider's view

Richard Kidgell

Background

My name is Richard Kidgell. I am 62 years old, I served seven years in the Royal Air Force (RAF), and I have combat-related Post-Traumatic Stress Disorder (PTSD). If this sounds like a drinker introducing himself at a meeting of Alcoholics Anonymous then it is no coincidence, because PTSD is a condition that causes feelings of embarrassment, even shame, and self-condemnation, just as alcoholism can. I had an extra difficulty in being open about my problems because my trauma happened in *combat-like* circumstances in Britain, rather than actual combat, so I have no military campaigns to point to as an explanation, no medals to wear with pride; just private memories of bad things – several of them 'forgotten' by my conscious mind but corrosively remembered at a deeper level. Even my brothers (both ex-servicemen) voiced disbelief that I could have been traumatised by 'home service'. It is a testament to the treatment I have received from the veterans' charity Combat Stress, especially the art therapy, that I am now able to talk openly about my condition and my experiences.

I served on a small air-weapons range for over three years in the early 1980s. There were very few staff, so I had to perform many duties that I had not been trained for, and it was a dangerous place to work. The details are not relevant, but I came close to death on several occasions and I saved colleagues from injury or death on others, although my first aid failed to save one friend's life. Strangely, that posting was very enjoyable: everybody developed a peculiar sense of humour and I felt incredibly alive. We had a job to do, and we were determined to do it well – it was our duty, and our tool was self-discipline. Quite soon I found that I stopped feeling fear; caution and self-preservation remained, but the emotion was gone – or, rather, it was heavily and automatically suppressed.

I went from the range directly to officer training, not realising that I was suffering from the effects of trauma. It was a tough course and, although it was not bullying, it had some of the same characteristics, and I had to inflict even harsher self-discipline on myself. Instinctively protecting the painful, wounded areas of my mind, I felt constantly under siege and derived no satisfaction from my successes; I found it a miserable experience but I kept going for eight months through sheer stubbornness before I withdrew from training. A few months after I finished training I had what I would call a breakdown, although it was not professionally diagnosed. At the time, I judged the symptoms to be unacceptable weakness, and got myself functioning again by imposing yet more self-discipline, and then returned to civilian life. I survived by building a mental 'suit of armour' that shut out negative emotions; I was 'safe' and I could function, but I felt isolated from the world.

During my last few months in the RAF I had two incidents that I now know were 'flashbacks'. One moment, so it seemed to me, I was working on the gun targets at the air weapons range, the next moment I was standing on an airfield that I did not recognise, with no knowledge of how I had suddenly changed place. I was utterly lost and confused, and it took every shred of my self-control to stay calm and work out what was happening to me, until I could suddenly recognise my present surroundings and the intervening memories instantly snapped back into place. I was then able to continue with my tasks, but the return to the present was a quite terrifying experience.

Post-traumatic stress

I made a successful civilian career, becoming a principal systems engineer designing radar systems for GEC-Marconi and BAE Systems, and I had a reasonable social life, getting married and becoming an instructor in the Air Training Corps and the St John Ambulance Cadets. But I was always rather illogically vigilant, being very careful where I placed my feet, to avoid non-existent unexploded weapons, and scanning the sky for non-existent attacking aircraft. I prepared meticulously to be ready for all foreseeable problems and hazards in life, and I felt responsible for the security of everybody around me. I was patient and tolerant of limitations and errors in other people, but I was very intolerant of any failings or weaknesses in myself, and my self-criticism could be quite merciless. I rarely got angry or upset with other people, and I could be remarkably calm and logical in genuine emergencies, but I could explode with self-directed anger and frustration when I made an unimportant mistake or error.

I could still feel happy, but usually in a guarded and muted way; I would rarely allow myself to feel euphoric because I knew that happiness could be snatched away. In the other emotional direction, I could feel threats and danger but I did not feel fear, as I had known it when younger. In 1998, for example, I was involved in a road traffic collision where my car was written-off, with the door being ripped off beside me. I calmly got out of the car, made sure the area was safe and nobody was injured, took necessary actions including making a statement to the police, made arrangements for the car to be recovered, and then caught a bus to work about three hours after the accident. This was not praise-worthy stoicism – I simply did not feel emotionally troubled. In another example of emotional detachment, when my parents died, although I loved my parents and was saddened when they passed away, I again did all the necessary things efficiently and effectively and I did not shed a single tear – I did not seem able to actually grieve. Some people may see this emotional detachment as an advantage, and it certainly makes it easier to deal with problems and emergencies, but now it makes me sad because I lost an aspect of what it really means to be me.

My crisis came in 1999 when my wife had breast cancer. Not, strangely, during the life-threatening phase of her illness but, rather, when she was told that no remaining trace of her cancer could be found and that she would progress to hormone-therapy and monitoring. I gratefully relaxed my self-control and, within two weeks, my wife's Macmillan nurse ordered me to report to my doctor because I had depression. I was immediately prescribed antidepressants and was diagnosed with anxiety and depression by a psychiatrist. I was given a course of relaxation therapy followed by several sessions of one-to-one psychotherapy, and then had to wait around a year for a vacancy for group psychotherapy. This National Health Service (NHS) treatment helped to some extent in keeping me functioning but I continued to deteriorate. Concentration became very difficult, my memory became extremely poor, and there seemed to be threats and potential enemies everywhere. I became hyper-vigilant even though I knew it was unrealistic: crowded places could hide terrorists; unexploded weapons could be lying on the ground; I couldn't stop myself scanning the sky for non-existent attacking aircraft; fireworks were a horror that would send me diving to the ground. I felt ridiculous because I knew it was unreal in the present-day world, but I was locked into a previous time in my life.

I continued to perform well in work, but only by sacrificing my spare time and enjoyable activities, and there were only a few select people that I felt I could trust. I developed a 'siege mentality', even fitting a mirror to my desk so that I could see anybody approaching from behind. And I had frequent, powerful thoughts of killing myself, which was the only way I could see of stopping this mental pain. Here, at least, my excessive self-control worked in my favour because it seemed unfair and dishonourable to cause such upset and grief to the people I cared for just to relieve my own pain. I suffered frequent flashbacks to episodes in my RAF service – not simply vivid memories but episodes where I was living back in the past with no knowledge of my present self. At the worst times, I was getting flashbacks almost every day.

I struggled to keep working and functioning socially, and it was hard. I was tired, depressed, frequently confused and, just in order to survive, I suppressed my emotions with a quite brutal self-discipline. The face I showed to the world, however, convinced everybody, except my wife, that I was cheerful and dealing well with all problems of work and life. I was not. I often felt isolated from the world around me, even when surrounded by colleagues and friends. I felt that my eyes were glass windows and that other people were outside while I was inside, just observing them but not among them. I nicknamed this 'the goldfish bowl effect', but I have since learned that it is termed 'dissociation'.

My life started to change for the better when I approached the charity Combat Stress for help in 2004. I was given a diagnosis of PTSD and started to receive several different kinds of therapy and education. Most importantly, I experienced art therapy, which led me on an incredible journey of discovery through an internal landscape of suppressed emotions, buried memories and internal conflicts. The images I produced over the course of several years led me to discover that my mind had dissociated, and what that entailed. The images even led me to discover mental tools that I could use to help my mind to function properly again. It came too late to save my career (I was medically retired in 2006) but it is helping me to adjust and to function better socially, and I feel that I am again contributing usefully.

The experience of psychological dissociation

I spoke about 'the goldfish bowl effect' earlier, where my eyes seemed to be glass windows, but the effect was actually so strong that I often visualised myself walking up to those windows and tapping the inside of the glass with my hand. When I was in this state, the world outside seemed to be a flat, almost two-dimensional place that had no real meaning for me; sounds seemed muffled and I had little emotion other than a rather detached interest. Strangely, other people did not seem to notice anything unusual about me, but I came to recognise it as a warning sign that I was heading into 'flashback country', as I called it. If I didn't take immediate action to remove myself from the current stressful situation and ground myself in the present, the next phase of the dissociation would be a stream of uncontrollable vivid memories that would scroll past faster and faster, like a film show on fast-forward, and then suddenly stop on one scene. At this point I had only seconds left to ground myself in the present before that memory would take over my whole reality and I would be lost inside a flashback.

People often use the term 'flashback' to describe the experience of uncontrollably recalled vivid memories, but my flashbacks are something else entirely. When in flashback I still have awareness of the things currently around me, but they become incorporated into the memory that I am trapped in, and are interpreted and modified in terms of the mental image caused by that memory. Usually I am on the air-weapons range in the early 1980s wearing RAF uniform; if I am near a car in the current world, it will be an RAF Land Rover in my reality, and carpeted floors will be sandy tracks among scrubland. While in flashback my present time is the date of the memory, and I have no knowledge of my older self or later times.

On one occasion, I had not removed myself from my workplace quickly enough and I entered flashback while still in the car park but, unusually, a tiny part of my present-day conscious mind remained, observing as though from a great distance. In the outside world, I was standing next to my car, a grey Vauxhall Agila, but in the reality of my flashback I was outside the control tower on the air-weapons range; I was in RAF working uniform and I was standing next to an olive-green RAF Land Rover, about to drive out to the targets. The remaining fragment of my conscious mind knew that it would be disastrous to drive in that delusion, but could not penetrate into the flashback to take action. Then I stopped and looked at my hands in puzzlement because I could not bend them; I was wearing, so I thought, my canvas and leather RAF working gloves and all looked normal – but my wrists were locked, and I started to get very worried. In the real world, I had developed repetitive strain injuries a few months earlier from using a computer and I was wearing rigid wrist splints; but the younger me of the flashback knew nothing of this. The remnant of my conscious mind managed to wrestle enough control back to shout one imperative order: 'Run!' And I did. And as I moved away from the situation, the flashback faded and I gradually returned to being my older self. It was a very unpleasant experience.

I had one particular experience of flashback that gives, I think, a valuable clue about what is happening in the brain during this phenomenon. One day in late 2005, I was walking down a corridor in work, returning to my office after a difficult and stressful technical meeting, when I found myself drifting into a flashback. But the interesting thing about this occasion was that I found myself simultaneously in two different realities. In one reality, I was in the present day walking down the corridor and about to turn left to my office. In the other reality, I was in flashback on the air-weapons range, walking down a sandy track and about to turn right to the electronic gun target that I had to repair. As I reached the turning point, my right leg turned left and my left leg turned right! I fell flat on my face, of course, and began laughing like an idiot because I found my situation both ridiculous and hilarious! My feelings of stress disappeared with my descent into comedy, and my mind snapped back completely to the present. I think that the important feature of this episode was that my right leg acted correctly for the present-day situation, while my left leg reacted according to the needs of the flashback. My conclusion from this is that the flashback originated in my right brain hemisphere, the emotional source of the subconscious mind. If I had not fallen over and snapped back to reality, I believe that the flashback would have swiftly overwhelmed the left brain hemisphere also, and I would have missed this insight.

Another symptom I have of dissociation is 'lost time', which usually happens when I am relaxed in a quiet period without stresses or pressure. I suddenly become aware that time has passed that I have no awareness of; perhaps the clock will seem to have suddenly jumped forward by half an hour or more, or the room will appear to have suddenly got darker in the evening. I have an awareness that I have not been asleep, and sometimes tasks will have been done without my apparent knowledge. It is as though my conscious mind has 'stood down' for a while and left my subconscious in charge.

Luckily, art therapy has not only led me to an understanding of dissociation and its cause, but it has also suggested mental techniques and tools to help me reduce the frequency and effects of dissociation.

My experience of art therapy

I am neither a medical nor a therapy professional, so I can only talk about art therapy from my personal experience as a client. But I hope that my personal insight will be useful to readers of this book. I have experienced two different types of artistic therapies at the Combat Stress treatment centre: art therapy and art as occupational therapy. Laypeople tend to assume that these are the same thing but, although they are both valuable in their own ways, they are not the same. Occupational therapy uses art, along with other activities, to develop skills, to practice concentration, to foster self-confidence, and give a sense of achievement. Art therapy proper uses creative media as a tool to gain access to hidden and suppressed aspects of the mind and memory. I usually finish a session of occupational therapy less tense, and feeling good at having achieved something worthwhile. I am much more likely to finish an art therapy session feeling shaky and rather stunned by what has been revealed – and in great need of a sit-down with a nice hot cup of tea! I know several other veterans who have tried art therapy once and have declined any more sessions because they did not feel an immediate benefit. This is a great pity because I have found that it may take days or even weeks for art therapy's very real benefits to begin to show.

The art therapy room at the Combat Stress treatment centre has a variety of art materials such as modelling tools, different types of paint, pencils, pastels, chalks, and even a box of assorted 'bit and pieces' (small stones, snail shells, nuts and bolts and many other things that can be found for zero cost but may trigger a memory or thought). This variety allows me to clear my mind and allow my subconscious to select whatever feels right at the time. In the past, I have made images in paint, finger paint, pencil and coloured pencil, pastel and collage using the bits and pieces. Also, I have made several responses through written words – poems, short prose, or written comments on a picture. But all of these images have two things in common: I always try to first clear my mind of conscious, verbal thoughts, and I try to work in a quick, simplistic and unskilled way. I find that consciously trying to decide and plan the image and trying to work in a skilful manner will both trigger the logical left brain to interfere with the process, and it will then censor and block messages from the subconscious right brain. I describe my technique in art therapy as 'stick-man and blob drawing'!

The first images I made in art therapy were simple pencil sketches that displayed some troubling events in my past in a very literal way, but symbolism soon started to feature and colour became more significant. To me, symbols together with feelings are clearly the language of the subconscious right brain, and their invocation in art therapy has a similarity to dreaming; but whereas dreams are difficult to comprehend because they are uncontrolled, broken and difficult to remember, art therapy images are generated while fully conscious and have a concrete nature that can be analysed and reviewed at leisure, sometimes even years later.

Art therapy images have triggered the recovery of several memories that I had previously 'lost'. Some of these had simply disappeared from my recollection without even leaving an awareness that anything was missing; some had disappeared from recall but left a feeling that there was something that I should remember; others left a false memory of being told about an event that I was not personally involved in. All, however, left confusing 'jumps' and inconsistencies in my personal narrative history that I could not explain, and that left me worried, especially as I was apparently getting emotional reactions to nothing. Several times in art therapy sessions I would find that a symbolic or allegorical image would appear that I could not explain, rather similar to having a disturbing dream. However, unlike a dream, I had a concrete image that I could review and think about later, and then, sometimes after a period of days or even weeks, I would suddenly realise the meaning of the image and the memory would reappear in my recall, feeling as though it had never been missing. Strangely, all of the lost memories that I have so far recovered have been of unpleasant events where I did the right thing and had no reason to feel ashamed. I have no idea why I should have quarantined these memories, but I feel better for having them returned to my personal narrative.

Another difference to dreams that I have found is that art therapy images do not only indicate what is wrong, they can also suggest ways to improve, and can offer mental tools to deal more effectively with difficulties, such as through compassionate imagery (as discussed in Chapter 7). For example, one of my images showed that I faced a stark choice between two directions; I could take the 'easy' route and accept mental 'immobility until death' or I could exert myself to re-join the 'Dance of Life' and one day re-emerge into the sunlight (I don't know whether the term 'Dance of Life' was unconsciously inspired by the title of the famous painting by Munch but, to me, it just seemed to be a spontaneous metaphor). The choices and consequences were suddenly very clear, and I decided on the painful and harder path to re-join the Dance of Life. The most powerful and useful 'compassionate image' that I have produced seems quite strange at first sight because it is a large pink dragon named Taffy the Friendly Dragon that represents my complete self when my left brain and right brain (or conscious and subconscious minds) are working in harmony. Plate 9.1 is a picture of Taffy that I painted to make him more 'real' to me. When I face a challenging task, such as walking through a crowded street or travelling on public transport, I will visualise Taffy next to me reminding

Figure 9.1 Left and Right by Richard Kidgell

me that I still have the strength and determination to do what must be done. When my mind dissociates and I find it hard to function because my two minds disagree, I see Taffy within myself and I talk to the two warring minds through him, encouraging and persuading them to co-operate. And it works.

Figure 9.1, drawn in 2013, is an important example of my art therapy images because it explained to me, as a strip-cartoon running from top left to bottom right, how my dissociation came about. The logical, disciplined conscious mind of the left brain is drawn as a plain black figure, while the creative, emotional subconscious mind of the right brain is drawn as a brightly coloured figure. In the days before trauma they are shown as good friends who are happy to work together; but when traumatic danger struck, the conscious mind knew that I had to be logical and disciplined to survive, so it suppressed the emotional subconscious mind and hid it in a place of safety buried by discipline, standard responses, logic and rules. This was the right thing to do in the time of danger because it ensured my survival but, like an old warhorse, the left brain could never accept that the danger was past and stand down. It remained permanently on guard, and would never let the subconscious leave its shelter. The shelter became a prison to the subconscious mind, which was only allowed to peep out briefly when the conscious mind needed assistance for intuitive thought, creativity or decision-making, and was then pushed back down again. Not surprisingly, the subconscious mind became angry, resentful and afraid.

Figure 9.2 Mind and Body by Richard Kidgell

Figure 9.2 appeared during my next admission at Combat Stress, about six months later, in response to the given topic 'Mind and Body'. I had begun to tell myself that I had identified all the major problems in my past, and could move forward more rapidly towards recovery as a more integrated person, but this simple image warned me that I had still deeper and more troubling levels of my psyche that must be explored. The image is stark in black and white, with a road leading back through my life to a time when the sky was even blacker than the black paper I have drawn on. The big human figure is me in the present day, and I have turned around to see how far I have travelled. But farther back along the road I can see another human figure, and I realise that this is a part of me that is still stuck in the past, and he is covered in a black pall of sorrow and depression. I think of the present me as 'I' and the me lost in the past as 'him', and whereas I have looked back by choice, he is compelled to look back all the time in fixated horror. I feel real sorrow and compassion for him, and a great need to rescue him from his nightmare, which seems strange since I know that he is 'just' a split-off part of me.

Figure 9.3 is a landmark image that I made just a few days later. Ever since I made the decision in 1984 that I would leave the RAF, I had been haunted in my mind by a devilish presence that I named 'The General'. Logically, I was certain that his existence was impossible, but he felt absolutely real

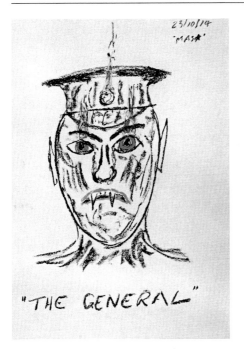

Figure 9.3 The General by Richard Kidgell

to me and I knew that if I put my thoughts into words then he would hear them inside my head and intervene to wreck my plans. I had no doubt that I would be marked down as having paranoid delusions if anybody found out about The General, and this would wreck my plans just as effectively – but I also knew that this would be a wrong diagnosis. I knew absolutely that The General had a real existence, even though I could not explain him, but I was well aware of the devastating effect that a label of 'paranoid' would have on my career and personal life, so The General remained my tightly guarded secret.

But as my dissociation was gradually disclosed to me through art therapy I began to suspect that The General was the right brain's symbolic view of the left brain, with its discipline and rigid control, and its demands for performance no matter what the personal pain and grief, and I started to think that there may even be some sense of fear. And it explained the idea that my thoughts could be read once I had put them into words – the left brain is, after all, the hemisphere that produces and uses language; it's just that without dissociation we do not perceive two people in one mind.

Then this image of The General appeared in an art therapy session, though the mental image in my mind was even more demonic and evil than could be captured in this quick sketch. I was left in no doubt that it was how the

Figure 9.4 Dead Eye by Richard Kidgell

subconscious saw my conscious mind, and it was a big shock. How could one part of my mind be so afraid of another part of my own mind? After the session, I fell asleep for three dream-filled hours and, when I woke, I actually heard an internal conversation in words:

> Conscious mind (in a worried tone): Is that really how you see me?
> Subconscious (sounding a bit embarrassed): Well ... not really. Not now.
> Conscious mind: So, how do you see me now?

And a new image flashed into my mind; complex, in full colour, and accompanied by a description in words suitable for a schoolboy adventure story! I drew this image as clearly as I could while it was fresh in my mind, and this image is reproduced in Figure 9.4. The verbal description I heard was, 'Squadron Leader Richard ("Dead Eye Dick") Kidgell, known to his friends as "Dead Eye", Scourge of the Black Dragons!' and my conscious mind has been 'Dead Eye' ever since. I was haunted by The General for 30 years; it took one session of art therapy to kill him forever.

Although I still have dissociation, the excessively self-critical, over-disciplined and self-controlling aspect of myself, which manifested as a response to trauma, has now been largely replaced by a willingness to cooperate internally (though not always successfully). My subconscious mind has also become more assertive when my conscious mind tries to act aggressively, and Dead Eye has become another compassionate image – ready to step in and fight the 'Black Dragons' that are the problems caused by traumatic memories.

My experience of the value of art therapy

All the types of therapy I have experienced have been valuable in their own ways but, for the sheer depth and speed of penetration, art therapy stands head and shoulders above the others for me. By the very nature of language, the subconscious mind must work through the left brain hemisphere to hold a conversation, and this gives the logical conscious mind a perfect opportunity to censor the information released. Old habits, fears and questions of public image can all prevent the subconscious being heard in the spoken therapies, whereas art therapy, as long as great skill is not demanded, gives the subconscious a voice of its own to speak without censorship in its own symbolic language. And I have found that its revelations can be both surprising and shocking to the conscious mind.

My conscious mind has suppressed many problematic memories that remain accessible to my subconscious, causing emotional problems that surface in dreams … and in art therapy! I have recovered several 'lost' memories through art therapy, but none through the spoken therapies I have engaged in. By presenting subconscious images in a concrete form that must be viewed and analysed by my conscious mind, art therapy is forcing my two minds to communicate and, as a result, they are coming to gradually reconnect and reintegrate.

Chapter 10

Bypassing the sentinel

Janice Lobban

It can be a challenge to tease out the specific contribution of art therapy in treatment outcomes when it is part of a multi-disciplinary programme. Feedback from veterans with Post-Traumatic Stress Disorder (PTSD) through group evaluations and questionnaires at Combat Stress, the veterans' mental health charity, suggested that art therapy might be able to help to overcome avoidance and assist therapeutic engagement. With this in mind, it was posited that by providing a channel of expression for non-verbal operations of the brain associated with emotions, visual imagery and body sensations, it might be possible to circumvent restrictive cognitive and language centres of the brain that can present a rigid and inflexible stance. In this way suppressed, unconscious or avoided material might be accessed to enable wider perspectives to be considered. To explore these possibilities, a sample of veterans were offered individual art therapy sessions on an outpatient basis. They were receiving no other psychological interventions, so it was more likely that any changes would be related to the art therapy sessions. Emerging symbols of resistance were found to be experienced with surprise as veterans gained deeper insight into their personal barriers to recovery. The following text provides an overview of the pilot study. To stay in keeping with the rest of the chapters, the material is not presented as a traditional research report but as a more general discussion.

Background

Avoidance is one of the four clusters of PTSD symptoms and manifests as 'Persistent avoidance of stimuli associated with the traumatic event(s)' either through thoughts and feelings, or external reminders such as people or places (American Psychiatric Association, 2013, p. 271). As such it can present a significant barrier to engaging in treatment. It can take time to establish enough trust to start opening up in therapy, which is not always possible with limited resources and austerity measures in place. Even then, avoidance can have a strong hold that is hard to overcome. When compounded by guilt or shame, resistance to overcoming avoidance might present a seemingly insurmountable block. Safety behaviours like avoidance, if left unchallenged, can create restrictions that have a profound effect on daily life functioning. Avoidance can maintain psychological distress and affect spontaneity (Kashdan, Barrios, Forsyth & Steger, 2006). It is a key concept in many theoretical approaches but different terms of reference might be used. It could be compared with the psychoanalytic concept of repression with resistance to treatment, although avoidance is often a conscious choice (Lobban, 2016).

Sometimes avoidance presents in art therapy imagery through symbols of isolation, detachment or perhaps aggression. Figure 10.1 gives the message 'keep out' or perhaps 'handle with care', with pins ready to pierce unwelcome approaches. The contents of the box are sealed inside out of view, with the suggestion of an unexploded bomb primed and ready to be detonated. Veterans might 'show their claws' to keep people at a distance both to protect the person and themselves. There can be fear of opening up emotionally and getting hurt again, for instance after losing a close comrade.

The task then is to find ways of overcoming avoidance and fostering therapeutic engagement. There is no universally agreed definition of 'therapeutic engagement' and measures tend not to be generalisable across contexts and populations (Tetley, Jinks, Huband & Howells, 2011). So, for the purpose of the pilot research, the concept of therapeutic engagement was understood as: (i) attendance; (ii) active participation involving art-making and reflective discussion; (iii) emotional tolerance of the material shared; (iv) signs of new learning; and (v) completion of the treatment.

Figure 10.1 Pin Box

In order to construct a research question, veteran art therapy group evaluations and surveys were studied for indication of any mechanisms that might be in play. An analysis of the veteran feedback for art therapy groups will be presented in Chapter 11, but it is relevant to include some references at this point. Veterans expressed surprise by the strength of feeling stirred and by the symbols that emerged through art therapy. There were comments about making new discoveries and learning more about themselves. Respondents found that art therapy brought out things in them that they did not know were there, and that they were unexpectedly able to express their emotions (Lobban, 2016). These comments seemed to indicate that veterans were exposing material that had been unconscious or suppressed, and that they were able to manage the strength of feeling stirred, thereby increasing emotional tolerance. To explore these ideas in more depth, the research question for the pilot was: In what ways might art therapy be able to assist the overcoming of avoidance among veterans and facilitate therapeutic engagement? In order to address this question, veteran referrals were sought.

The research framework

Potential participants were approached on the basis of fitting various criteria, including having a diagnosis of chronic PTSD and not being ready, willing or able to attend the six-week, inpatient Intensive Treatment Programme. Veterans had to be available to commit to 14 weekly or fortnightly sessions and be able to travel to the treatment centre. Many veterans with PTSD are unable to use public transport due to the anxiety it causes, or might be unable to afford the cost of travel. In all, nine veterans began the research pilot but only five completed the full course of sessions. Transportation problems played a significant part in the dropout rate. Several veterans had to rely on getting lifts from friends or family members, but that was not always possible. Four participants had return journeys of between 116 and 178 miles to make due to the geographical spread of the catchment area. Two of the four veterans eventually dropped out of the pilot.

The research pilot comprised a baseline session during which two psychometric measures, the PTSD Symptom Scale-Interview (PSSI) and Dissociative Experiences Scale-II (DESII), were used to determine symptoms measurement at that point. Individual semi-structured interviews were also conducted to establish personal aims and objectives relating to the sessions. These interviews were recorded and later transcribed verbatim for analysis. Finally, an art therapy task was set. Each veteran was asked to describe the image that they produced during the task, and these descriptions were recorded for subsequent analysis. This baseline session was followed by 12 art therapy sessions that were spread over 5–9 months according to circumstances. Each participant had a review session during which the PSSI and DESII were repeated, a semi-structured interview was recorded and later transcribed verbatim, and the art therapy task was repeated and the description recorded.

The art therapy task was to make a creative response to the theme 'mask'. A mask is an internationally recognised symbol, sometimes associated with ritual or ceremony. The concept of presenting a disguising mask that hides inner experience repeatedly finds expression during art therapy groups. The military role involves presenting a fixed expression in certain circumstances, such as when on parade or guard duty, that gives no indication of inner thought processes. In a thematic analysis of a filmed Combat Stress art therapy group, the theme of 'mask' emerged and associations were made with structural dissociation of the personality, whereby an apparently normal personality presents to the world covering an emotional personality trapped in trauma time (Lobban, 2014; Nijenhuis, van der Hart & Steele, 2004). The analysis identified 'the dichotomy of hiding the emotional self behind a coping mask, the effort involved and the fragility of the man inside' (Lobban, 2014, p. 8). In the current study, repeating the task at the end of the course of sessions enabled a comparison between two different interpretations of the same theme by the same veteran, and observation of any changes.

Comparison between the mask images made at the beginning and end of treatment

This section features a descriptive analysis of images created in response to the theme 'mask'. Pseudonyms are used to protect the identities of participants, and veterans' own words are used to enhance the text.

John's response to the theme in the baseline session was to create a three-dimensional collage to express his well-defended position (Figure 10.2). It was difficult to construct and kept falling down but he persevered, which gave a sense of the instability of the front presented and of the effort needed to maintain the lines of defence. He explained 'you've always got this fear that everything around you is just gonna fall apart'. Represented by a small plastic soldier lying prone on guard with rifle in hand ready to respond to approaches, he erected a huge barricade to protect himself and to hide behind. John described his position as 'keeping myself away from everything I don't have to deal with', which seemed to highlight the force of avoidance. There are a number of obstacles to negotiate before being able to reach John. Four large boulders at the forefront represent buildings, with trees and a wall behind. People try to come in from the side and bypass this initial line of defence. This is shown by the footprints left in the sand. John can observe approaches through a tiny crack in the barricade but no one can see him. The blockade was constructed of natural materials suggestive of the use of camouflage in operational duties where soldiers play the waiting game ready to attack or defend their position.

By contrast, in the image created by John in the review session after 12 art therapy sessions, the mask has been removed (Figure 10.3). The coping, smiling front that says 'everything is good' has been pulled off revealing a charred, black, suffering inner self. The alliterative quality of the accompanying rhyme

Figure 10.2 Mask 1 by John

'a projection of protection to mask the task' seems to act as an amusing buffer that simultaneously identifies the purpose of the defence while deflecting from the painful exposure. This shift from blockade to exposure demonstrated the progress made by John while also revealing the considerable work yet to be done to assist that damaged inner self in beginning to repair. The pulling away of the mask had a shock factor that reinforced a need to take paced steps towards trauma work.

Steve's response to the unexpected theme of the baseline session was also three-dimensional (Figure 10.4). He rolled out clay and then placed it over his own face to form the shape of a mask with the intention of embedding an impression of the real self inside where no one sees it. He explained that no one can really know what is going on inside you by looking at the outside. Even looking at it from the outside himself, as though a mirror image, it was 'not a true reflection' but an 'unrecognisable distortion'. The softness of the clay made it susceptible to tearing as he tried to maintain the form created. The mouth appears to be crying out and the tilted eye areas add to the emotional expression, but any signs of anguish were batted away by humour and comments that he had almost suffocated himself during the creative act. Steve commented that the eyes were open but 'not necessarily seeing' because of distorted perceptions. The artwork resembles an ancient Greek warrior

Figure 10.3 Mask 2 by John

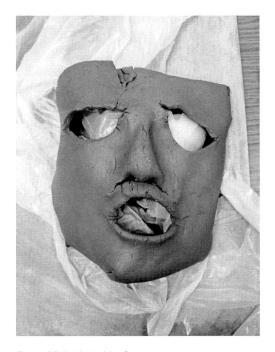

Figure 10.4 Mask 1 by Steve

theatrical mask. Steve was later to speak about the theatre of war and playing his part. The art therapy mask had expression but it was not set. The soft malleability of the clay made it fragile and susceptible to damage, yet also offered potential for remoulding and changes.

After the series of individual art therapy sessions, Steve took a different approach when revisiting the theme in the review. He used pastels on paper to create an elaborate colour-coded image that could barely be contained within the sheet of paper (Plate 10.1). It formed a timeline of emotional responses to life circumstances. He gave a detailed account of situations faced and the emotional impact of events, noticing patterns and cycles, explaining codes and giving shape and form to experiences both good and bad. This opening-up enabled joint viewing and observations from shared perspectives of his 'life on a piece of paper'. The smudged line across the middle of the image was to convey the blurring experienced at the time, it was only now from a distance that responses began to make sense.

Brian was apprehensive about responding to the theme during the baseline session. He presented as anxious and guarded but wanted to find a way to begin to open up. His desire to vent feelings was measured by his resistance to letting those feelings find release for fear of becoming overwhelmed and suicidal. His small hesitant pencil drawing shows him behind a mask that resembles a shield or visor (Figure 10.5). Beside the small figure he wrote

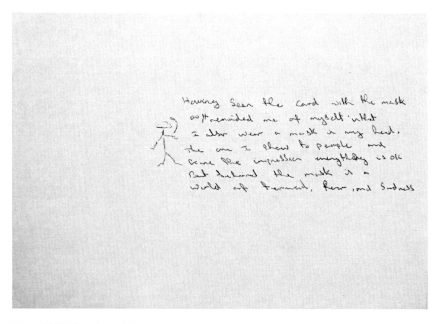

Figure 10.5 Mask 1 by Brian

having seen the card with the mask on, it reminded me of myself in that I also wear a mask in my head. The one I show people and give the impression everything is okay. But behind the mask is a world of turmoil, fear and sadness.

The card he referred to was one of a selection of different art postcards available at a previous art therapy group. It was of the golden funeral mask of Agamemnon. After making the image, Brian had little more to add verbally to the words written on paper.

As part of the review session, Brian created another interpretation of the mask (Figure 10.6). This time a self-portrait fills the paper, which meets the viewer's gaze. The image shows Pandora's Box, which holds memories of trauma, in a black shroud that intrudes into the present. The right-hand side of the face in this mirror image disintegrates into a shadowy form that conveys the sensory quality of trauma re-experiencing. Brian was able to convey abstract, sensory material through his work, giving the viewer a sense of the duality of his experience. Pandora's Box is closed and strapped down, as he likes it to be – under his control. There are little figures in battle. Some represent the 'bad stuff' while others representing the 'good stuff' in life are pulling back the shroud. In this work he seems more confident and he identified his expression in the image as 'calm'.

Figure 10.6 Mask 2 by Brian

The art therapy images provide visible evidence of the changes in approach to the concept of the mask and progress made towards overcoming avoidance. By the end of the course of art therapy sessions, John removed his mask and exposed the darkness he felt inside; Steve's mask had gone and he was examining the person behind the mask; and Brian revealed the next challenge to accessing the source of his 'turmoil, fear and sadness' but also provided symbolic resources to help. The other two veterans who participated in the full programme of sessions, Ian and Rob, also changed their approaches to masking difficulties and referred to specific experiences in their work. Art therapy was able to facilitate a gradual exposure of underlying fears and an increase in self-confidence that any feelings and trauma material touched upon would be within their own control and at their own pace.

The inner critic or self-saboteur – seeing resistance through art therapy images

In Chapter 8, veterans' experiences of having 'two minds' was explored using frameworks such as dissociation, trauma intrusions and differences in brain hemisphere information processing to make sense of this concept. Another aspect in play seems to be more associated with the negative changes in cognition cluster of PTSD symptoms. Once trust is built, veterans frequently begin to acknowledge and refer to an 'inner critic' that undermines progress. Achievement and hope can be swiftly destroyed by attacks of guilt and self-loathing. It is not unusual for veterans to admit that they had been covering up the presence of this inner critic in the knowledge that exposure would be followed by unbearable reprisals by this split-off part of themselves. *Moral injury* (Litz et al., 2009) can play a part in this form of resistance to recovery. Veterans might judge that witnessed or experienced acts of omission or commission violated their personal values and beliefs, shattering deeply held assumptions, and seemingly creating irreparable damage to their ability to think kindly of themselves ever again, or to contemplate self-forgiveness. This subject is explored in more depth in Chapter 5.

During the art therapy outpatient sessions, there were occasions when resistance was revealed through the image-making either manifesting by surprise or through direct targeting. Plate 10.2 was made jointly by Ian and the art therapist. He had been experiencing distressing feelings and body sensations prior to the session but did not know how to begin to work with this. Usually after a discussion of presenting circumstances, Ian would use the materials to express his associations and insights would be gained. However, he felt blocked and uncertain. For the first time in their work together, the art therapist suggested that joint painting might help to find a way forward. He was open to this suggestion as he felt something different needed to be done. In such circumstances, the art therapist follows the lead of the veteran painting reflections of his/her work, for instance an echo of a colour or a balancing mark. Silent turn-taking ensued and a divided landscape emerged with Ian leading its form. The figure of Don Quixote and a dragon appeared. The art therapist painted a flagpole to echo the shape of Don Quixote's lance, linking it with a band of red and yellow to give the appearance of a flag. To Ian's surprise he responded by painting another figure, this time kicking the flagpole. He had interpreted the therapist's marks as the flame of a lamp casting light into a bleak, dark landscape and he saw the figure as his subconscious mind angrily rejecting the light and forcefully saying, 'Go away! I want to stay here'. Ian was surprised by his angry response and this recognition of his own resistance was a shock to him, which opened up new areas to explore. He later observed that there had been signs in earlier work but he could not or would not recognise them at the time.

It became evident through sessions with John that opportunities to reclaim his life were undermined by self-sabotaging thoughts and behaviour. He described having to hide progress from himself by not acknowledging gains because the guilt stirred up could be overwhelming. Taking a compassionate mind approach, John was encouraged to develop a third-party compassionate image that might enable him to view his situation from an alternative, non-judgemental perspective. As progress was made with this suggestion, John was invited to create an image of the self-sabotaging aspect of him to try to understand more about it. He created Figure 10.7 in response. Having

Figure 10.7 Inner Saboteur by John

a resonance with Figure 10.2, John's initial response to the mask theme, it shows a barrier separating the saboteur from the viewer. However, this time the barrier is much smaller than the figure, who peeps over the top looking surprised and anxious. With its crenellations, the wall appears castle-like but its curve gives the impression that the viewer is inside and the figure is outside. He wrote 'you may see but you cannot pass' on the image, emphasising that there would be much more work to be done before change could be made. The self-sabotaging figure is no fierce demon but has more of the appearance of a frightened child. This offered new perspectives to work with.

Seeing images from a different perspective

In session 12 of each of the cases, the veteran and the art therapist looked back over all the work created during the previous sessions, spread out over tables like an exhibition. The majority of the veterans had forgotten several of the images they had made and were able to look at them as though for the first time from a third-person stance. Rob did not recognise his work at first and then was shocked by how chaotic the images were. He chose to write poems in many of the sessions. When he did choose art materials, he used pencils, pens and a ruler to provide structure to his image (Figure 10.8). Nevertheless, looking back all he could see was chaos and gaps that made him realise that

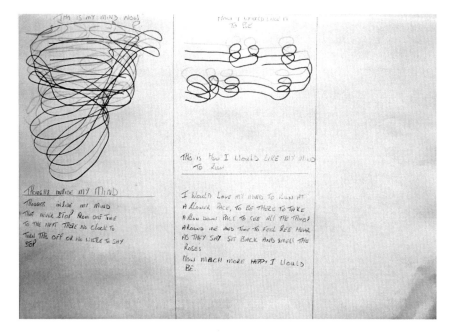

Figure 10.8 My Mind by Rob

something had to be done to enable change. It seems he was too close to see this when he first created the images and needed to take a step back to view them from a wider perspective. The work captured undeniable proof that he was no longer able to hide from himself, which he could only recognise over time, and he had built sufficient self-compassion to want to do something about it.

Looking back, Steve observed repeating patterns in his work, particularly circles, seemingly trapped in repeating the same cycle. Notably his last image broke that pattern and offered an open-ended viewpoint, although accepting there would still be ups and downs (Plate 10.1). Brian chose to create repeated images of one of his traumas in the sessions, but each time his tolerance of the memory increased. Initially there had been a reluctance to open up about the experience, but progressively he was able to say more about the trauma. He added adaptive information and details to the scenario, seeing the situation from different perspectives. His intrusions decreased and he reported that the memory now felt manageable. He also experienced a shock of recognition that he was reluctant to let go of that trauma as it was keeping other traumatic memories at bay, the next step being to face those memories.

Veteran interviews

The transcribed interviews were explored using inductive content analysis, a qualitative research approach. Some of the shared themes that arose are presented here, along with changes seen through psychometric measures, with quotations from participants to illustrate their observations.

Overall, the PSSI measures showed a decrease in the frequency and severity of avoidance subscales related to the prevention of engagement with life goals and the ability to experience a whole range of feelings. There was a slight increase in hyper-arousal and physical symptoms in some cases, seemingly related to exposure to difficult material and the reduction in avoidance. The DESII measures revealed a decrease in dissociation scores, which suggest an increase in emotional tolerance.

Behind the mask

Baseline interviews revealed that 'wearing a mask' was seen as a way of protecting others and oneself. This might be due to: fear of losing control and contaminating others with unspeakable knowledge, or causing damage to the self or others; fear of being judged and recognised as unworthy; or as a way of deceiving oneself or others. The masked self was described as 'defective, weak, incapable, vulnerable' and 'unacceptable', but also in some cases as 'angry' and 'dangerous'. Fear was expressed over the capacity to meet threat with cold and remorseless detachment. The character behind the mask was described as 'a demon' in some cases.

A mask provided an 'appearance of confidence' but also gave nothing away by having a fixed expression. One participant said that he could 'scream behind it and nobody can hear', recognising that he could 'love but the mask stops it'. A mask conveys that 'there's nothing wrong with me' but inside the veteran knew that was untrue. There was a sense of hiding behind the mask and being caught up in a whirlwind inside. The mask was experienced as restrictive as 'you can't see your way forward'. It was also heavy and tiring to maintain.

Looking behind the mask through the art therapy sessions opened up new perspectives. One veteran expressed his relief at looking at the emerging symbol and knowing what he looked like. There were signs of self-compassion and a growing desire to understand the masked self and to rescue that part trapped in suffering.

The experience of art therapy

Participants reported that the art therapy sessions had been a revelation and they all discovered new insights. There was surprise: 'My response amazed me'; 'I was surprised how deep you could get by drawing'; 'really revealing'; 'surprised me to a very large extent'; 'art therapy seems to go straight to the subconscious without filtering and you get the full emotional impact'; 'then I suddenly realised what I'd drawn'. The emerging material had been unplanned: 'I didn't have the idea of coming and talking about it'; 'I wasn't thinking about what I was drawing, then I suddenly realised'; 'crossing boundaries into an unknown world'; 'I had something else in mind and all of a sudden something else came out'.

The veterans were able to regain a sense of control: 'I got things out'; 'I managed to get them all back in the box'; 'release a little bit at a time'; 'didn't let on at the time'; 'not having to go into depth [in words]'. The ability to use coding and to disguise material was seen as helpful: 'tricking your mind into letting things out'; 'put the message in there but surrounded it'; 'code and take it as far as you want to in the session'. This allowed participants to pace their own exposure to difficult thoughts and feelings.

There was a sense of self-discovery: 'it started to make sense'; 'I learned an awful lot about myself'; 'brought out things I didn't know were there'; 'sometimes you didn't know until you'd almost finished'; 'things that I've never really thought about before make perfect sense as to why I do certain things or think certain thoughts'; 'freed up that part [of my mind] that had been censored'. Accompanying this was recognition of inner conflict: 'I hadn't realised that before; positive and negative having a punch-up'; 'seeing the self-criticisms'; 'in a very real sense [[that part of me] had been a damn bully'; '[recognising] the detached part of my personality stuck in the past'; 'angry and not wanting to come forward [into the present]'.

Significantly, there was increasing tolerance of the difficult material: '[my problems] haven't got the same power anymore'; 'I find myself letting go [of the events]'; 'not as bad as I thought it was going to be'; 'I thought I'd be completely overwhelmed but I wasn't'. The sessions had been like 'lancing a boil' whereby healing could begin. Behind the mask, experiences had been a 'blur', but art therapy helped veterans to find 'clarity' and 'see a wider picture'. From other perspectives, the veterans were able to begin to re-evaluate their positions.

Conclusion

All completing participants were able to tackle their avoidance of difficult psychological material and to increase distress tolerance, as shown by their responses to the theme of the mask. They also demonstrated therapeutic engagement, as defined earlier in the chapter. The work provided a gateway for further treatment as appropriate for each individual.

The research question explored in this study was: In what ways might art therapy be able to assist the overcoming of avoidance among veterans and facilitate therapeutic engagement? Findings suggest that art therapy can be an effective way of bypassing psychological defences, which could be viewed symbolically as a sentinel that had not been ready to stand down. Constantly on guard and with a view restricted by threat perception, defences were causing significant distress and life limitations. Experienced as less confrontational than verbal therapy approaches, art therapy allowed the emergence of underlying anxiety at a pace deemed manageable by participants. Using their own symbolic language, participants were able to 'trick' their own defences into exposing the crux of their inner conflict, and to use the insights gained to challenge perceptions and to begin to see their own material from different perspectives. Barriers to progress that were previously either masked or out of conscious awareness began to find expression through image-making, and once recognised, could be challenged. As participants were receiving no other form of psychological input at the time of the study, it is likely that these changes were associated with the art therapy sessions. This study suggests that art therapy is a promising approach for the treatment of psychological avoidance in PTSD. It also highlights the need to provide further treatment once avoidance is breached. This might involve more art therapy sessions or referral on for trauma-focused cognitive behavioural therapy.

Furthermore, as well as overcoming avoidance, both Brian and Ian were able to make significant progress towards reprocessing traumatic memories. There seems to be a general consensus of opinion between art therapists working within the field of trauma that art therapy can help with cognitive restructuring and the integration of trauma memories (Gantt & Tinnin, 2009; Hass-Cohen, Findlay, Carr & Vanderlan, 2014; Lusebrink & Hinz, 2016; Naff, 2014). In essence, art therapy is able to assist with the 'integration of nonverbal implicit memories stored in the right hemisphere with the left hemisphere verbal functions to form explicit, reconstructed, and coherent verbal memories' (Lusebrink & Hinz, 2016, p. 43). However, empirical evidence is needed to establish the effectiveness of art therapy as a trauma treatment. To add to this discussion, the following chapter is dedicated to the subject of art therapy research and evaluation in relation to PTSD and in particular work with veterans.

References

American Psychiatric Association (2013). *Diagnostic and statistical manual of mental disorders* (5th edn). Washington, DC: APA.

Gantt, L. & Tinnin, L. W. (2009). Support for a neurobiological view of trauma with implications for art therapy. *The Arts in Psychotherapy, 36*(3), 148–153.

Hass-Cohen, N., Findlay, J. C., Carr, R. & Vanderlan, J. (2014). 'Check, change what you need to change and/or keep what you want': An art therapy neurobiological-based trauma protocol. *Art Therapy: Journal of the American Art Therapy Association, 31*(2), 69–78.

Kashdan, T. B., Barrios, V., Forsyth, J. P. & Steger, M. F. (2006). Experiential avoidance as a generalized psychological vulnerability: Comparisons with coping and emotion regulation strategies. *Behaviour Research and Therapy, 44*(9), 1301–1320.

Litz, B. T., Stein, N., Delaney E., Lebowitz, L., Nash, W. P., Silva. C. & Maguen, S. (2009). Moral injury and moral repair in war veterans: A preliminary model and intervention strategy. *Clinical Psychology Review,* 29, 695–706.

Lobban, J. (2014). The invisible wound: Veterans' art therapy. *International Journal of Art Therapy, 19*(1), 3–18.

Lobban, J. (2016). Factors that influence engagement in an inpatient art therapy group for veterans with Post-Traumatic Stress Disorder. *International Journal of Art Therapy, 21*(1), 15–22.

Lusebrink, V. B. & Hinz, L. D. (2016). The Expressive Therapies Continuum as a framework in the treatment of trauma. In J. King (ed.), *Art therapy, trauma and neuroscience: Theoretical and practical perspectives* (pp. 42–66). New York, NY: Routledge.

Naff, K. (2014). A framework for treating cumulative trauma with art therapy. *Art Therapy: Journal of the American Art Therapy Association, 31*(2), 79–86.

Nijenhuis, E. R. S., van der Hart, O. & Steele, K. (2004). Trauma-related structural dissociation of the personality. Trauma Information Pages website, January 2004. Retrieved from www.trauma-pages.com/a/nijenhuis-2004.php.

Tetley, A., Jinks, M., Huband, N. & Howells, K. (2011). A systematic review of measures of therapeutic engagement in psychosocial and psychological treatment. *Journal of Clinical Psychology, 67*(9), 927–941.

Chapter 11

Research and evaluation

Alison Smith and Janice Lobban

Research is not only an essential ingredient in increasing understanding of art therapy processes but also a necessary way of establishing an evidence base that will promote the commissioning of services. Kapitan (2010) suggests that research itself is a reflexive and creative process allowing for the development of new research paradigms to explore outcomes.

Political interest in the arts, health and well-being agenda is growing across all health and community disciplines. Exploration of arts, humanities and well-being in health will culminate in the much-anticipated publication in England and Wales of the All Party Parliamentary Group Inquiry into Arts, Health and Well-Being (APPG) in 2017 (APPG, 2016). There is potential for the APPG report findings to mark the beginning of a policy and paradigm shift in creative methods and provision for health and well-being. This could provide a platform and opportunity for formal creative psychotherapies, including art therapy, to develop important contributions through evidence-based research. This in turn, will inform practice and accessibility for those individuals and groups that wish to participate.

Disciplines that would have formerly seemed to assume substantially differing professional stances regarding their contribution for health and well-being are collaborating and developing shared understandings of what can be beneficial. A clear example of this is the collaborative work being undertaken both in practice and research by King's College London, where artists are actively engaged in working with medical trainees using the arts (King's College, 2016). Collaborations such as this also present unique opportunities for art therapists to engage in research across disciplines in exciting and innovative ways, building and developing an evidence base to support practice.

We begin this chapter with a review of recent published literature on art therapy and trauma, including studies with veterans. The breadth of examples serves to illustrate key areas of ongoing interest and exploration. The subsequent text highlights further relevant studies from the US and the UK before communicating recommendations for future research.

Literature review

Compared with the general working-age population, veterans who have engaged in military action and return to the UK have an increased incidence of mental health problems requiring intervention (Murrison, 2010). Such problems are generally related to anxiety and depressive symptoms, or alcohol and substance use. In addition, veterans often experience psychosocial challenges associated with returning to civilian life, often associated with changes in family functioning, family breakdown, increased use of alcohol, poor employment outcomes and loss of contact with forces life (MacManus *et al.*, 2013). Furthermore, there has been an increase in diagnoses of Post-Traumatic Stress Disorder (PTSD) among UK veterans, which indicates increased recognition of the disorder and help-seeking by veterans (Combat Stress, 2016).

Current guidance for PTSD treatment in the UK recommends the use of trauma-focused Cognitive Behavioural Therapy (CBT) or Eye Movement Desensitisation and Reprocessing (EMDR) (NICE, 2005). In addition, veterans may be prescribed medication as part of a treatment strategy.

However, the recommended trauma therapies are not always effective for veterans with PTSD. It has been suggested that for this particular group success rates for CBT as a lone intervention have been as low as 50 per cent in a review of 55 studies (Schottenbauer, Glass, Arnkoff, Tendick & Gray, 2008). This may have something to do with veterans withdrawing themselves from therapy. Kar (2011) notes that there are multiple reasons for dropout in veteran groups with PTSD using CBT, including the time of engagement and the psychological state of the veteran concerned. Fundamentally, it appears that CBT completion is inversely impacted by symptoms associated with PTSD, such as hyper-arousal, avoidance and depression. Such outcomes would indicate that other therapeutic avenues should be explored in greater depth.

There is a rich history of veterans accessing relief from the distress of PTSD through the avenue of creativity. Using art therapy in particular, veterans have not only explored their immediate symptoms associated with trauma but also attempted to rebuild the narrative of the traumatic experiences in order to make sense of events. Provision available to veterans varies across settings. Lobban (2016a) gives an overview of art therapy provided by four US Department of Veterans Affairs Healthcare Systems and two Military Medical Centers, where art therapy is recognised as a valuable part of treatment. Veterans in the UK have also identified art therapy as beneficial to their recovery, indicating that it would be worth further examination of the role of creativity and art therapy, in particular for the veteran population with PTSD (Lobban, 2014).

A challenge to understanding the therapeutic processes and mechanisms of art therapy as a treatment for trauma, particularly for veterans with PTSD, is the current paucity of literature on the topic. A systematic examination of relevant literature and databases was therefore undertaken in preparing this chapter. This resulted in the identification of 11 key papers suitable for review. The majority of the papers were of a qualitative design (Avrahami, 2005; Collie, Backos, Malchiodi & Spiegel, 2006; Lobban, 2014; Pifalo, 2002). The remaining consisted of mixed methodologies (Kopytin & Lebedev, 2013; Rademaker, Vermetten & Kleber, 2009); two literature reviews (Gantt & Tinnin, 2009; Nanda, Gaydos, Hathorn & Watkins, 2010); and three quantitative studies (Chapman, Morabito, Ladakakos, Schreier & Knudson, 2001; Johnson, Lubin, Miller & Hale, 1997; Lyshak-Stelzer, Singer, St. John & Chemtob, 2007).

Using thematic analysis (Braun & Clarke, 2006), six key emerging themes were identified across these papers: the group; externalising the image and symbolic expression; from non-verbal to verbal processes; integration and processing of memory; containment; artistic pleasure and mastery. These will now be discussed in turn.

The group

Eight of the selected papers referred to the nature of group processes and the sharing of trauma and experiences in group settings. Kopytin and Lebedev (2013) noted that traditionally held views and constructs associated with masculinity and strength were dissolved in veteran groups. Humour used in the groups allowed for the dissolution of military hierarchy and facilitated sharing of trauma experiences. On the other hand, Lobban (2014) noted that previous experience of military cohesion aided the group in retaining its structures and identity. In Lobban's study, the shared culture of the forces led to veterans describing the feeling and experience of being part of a 'Band of Brothers'.

Rademaker *et al.* (2009) and Pifalo (2002) both noted that symptoms of trauma were reduced significantly following group interventions. Of note, the studies featured different participant groups but both identified the same reduction in symptoms of depression and dissociation. The groups appeared to operate as emotional 'containers' (Bion, 1962, 1970), creating an arena for the safe sharing of experiences. Young people who had experienced trauma talked of the group as a 'Circle of Believers', where there was shared understanding of experiences and therefore safety to share those experiences (Pifalo, 2002).

Both Lyshak-Stelzer *et al.* (2007) and Chapman *et al.* (2001) identified that their group members all mentioned a sense of safety. In addition, groups noted that the process and clear function of the group added to the feeling of being in a safe place to share. Chapman *et al.* (2001) felt that this was due to the art-making and therapy, whereas for Lyshak-Stelzer *et al.* (2007), the emphasis was on the group process itself.

Resonating with the ideas of Lobban (2014) and Kopytin and Lebedev (2013), Collie *et al.* (2006) noted that the group process allowed for self-esteem to increase. The sharing of experiences and challenging of memories were witnessed in a non-judgemental manner by those who had also been exposed to trauma; group members experienced this as validating their memories and therefore enhancing their self-esteem.

Externalising the image and symbolic expression

All 11 papers allude to this theme, with the concept of the trauma narrative being developed and then externalised seen as significant in all the studies (White & Epston, 1990). Avrahami (2005) notes that in two case studies the participants used the symbolism of the trauma, represented in the external-ised image, to gain mastery over its influence, thereby facilitating a new per-spective and options for recovery. Alternatively, Collie *et al.* (2006) and Pifalo (2002) suggest that the image being externalised allows emotional distance for the participant, reducing avoidance and facilitating gradual exposure to the image at the time the participant chooses.

Lobban (2014) describes the creation of a tangible image as powerful, and describes how both the group and the individual are then free to step back from the image and observe it. This position of observation allows the observer to walk away from the image if they so choose, thereby giving the viewer power over the image, maybe for the first time. Kopytin and Lebedev (2013) saw image creation and subsequent externalising as key in the narrative of trauma in the group. The group members were free to choose to engage with the image or not and to see the image from an alternative perspective. This allowed the participants to experience choice and empowerment in their relationship with the trauma and image.

Collie *et al.* (2006) propose a model of art therapy groups for veterans with PTSD. They identify that generation and externalising of the image is fundamental to the success of the therapy and group. As in the afore-mentioned studies, they suggest that the creation of the image allows for emotional distance and a reassessment of the image and its influence on the individual.

Nanda *et al.* (2010) explored the impact of visual art on veterans rather than discussing art therapy itself, however they note that the art had a positive effect by allowing veterans to project and externalise their internal experience on the art around them. It is suggested that close attention be paid to the art in the recovery environment, as there could be potential for additional sup-port for the veteran group.

The participant groups described in these studies were varied. However, despite these differences, it is evident that externalising the image and under-standing the symbolic content were significant for the participants.

From non-verbal to verbal processes

In a review of studies that framed trauma as a neurobiological issue, Gantt and Tinnin (2009) note that trauma is described as a non-verbal problem. It is posited that the art therapy process allows the participant to re-associate experiences and words with each other through creation of the image. Chapman *et al.* (2001) concur, describing how the creation of an image in an art therapy group facilitated discussion and, through verbalising, memory storage was positively reordered (van der Kolk & Fisler, 1996).

Lyshak-Stelzer *et al.* (2007) identified that art-making allowed a group of young people who had experienced trauma to use the image as the basis for beginning to verbalise their trauma. Collie *et al.* (2006) noted similar results, finding that non-verbal expression assisted verbal processes. The art therapists involved in the study also found that mastery over the perceived power of the image representing the trauma was felt by participants, adding a further dimension to the impact of the process.

As with discussion of other themes, it is essential to note that the studies mentioned are not all dealing specifically with veterans who have PTSD. The studies do, however, support current neurobiological ideas about integration and processing in trauma and how art therapy interventions could be beneficial (Hass-Cohen & Carr, 2008; Panksepp, 2012).

Integration and processing of memory

Memory processing and integration was a strong theme across the papers, reflecting contemporary thought related to the processing of traumatic memories (van der Kolk & Fisler, 1996). Lobban (2014) expands on key neuroscientific studies, as does McNamee (2004), to advance an understanding of the unprocessed memory involved in PTSD, and how this impacts on the manifestation of physical symptoms.

Lobban describes theories related to hemispheric brain activity in trauma, with differing activity in the right and left hemispheres and the need for memory integration (Hass-Cohen and Carr, 2008; McNamee, 2004; Panksepp, 2012). She posits that art therapy offers potential for improved hemispheric communication by combining non-verbal expression with narrative experience. Collie *et al.* (2006) also identify the potential for a coherent narrative to be developed through the art therapy process, again allowing for the reintegration of memory in the verbal processing areas of the brain. Gantt and Tinnin (2009) concur and identify that fragments of memory appear to be processed through the art therapy process.

Avrahami (2005) describes two case studies within which the process of memory intervention was a strong theme, suggesting that visual representation through the art therapy process facilitates processing in both hemispheres of the brain.

Containment

The concept of containment was proposed by Bion (1962) describing a process whereby an infant projects unmanageable feelings into the mind of the mother who is able to contain and transform them, reflecting them back in a form that is more tolerable for the infant. According to Fonagy and Target, central to this concept 'the mother not only reflects the baby's emotional state, but also her own capacity to deal with it, without being overwhelmed' (2003, p. 122). Bion (1970) later expanded the notion of container-contained into other contexts.

Containment as a psychological concept is discussed by Avrahami (2005) when describing two studies with individual veterans with PTSD. The process and experience of containment is seen as a fundamental and therapeutic aspect of the art therapy intervention. It is suggested that the containment and emotional holding inherent in the therapy is a therapeutic mechanism in itself. The therapist acts as the container and holder of the powerful feelings evoked by recall of the trauma.

Conversely, Collie *et al.* (2006) suggest that it is the *image* rather than the therapist that serves as a container. As with the earlier theme of externalising, it is suggested that the containment of the trauma offered by the image facilitates a sense of empowerment and mastery over the trauma memories and image.

Lobban (2014), Lyshak-Stelzer *et al.* (2007) and Pifalo (2002) regard the *group art therapy process* as acting as the container of the trauma experience and memory. This fundamental difference is very interesting, and may be the result of different philosophical perspectives and understandings of the concept of containment in each setting. Across all papers that refer to the concept, there is not an obvious agreed definition of containment, which presents a challenge when attempting to make clear interpretation of this theme, despite its obvious significance for each author. However, it underlines the multi-dimensional application of this concept possible through the art therapy process.

Artistic pleasure and mastery

The pleasure of the art-making experience is evident across all the papers described above. The shared experience of group art therapy has been found to increase feelings of pleasure in three studies: Kopytin and Lebedev (2013); Lobban (2014); Pifalo (2002). In the second of these, the veteran group identified their sense of achievement when an image was created that was admired by others and also by themselves (Lobban, 2014). The distraction afforded by the art-making process and the additional challenge of doing so was identified by Kopytin and Lebedev (2013) as pleasurable in itself. In addition, humour was a key component for this study and its use appears to have added to the pleasure of the group therapy experience.

Collie *et al.* (2006) note the mastery over symptoms associated with trauma due to both art therapy and image creation. The relaxation afforded by art-making also seems to have facilitated some relief from symptoms such as hyper-arousal.

Further relevant art therapy research from the US

Currently a randomised controlled trial (RCT) research collaboration between the Eastern Virginia Medical School and Hampton VA Medical Center is operating to test the outcomes of individual Cognitive Processing Therapy (CPT) sessions against individual CPT in conjunction with individual art therapy sessions, for veterans with combat-related PTSD. The results of the initial pilot study of 11 subjects were published in 2016 (Campbell, Decker, Kruk & Deaver, 2016). CPT is an evidence-based, manualised treatment for PTSD involving the completion of a written trauma narrative and the challenging of negative thought processes. The art therapy sessions also followed a protocol including a directive to 'depict six specific moments before, during, and after the traumatic event' (Campbell *et al.*, 2016, p. 4).

Although there were no statistically significant differences in outcome between the groups, possibly due to the small sample size, improved trauma processing and the suggestion of enhanced engagement was seen in the art therapy/CPT experimental group. All participants in the experimental group reported gaining insight or recovering memories that assisted healing, and they were all highly satisfied with the treatment (Campbell *et al.*, 2016). A subsequent larger research study, to be published in due course, will make an invaluable research contribution, as RCTs are held as the gold standard of evidence-based research.

Elsewhere, biological indicators are being used to gain objective, empirical data to assist art therapy research. In one study, 45 minutes of creative self-expression within an art therapy open studio format was found to lower cortisol levels in healthy adults, thereby demonstrating an association between art therapy and a decrease of cortisol level, with noteworthy implications (Kaimal, Ray & Muniz, 2016). Cortisol is an adrenal hormone that regulates the body's response to stress. Sustained elevation of cortisol level can cause a range of damaging effects such as impaired cognitive functioning and raised blood pressure (Lobban, 2016a). Implications of cortisol level in relation to the development of PTSD symptoms are discussed in Chapter 3 of this volume.

Additionally, there is increasing interest in the potential for using brain-imagining techniques to inform treatment matching (Lusebrink & Hinz, 2016). Konopka (2016) promotes the use of a person-centred, diagnostic approach to provide the optimal treatment choice for meeting the specific needs of an individual. He observes that clinical populations are usually defined by symptoms, not taking into account biological variability. By combining neuro-imagining with psychological assessment, history and observations, Konopka suggests that it is possible to gain a more precise understanding of the difficulties experienced, which would then inform the treatment most likely to be effective for that individual. The implications are that a range of treatment approaches need be available.

Konopka offers an example whereby abnormalities detected in a client's left mesial temporal lobe through the brain mapping of quantitative electroencephalography (qEEG), led to a change in treatment (qEEG is a non-invasive neuro-imaging technique used to measure and interpret electrical patterns in the brain). Realising that deregulation affected the client's perceptions and verbal expression, adjustments were made to the cognitive approach being taken and she was referred for art therapy (Konopka, 2016).

Art therapy research at Combat Stress

Chapter 10 of this volume features a qualitative outpatient study aimed at learning more about how art therapy might assist therapeutic engagement by overcoming avoidance. The following section offers the results of small mixed-method studies that used surveys to learn more about veterans' experiences of art therapy.

Service development questionnaires

Art therapy groups on the six-week Intensive PTSD Treatment Programme (ITP) at Combat Stress are mandatory as they are seen as providing an alternative way of accessing and processing information. Occasionally, veterans drop out of groups across the programme. In order to try to understand why this happened in the context of art therapy, a survey was designed and distributed to a cohort of veterans. The aim was to ascertain whether any specific changes could be made to increase engagement, but also to discover what art therapy was providing by understanding what was being avoided (Lobban, 2016b).

There were 19 respondents and the resulting data enabled the clustering of participants into three sub-groups: eight veterans attended all six groups (Full); six veterans attended five of the groups (Full-1); five veterans attended between one and four groups (Part). A full analysis of the data is beyond the scope of this chapter, but some of the findings that merit consideration are as follows.

The survey contained statements concerning possible apprehensions about attending art therapy and the experience of the art therapy groups, which participants could comment on using a Likert five-point scale graded from 'strongly agree' to 'strongly disagree', with a 'no opinion' option. An open text box for additional comments was provided. Responding to the comment 'I'm no good at art so there is no point trying', 60 per cent of the

Part cluster strongly agreed/agreed, suggesting that self-rated artistic competence was relevant to this group. To the statement 'I can't see the point of art therapy', 100 per cent of the Full and Full-1 groups strongly disagreed/disagreed, whereas 80 per cent of the Part group agreed/strongly agreed. In response to 'I got upset seeing the others' work and hearing the meaning of it', 100 per cent of the Part group agreed/strongly agreed with the statement, which would seem to indicate that this was a factor affecting attendance and engagement in art therapy. However, to several of the statements, the Part group gave completely polarised responses, suggesting that there was no specific change that could be made to improve their engagement.

The survey revealed certain areas of significance around barriers to engagement. Regarding apprehensions, there was concern about revealing too much and fear of losing control of emotions. The experience of art therapy caused some veterans to feel out of their comfort zone. For some, it brought out things that they did not want to think about. Others thought that the artwork revealed too much, and some had difficulty sharing their emotions in a group setting.

For the art therapists, the study underlined the importance of: flexibility; sensitivity to individual circumstances; the need to adapt each group to match the specific dynamics of the day; being available to discuss apprehensions; and offering support and guidance when necessary. There was also a desire to involve veterans in research as joint collaborators (Lobban, 2016b).

A further survey was designed to evaluate veterans' free-text comments about the benefits of art therapy, with 10 different respondents. The results showed that 100 per cent agreed/strongly agreed that: the atmosphere was relaxing; the art therapy process had brought out things in them that they did not know were there; they were surprised how much they got out of the art therapy group; they found it useful to hear other peoples' interpretation of the themes; they saw a different side of their peers through their artwork; it helped with group bonding and helped them to realise that they were not alone with their problems (Lobban, 2016b).

Art therapy group evaluations

At the end of each group, or course of groups, on the inpatient programmes at Combat Stress, veterans are asked to complete evaluations to provide feedback to the facilitators. Questions are on a five-point Likert scale with options ranging from 'strongly agree' to 'strongly disagree', with a central option of 'just right'. The questions ask for opinions on group pitch, learning, whether gains will be applied at home and usefulness of handouts. There are also free-text boxes inviting comments on 'what you liked most about the group' and 'what could be improved'.

An analysis of the questionnaire data for art therapy groups across all three treatment centres over the span of one year (2015) was presented in a recent study (Palmer, Hill, Lobban & Murphy, 2017). There were 547 respondents of which 404, or 74 per cent, provided free-text comments. The interdisciplinary study explored the acceptability of art therapy as treatment. It revealed that the veteran sample highly rated the usefulness of art therapy, with a mean score of 4.43 out of a maximum of 5. Themes emerged from the free-text comments, with content analysis revealing the importance of three key areas: the experience of sharing with others; accessing and exploring difficult feelings; and environmental aspects.

Experiencing art therapy within a group was seen as assisting communication and facilitating bonding, which suggests promise for increasing veterans' ability to connect with others. The expression and discussion of difficult feelings helped to normalise mental health problems. Art therapy helped to 'unlock' feelings that had been out of awareness and provided an alternative, non-verbal way of expressing difficult feelings. The soothing art therapy environment created by the therapists was revealed as playing a positive role, along with the range of materials available.

The findings demonstrate a high level of acceptability of art therapy from the sample group, which has implications for the inclusion of art therapy in programmes for veterans. The veterans' references to the psychological mechanisms valued in art therapy suggest therapeutic engagement, which further supports the inclusion of art therapy in treatment programmes. Furthermore, veteran descriptions of being able to access and express difficult feelings highlight how art therapy might play a valuable role with veterans who are unable to engage in verbal therapy approaches.

Recommendations for further research

Smith (2016) suggests a need for increased research into the role of art therapy in the recovery of veterans with PTSD. Although the study begins to identify the therapeutic mechanisms that are at play in the art therapy process, it does not begin to identify the art therapy process in isolation to other therapies. Multi-modal treatment packages tend to be the standard for veteran groups who are receiving other therapies, such as CBT, in tandem with art therapy. It would seem clear that increased direct engagement with veterans to develop further understanding of the role of art therapy in recovery from PTSD is required in the near future.

With the expectation from service users, practitioners and research funders alike that good research is identified by its collaborative nature (ESRC, 2016), it is essential that research into art therapy for veterans is interdisciplinary. Such research offers the opportunity for exciting creative partnerships, drawing on the combination of skills and experience of all involved. Differing theoretical stances can build depth and rigour to collaborative research, allowing for the voice of all concerned to be heard with the emphasis of the experience of those who have used art therapy interventions in their recovery.

Studies discussed here have aimed to engage the veterans at all stages, both in development and in participation with the aim of allowing the voice of the service user and their creative experience to be heard and thus elaborated on.

References

APPG (2016). www.artshealthandwellbeing.org.uk/APPG 2016.

Avrahami, D. (2005). Visual art therapy's unique contribution in the treatment of Post-Traumatic Stress Disorder. *Journal of Trauma and Dissociation*, 6(4), 5–38.

Bion, W. R. (1962). *Learning from experience*. London: Heineman.

Bion, W. R. (1970). *Attention and interpretation*. London: Tavistock.

Braun, V. & Clarke, V. (2006). Using thematic analysis in psychology. *Qualitative Research in Psychology*, 3(2), 77–101.

Campbell, M., Decker, K. P., Kruk, K. & Deaver, S. P. (2016). Art therapy and cognitive processing therapy for combat-related PTSD: A randomized controlled trial. *Art Therapy: Journal of the American Art Therapy Association*, 33(4), 1–9.

Chapman, L., Morabito, D., Ladakakos, C., Schreier, H. & Knudson, M. (2001). The effectiveness of art therapy interventions in reducing Post-Traumatic Stress Disorder (PTSD) symptoms in pediatric trauma patients. *Art Therapy: Journal of the American Art Therapy Association*, 18(2), 100–104.

Collie, C. A., Backos, A., Malchiodi, C. & Spiegel, D. (2006). Art therapy for combat-related PTSD: Recommendations for research and practice. *Art Therapy: Journal of the American Art Therapy Association*, 23(4), 157–164.

Combat Stress (2016). *The veterans' mental health charity*. Retrieved from www.combatstress.org.

ESRC (2016). *Economic and Social Research Council*. Retrieved from www.esrc.ac.uk/collaboration/guidance-for-collaboration/.

Fonagy, P. & Target, M. (2003). The Klein-Bion model. In *Psychoanalytic theories: Perspectives from developmental psychopathology* (pp. 118–136). London: Whurr.

Gantt, L. & Tinnin, L. (2009). Support for a neurobiological view of trauma with implications for art therapy. *The Arts in Psychotherapy*, 36, 148–153.

Hass-Cohen, N. & Carr, R. (2008). *Art therapy and clinical neuroscience*. London: Kingsley.

Johnson, D., Lubin, H., Miller, J. & Hale, K. (1997). Single session effects of treatment components within a specialized inpatient Post-Traumatic Stress Disorder program. *Journal of Traumatic Stress*, 10(3), 377–390.

Kaimal, G., Ray, K. & Muniz, J. (2016). Reduction of cortisol levels and participants' responses following art-making. *Art Therapy: Journal of the American Art Therapy Association*, 33(2), 74–80.

Kapitan, L. (2010). *Introduction to art therapy research*. New York, NY: Routledge.

Kar, N. (2011). Cognitive behavioural therapy for the treatment of posttraumatic stress disorder, a review. *Neuropsychiatric Disease and Treatment*, 7, 167–181.

King's College (2016). *Connecting through culture*. Retrieved from www.kcl.ac.uk/Cultural/ConnectingThroughCulture-2014-15-WEB-(1).pdf.

Konopka, L. (2016). Neuroscience concepts in clinical practice. In J. L. King (ed.), *Art therapy, trauma and neuroscience: Theoretical and practical perspectives* (pp. 11–41). New York, NY: Routledge.

Kopytin, A. & Lebedev, A. (2013). Humor, self-attitude, emotions and cognitions in group art therapy with war veterans. *Art Therapy: Journal of the American Association*, *30*(1), 20–29.

Lobban, J. (2014). The invisible wound: Veterans' art therapy. *International Journal of Art Therapy*, *19*(1), 3–18.

Lobban, J. (2016a). *Art therapy for military veterans with PTSD: A transatlantic study*. Retrieved from www.wcmt.org.uk/fellows/reports/art-therapy-military-veterans-ptsd-transatlantic-study#downloads.

Lobban, J. (2016b). Factors that influence engagement in an inpatient art therapy group for veterans with Post-Traumatic Stress Disorder. *International Journal of Art Therapy*, *21*(1), 15–22.

Lusebrink, V. B. & Hinz, L. D. (2016). The Expressive Therapies Continuum as a framework in the treatment of trauma. In J. L. King (ed.), *Art therapy, trauma and neuroscience: Theoretical and practical perspectives* (pp. 42–66). New York, NY: Routledge.

Lyshak-Stelzer, F., Singer, P., St. John, P. & Chemtob, C. (2007). Art therapy for adolescents with Post-Traumatic Stress Disorder symptoms: A pilot study. *Art Therapy: Journal of the American Art Therapy Association*, *24*(4), 163–169.

MacManus, D., Dean, K., Jones, M., Rona, R. J., Greenberg, N., Hull, L., Fahy, T., Wessely, S. & Fear, N. T. (2013). Violent offending by UK military personnel deployed to Iraq and Afghanistan: A data linkage cohort study. *The Lancet*, *381*, 907–917.

McNamee, C. (2004). Using both sides of the brain: Experiences that integrate art and talk therapy through scribble drawings. *Art Therapy: Journal of the American Art Therapy Association*, *21*(30), 136–142.

Murrison, A. (2010). *Fighting fit: A mental health plan for servicemen and veterans*. London: Department of Health.

Nanda, U., Gaydos, L., Hathorn, K. & Watkins, N. (2010). Art and post-traumatic stress: A review of the empirical artwork for veterans with Post-Traumatic Stress Disorder. *Environment and Behaviour*, *42*(3), 376–389.

NICE (2005). *Post-Traumatic Stress Disorder: Management*. Retrieved from www.nice.org.uk/guidance/cg26.

Palmer, E., Hill, K., Lobban, J. & Murphy, D. (2017). Veterans' perspectives on the acceptability of art therapy: A mixed methods study. *International Journal of Art Therapy*, 1–6. Retrieved from www.tandfonline.com/doi/full/10.1080/17454832.2016.1277250.

Panksepp, J. (2012). *The archaeology of mind*. New York, NY: W. W. Norton.

Pifalo, T. (2002). Pulling out the thorns: Art therapy with sexually abused children and adolescents. *Art Therapy: Journal of the American Art Therapy Association*, *19*(1), 12–22.

Rademaker, A., Vermetten, E. & Kleber, R. (2009). Multimodal exposure-based group treatment for peacekeepers with PSTD: A preliminary evaluation. *Military Psychology*, *21*, 482–496.

Rauch, S., van der Kolk, B., Fisler, R., Alpert, N., Orr, P., Savage, C., Fischman, A., Jenike, M. & Pitman, J. (1996). A symptom provocation study of Posttraumatic Stress Disorder using positron emission tomography and script-driven imagery. *Archives of General Psychiatry*, *53*(5), 380–387.

Schottenbauer, M. A., Glass, C. R., Arnkoff, D. B, Tendick, V. & Gray, S. H. (2008). Nonresponse and dropout rates in outcome studies on PTSD: Review and methodological considerations. *Psychiatry*, *71*(2), 134–168.

Smith, A. (2016). A literature review of the therapeutic mechanisms of art therapy for veterans with Post-Traumatic Stress Disorder. *International Journal of Art Therapy*, *21*(2), 66–74.

van der Kolk, B. & Fisler, R. (1996). Dissociation and the fragmentary nature of traumatic memory. *British Journal of Psychotherapy*, *12*(3), 351–361.

White, M. & Epston, D. (1990). *Narrative means to therapeutic ends*. London: W. W. Norton.

Part IV

Taking a wider perspective

Chapter 12

Cultural collaborations

Janice Lobban and Liz Ellis

This chapter discusses a collection of three studies with the common theme of 'partnership working'. The first section describes a collaboration between the Tate Modern Community Learning Programme and the veterans' mental health charity Combat Stress. The next section explores the contribution of gallery workshops in a pilot art therapy-focused, short-stay admission programme at Combat Stress. In the final section, a discussion surrounding the display of veterans' art therapy images in public places is presented, with reference to three exhibitions.

National galleries and museums in the UK offer public access to cultural heritage, arts and sciences, usually within impressive architecture and often free of charge. Growing evidence suggests that engaging with galleries and museums can improve health and well-being in many ways, for instance by providing a safe environment for meaningful pursuits, fostering social capital, sanctuary and a sense of connection, and that they can offer an alternative form of healthcare venue for partnership working (Camic & Chatterjee, 2013; Chatterjee & Camic, 2015; Shaer *et al.*, 2008; Wood, 2007). Studies have shown that museum engagement can help reduce anxiety, promote self-esteem, increase positive emotions and reduce social isolation (Chatterjee & Noble, 2013). By interweaving art therapy with cultural experiences, it is possible to provide enriching possibilities that reach beyond traditional treatment boundaries.

A bubble of trust: a space within a space

Introduction

What follows is a case study of a long-term, interdisciplinary partnership between Tate Modern and Combat Stress involving veterans experiencing Post-Traumatic Stress Disorder (PTSD). The aims, processes and outcomes of the partnership are described and some benefits associated with interdisciplinary projects are identified. By exploring modern and contemporary artworks at Tate Modern as part of a group informal learning process, recovery was supported for veterans using Combat Stress services. The collaboration involved commitment to developing an understanding of the differing disciplinary contexts between the organisations.

The four-year partnership took place at Tate Modern in the context of the existing 'Art into Life' adult workshop programme, led by Community Learning staff within Public Programmes events (Tate, 2016a). This free weekly workshop programme is associated with informal adult learning partnerships, including public and voluntary sector organisations. Funded by a range of charitable trusts since Tate Modern opened in 2000, the Art into Life programme has engaged over 15,000 participants.

The methodology of small group work at Tate Modern is within the context of experiential approaches to learning, whereby each individual's contribution is encouraged and contributes to overall group learning. For Tate Learning across the four national Tate sites, the pedagogic methods of Kolb (1984), Piaget and Friere are used. The differing life experiences of the learning cohort are identified as core to the learning process (Pringle, 2009). Art into Life is particularly informed by the principles of Brazilian educator Paolo Friere in his approach to education as an emancipatory process, where the adult learner is identified as active in shaping the content and pace of learning (Friere, 1998). In preparation for working with Combat Stress veterans, Tate Modern staff were given a basic understanding of responses to traumatic experiences by art therapist Jan Lobban.

In late 2008, Jan approached Curator of Community Learning, Liz Ellis about a potential Art into Life workshop for veterans. The enquiry arose as a result of a public exhibition of Combat Stress veterans' art and art therapy images at a London gallery that year. The exhibition seemed to capture veterans' interest and many veterans travelled a great distance to see it. In order to offer further creative opportunities for veterans outside of the treatment centre, possible options were explored and the Tate Modern workshops seemed well suited to fulfil a range of treatment objectives.

In preparation for the first workshop, the curator and art therapist discussed the treatment aims of Combat Stress, in particular the arts-based approaches, and the overall group profile of veterans attending the programme. Potential challenges and opportunities inherent in visiting the busy public context of Tate Modern were explored. It was essential to discuss areas of potential stress in order to plan and identify solutions in advance of the gallery workshop. As part of careful planning, the hyper-arousal, hyper-vigilance and intrusive characteristics of PTSD were considered. It was likely that the journey to Tate Modern in itself would be a source of stress, while also providing the potential for developing confidence and regaining skills. Once at Tate Modern, a popular tourist destination with international status, it was also important to recognise the challenge for veterans in experiencing this spacious, unfamiliar and, for some, potentially stressful environment.

The crucial role of a shared commitment to high-quality practice recognising differing interdisciplinary contexts, the importance of reflective practice from Tate Modern and Combat Stress staff, and the creative engagement of veteran participants has been core to the success of this partnership project.

Process and content of the workshops at Tate Modern

Between January 2009 and October 2013, veterans and staff from Combat Stress participated in seven Art into Life workshops, led by Curator Liz Ellis, with up to 15 participants in each group. Although the veterans attending varied over this time, a core group remained over the four years. Participants in every workshop included up to 10 veterans, occasionally veterans' partners, at least two Combat Stress staff members and sometimes additional Tate Modern staff. Initially, the workshops were offered to veterans during inpatient admissions while at the Surrey treatment centre. The group travelled to London together in a minibus. However, over time, some veterans made their own way from their homes to the workshops. This presented challenges of using public transport, which veterans were prepared to face in order to participate in the workshops. In this way, veterans were able to overcome avoidance of public transport and increase distress tolerance.

Recognising the considerable energy and motivation required of the veterans in attending Tate Modern, Liz aimed to ensure each felt welcome, their experiences valued and that the workshop pace allowed time for differing responses to the gallery and selected artworks. These workshops were not art history tours, but experiential opportunities to share observations and responses to selected artworks, directly in front of the artworks in the public galleries. Shaping the group dynamic by welcoming everyone, learning participants' names and ensuring space was made for individual contributions were essential aspects of building trust.

The workshop group became a 'safe oasis' within the wider gallery space. The crucial importance of establishing trust and valuing each other's differences in life experience needs to be emphasised here. The workshops were not about 'a day out' but about informal shared learning contexts using carefully selected artworks. In preparing for this informal learning, time was made before, during and after each workshop to manage emotions such as anxiety and excitement raised by travelling and by being in a busy public space; and sharing potentially difficult feelings and experiences in a group context with Liz, an unfamiliar colleague.

Military training entails watching out for each other in the field. This was enacted during the workshops as the group moved around the large complex of Tate Modern galleries over a number of floors. Some veterans could not tolerate the enclosed space of a lift, so used the staircases or escalators. Veterans did not travel alone but would be accompanied by peers, enabling mutual safe-keeping. Participants carried lightweight, collapsible stools provided by Tate, which were set up in a semi-circle around the selected piece of artwork. The galleries were packed with visitors, which was the type of environment that many veterans with PTSD would avoid. A 'bubble of trust' was created by all involved during the course of the sessions, whereby the veterans felt safe enough to engage creatively, focusing on the artwork while managing hyper-arousal responses.

A simple concertina book-making activity started the session as we shared our names. These books were then used in the gallery as each participant wished; to record notes, drawings, observations and details of artworks. Liz encouraged the opportunity to slow down, using handling materials to facilitate observations and enrich experiences of artworks. At all times participants were encouraged to think critically and reflect. There was no expectation to 'like' the artworks selected. Values of sharing differing views and recognising the participants' differences of opinion and life experiences were established from the outset.

When invited to participate in a workshop at Tate Modern, veterans would sometimes respond with interest but state that they 'didn't like modern art'. Having completed the workshop, they might feedback that they still didn't like modern art but that the experience had got them thinking. This is important because developing new ideas and challenging fixed perceptions is key to facilitating change as rigid, repetitive thought patterns can hamper recovery from PTSD.

The supportive group atmosphere already created within the Combat Stress programme was further supported by the experiential learning approach, which underpins the Art into Life methodology. A small group of themed and selected artworks are discussed during the 90-minute workshops; usually four or five artworks that are in the public galleries. Tate Modern displays wide-ranging work by international artists from 1900 to the present day. Consequently, there is a generous selection of paintings and sculpture that could be the focus for workshops. Prior to each of the Combat Stress sessions, much discussion was had over the choice of artworks in reflecting overall goals for the workshop. Emails and telephone calls between the curator and art therapist helped to define choices and plans for each workshop, in anticipation of potential areas for discussion, and to manage inevitable areas of anxiety raised by sharing differing experiences in a busy public gallery. In this way, the workshops could be tailored specifically to suit the objectives of each group.

Selected artworks included experiences of conflict, for example *Forest and Dove* made by Max Ernst in 1927. Ernst, a German artist, frequently portrayed himself in the form of a bird. In this painting, many viewers interpret the bird as caged, in a deep and for some potentially frightening forest. The bird appears to have the blue sky above to fly away into and thus escape the cage. Liz introduced the painting early in the workshop series as she knew from experience that many visitors identify with the bird and its possible choices. Many of the veterans found this a fascinating painting, not only with its adventurous techniques of scraping and layering to reveal texture and create mood, but also for the opportunities to discuss personal fears and the experience of anxiety, through the metaphor of the bird.

A contemporary British artist, Chris Ofili, whose work *No Woman No Cry* (1998) was made in response to the racist murder of Stephen Lawrence, was selected in a later workshop as an exploration of grief and a response to violence. At the same time, discussion was also led on the innovative and exhilarating techniques used by Ofili in achieving such powerful visual impact in this artwork. This shift of focus between meaning and technique helped to moderate any possible emotional identification that might become too distressing for participants.

The veterans responded openly to each work of art in focus, making observations and building on each other's comments. Tasked to explore the handling resources in relation to a specific piece of work, they came up with new and inventive ideas. Sometimes the sensory aspects of the materials had a resonance with military service. For instance, in one workshop based in the Arte Povera gallery display, a veteran who served in the Merchant Navy selected one of the handling materials, a section of rope, and spoke about the memory of knot-making and the bonds made during service. This link between both the literal nature of the rope and the relational connection between him and other veterans is an exemplar of the metaphorical and symbolic richness that the artworks prompted in many of the workshop participants.

Exploring differences and challenges between the contexts of Tate Modern and Combat Stress

Having described the partnership, it is important to underline the differing contexts that inform Tate Modern and Combat Stress. On one hand, Tate Modern is a busy national and international public gallery, whereas the veterans visiting came from a psychotherapeutic inpatient programme taking place within a treatment centre. However, mutual respect for these differing contexts informed the partnership and increasing knowledge was gained through invitations made to Liz to exhibitions at the treatment centre, and a public exhibition in London in 2013.

As a national gallery collection, Tate Modern is free at the point of entry with 4–5 million visitors a year. Open 7 days a week for 362 days of the year, it is a busy environment, at times holding unexpected challenges in terms of finding quiet spaces for reflection and discussion. As an experienced Curator at Tate, Liz ensured that a calm meeting space was used on arrival for introductions and the brief warm-up activity. It was agreed at the outset of every workshop that at any point participants could leave the workshop, sit in a quieter area with a staff member, walk outside the building or re-join the group later. In fact, this rarely happened, but it was crucial that there was an open and consistent recognition given by staff that the gallery environment, unfamiliar for many, could trigger anxiety and that there were anticipated options to leave the workshop if this occurred.

Similarly, at the end of the workshop, a private meeting space was found for the group to have a packed lunch together, without having to use the busy public café facilities or shared lunch space. This lunch break also functioned as a time for the facilitators to discuss the workshop experience with veterans before leaving the gallery for the journey home or back to the residential centre. Having a private, safe base within the vast Tate Modern building enabled veterans to manage anxiety.

The trust developed between the two organisations enabled continuous reflective learning. Liz was invited to visit Combat Stress on Open Days at the Surrey base when veterans hosted public exhibitions. Artwork and writing created in the activities room or during art therapy sessions were displayed. Some of the veterans also chose to experiment with ideas and techniques discussed within Tate Modern workshops. This 'bridging' of the two contexts was recognised as valuable for all involved in the partnership.

For Liz, these exhibitions provided more knowledge of the veterans' context, while the veterans took the opportunity and risk to share personal creativity by publicly exhibiting their artworks. The resulting interest and feedback that all artists enjoy when exhibiting work further aided recovery for some veterans who had been experiencing extreme isolation and depression. Many were surprised that visitors were interested in their creativity. The knowledge and sensitivity of the veterans were very much in evidence at these exhibitions, with a sense of solidarity and compassion in supporting each other. Liz and Combat Stress staff recognised the healthy risk that being part of an exhibition includes, thus further supporting each other's differing disciplinary context.

Bringing something back to Combat Stress

Surrounded by extraordinary, international artworks from the last 100 years, discussions were often had on how selected media or techniques gave further impact to the artworks and how some of the veterans might include or adapt such techniques in their own arts practices. This type of direct learning, familiar for art students, was often a revelation for veterans, who were used to experiencing art through the media or reproduced in books. The emotional and conceptual impact of direct contact with the artworks at Tate Modern led to profound discussions on the meaning and nuance of specific works.

For example, *Staircase-III* (2010) by Do Ho Suh (Tate, 2016b) was a work of huge impact to many participants when discussed later in the partnership in 2011. Many veterans saw this artwork as full of potential hope and opportunity, and their filmed observations enabled other members of the public to see the power and beauty of this woven installation. Coincidentally, this workshop was filmed by BBC Scotland in 2011 as part of *The Culture Show Special* that featured art therapy at Combat Stress, within a discussion of PTSD (McArdle, 2011). Re-watching this film, noting that this was approximately halfway through the partnership, the confidence and skills of the veterans in responding to this artwork is apparent, adding their own thoughtful interpretation in the group discussion. The recognition of a sense of opportunity by some of the veterans in their reading of this artwork seemed to reflect a sense of personal optimism.

Each workshop contained opportunities for creative work in different formats. Some veterans chose to take photos. Others chose to use the simple concertina book introduced by Liz at the start of the session to make sketches or to note key words or artists discussed to follow up later at home or at Combat Stress, thus transforming it into a research notebook. It is important to note how these personal responses enabled participants to make connections across different personal histories within the context of modern and contemporary arts practice, through cultural engagement. These workshops and the integration of these experiences during treatment at Combat Stress enabled the veterans to share Tate as a national resource.

Although Tate had always belonged to them (as in common with all UK citizens, the veterans had contributed to the public gallery through their taxes), previously many in the group would not have experienced the gallery as relevant in their lives. By this shared group experience, including holding the anxieties and fears raised over travel and exposure to public spaces, the group experienced growing confidence in expressing views and differing opinions.

Lessons learned and recommendations for future partnerships

Veteran participants were given evaluation forms to complete by Combat Stress and asked to rate the relevance of a number of possible outcomes from the workshop. Options included: 'I learned something new'; 'I gained a sense of achievement'; 'I intend to use what I learned today'; 'It was no use to me'. Feedback was favourable and veterans were generous with their additional comments.

Broken down into categories, the feedback highlighted some key points around: creative engagement; overcoming environmental challenges; the importance of welcoming, attentive staff; future potential. The feedback suggested that many veterans felt creatively engaged, sharing comments like 'it was magical' and 'good to *see* rather than just look (I would have just walked past)'. One veteran felt inspired to write a poem for the first time upon returning to the treatment centre. He reflected on the great pleasure of being part of the cultural group experience.

As anticipated, the environment and travel presented problems for some veterans, who commented 'crowd and noise level difficult' and 'everything was good but the journey was bad'. In order to access this leading gallery, it was necessary to travel to London through heavy traffic. Smaller, provincial museums and galleries also offer community workshops that could be more appropriate for collaborative projects depending on treatment objectives.

There were many comments on the value of staff interactions, such as 'made welcome', 'felt safe and valued' and 'helpful staff'. As usual with the Art into Life methodology, Liz learned the names of all in the group and used individual names throughout the workshop. While this is standard good educational practice, this was of particular significance with the Combat Stress participants, many of whom had struggled to feel valued and respected as part of their experience of PTSD. Being held in mind is likely to have assisted with anxiety management in the vast space of the gallery, providing a sense of connection.

The importance of having access to a private space was acknowledged – 'appreciated the seminar room'; 'quiet space'. Sometimes after a workshop the group would sit silently eating the packed lunches as though assimilating all the stimuli from the gallery space. Eventually, banter would recommence and reflective discussion ensued. Occasionally veterans did experience panic attacks or flashbacks during the workshops, and it was invaluable having the private space to put into practice affect management and grounding techniques.

Significantly, many participants commented on the potential effects of the workshop, such as: 'inspired by looking at other people's artwork'; 'I came away with lots of ideas for artwork'; 'an important gateway for exploring art'. As part of two of the workshops, veterans, partners and Combat Stress staff had the option of using the private space for art-making. This provided an opportunity to make an immediate response to the gallery experience. Those who made a creative response fed back their enjoyment of the art-making. Other participants chose to use that time to explore the Thames-side view or revisit the galleries.

The perceptions of some veterans seem to have been challenged, as there were comments such as 'feared it would be over my head' and 'it was not what I expected'. This reflects observations made in a study by McKeown, Weir, Berridge, Ellis and Kyratsis (2015) that examined the experience of mental health service users who engaged in Tate Modern's Community Learning Programme. There were perceptions of elitism that were overcome through participation.

Core to the success of this interdisciplinary partnership was the recognition and discussion of difference from the outset of the partnership, enabling clarity of roles and objectives. For example, Liz was clear she was leading an adult informal learning workshop in the busy context of a national gallery. For Jan and her colleagues from Combat Stress, the workshop programme was in line with veterans' individual treatment objectives, which might include increasing self-awareness or stimulating creative thinking. The workshops provided additional work in preparing, supporting and following up the veterans on their experiences after the workshop. The external context of the workshops taking place away from the treatment centre enabled other aspects of recovery, including travel skills, building social confidence and using external cultural resources.

As the relationship between the two organisations developed, participants, and at times supporting partners or relatives, began to appear more comfortable at Tate Modern. This reinforced the overall recovery goals, with a national gallery belonging to everyone being a resource that was perceived as welcoming and accessible.

A pilot short-stay art therapy inpatient admission with gallery workshops

As part of a pilot art therapy inpatient admission at Combat Stress in 2016, two gallery workshops were organised to complement the art therapy groups and individual sessions that were provided within the treatment centre. The admission was for a group of five veterans with art therapy as the core treatment, without cognitive behavioural group input. The workshops were in collaboration with staff at The Lightbox, which is an innovative art gallery and museum in Woking, Surrey. This section of the chapter provides an overview of the specialised admission, with discussion around the benefits of incorporating gallery work into the programme.

A questionnaire was sent to all potential participants during the planning stage of the pilot programme for input into structuring the admission. All the veterans responded positively to the option of gallery visits, so a suitable venue was found. As well as having a permanent local history museum, The Lightbox has three galleries with regularly changing exhibitions. The lead art therapist visited The Lightbox and together with gallery staff, a structure was agreed for the workshops.

The themes of the pilot art therapy groups were tailored to fit an exhibition at The Lightbox entitled 'John Constable: Observing the Weather'. The overall aim was to encourage veterans to explore the interplay between inner and outer landscapes. The themes were devised to progress from identifying and reflecting on presenting circumstances and perceptions to exploring change. Beginning with 'My Planet' in the first group, participants responded to 'Frozen' in the second group and 'Moonlight' in the third before attending the first workshop off site. This was new ground, as there had not been an opportunity to work as a closed group with an art therapy focus over a two-week admission before.

It was clear as participants shared their responses to My Planet that they had much in common. The veterans took turns to show and explain the personal meaning of each image created. Discussion developed during the image-viewing and subsequently as they shared further observations and insights. One veteran had been inspired by recalling *The Planets Suite*

by Gustav Holst. His image showed Mars dominating, with its connections
with the god of war. It cast a shadow over the veteran's planet that clouded its
atmosphere, and it had a strong gravitational pull, symbolising the influence
of combat trauma (Plate 12.1). Other images expressed ideas around alienation, isolation and disconnection. A veteran explored the type of atmosphere
necessary for survival, and concluded that due to the inflexibility of his protective spacesuit in the image, i.e. the limitations caused by PTSD symptoms,
he was unable to see all the good things around him. There was a desire to
return to a pre-trauma way of thinking, before trauma affected perceptions;
to return to a time of curiosity and optimism.

The theme Frozen stimulated further striking images, several with sensory
associations. One veteran drew frozen clocks to convey how trauma memories become frozen in time in the same anxiety-provoking form (Figure 12.1).
Another veteran drew himself in terror awaking from a nightmare. It showed
him without a mouth or nose to convey how the smell and taste of past
trauma cannot be expressed verbally, and how terror is wordless. Through an
image of his own profile showing a dissection of his brain, another veteran
referred to an embedded 'Pandora's Box' that holds his trauma memories. It
was surrounded by frozen tissue, representing the intact preservation of the
trauma. It was also suggestive of the psychic numbing associated with PTSD,
which causes a reduced ability to experience positive emotions such as joy or

Figure 12.1 Frozen Clocks

tenderness. Another rich discussion ensued, peppered with humour to make the content more manageable.

By the third art therapy group it was clear that the veterans were taking sessions to a deeper level. In later discussions, the veterans confirmed that the trust built and sense of continuity had helped them to express issues usually kept private. Through the theme Moonlight, group members expressed what they called the 'subterranean history' of military life; an alternative version that does not go into history books. Along with that, there was total agreement that none wanted to contaminate, or infect, their loved ones with details of their experiences. This linked with what they discussed in the first session about a pre-trauma way of seeing the world, with a desire to maintain that state of mind within others. The imagery and discussion explored aspects of military life. Moonlight is a dangerous and vulnerable time in the field, when there is a possibility of being exposed to the enemy. This seemed to have a resonance with the pace of the group, as participants were revealing more of their censored or suppressed feelings.

The first workshop at The Lightbox provided a balance to the emotional content of the art therapy groups, and an opportunity to look together at artwork created by someone else, in this case, John Constable (1776–1837). There was apprehension beforehand from those veterans who tended to isolate and avoid public places. It would involve going out of their comfort zone into an unfamiliar place. We travelled there in a minibus with the journey taking about 40 minutes.

The veterans brought different aspects of their knowledge and interests into the workshops, enabling more rounded interactions. Two of the veterans had art qualifications and were fascinated by techniques they observed in Constable's work. Participants had lively discussions with gallery staff. One veteran with visual impairment experimented with different angles of viewing the work and made interesting discoveries. This act was later discussed as representing a key objective of the programme – to open up new ways of seeing and perceiving. Participants were intrigued by the structure of the building and investigated areas that had interesting light effects. During that time the veterans seemed able to view what was around them playfully and with curiosity rather than looking for potential threat. The gallery staff facilitated the art-making time. Veterans and staff, including the art therapists, experimented with watercolour techniques. The focus was on creating art together for its own sake, not for interpretation. With a further workshop to follow in week two, the veterans said that they would look forward to returning.

After a weekend break, the group reformed for an art therapy session on the Monday morning, which began with a discussion about week one of the programme. All had enjoyed visiting the gallery and one veteran in particular reported that he had found creative inspiration, which had enabled him to re-engage fruitfully with art-making in the activities room over the weekend. The theme 'Clouds' was set for the group and the veterans engaged in art-making.

The images expressed experiences of depression, represented by heavy, dark clouds that disable and obscure connections with the surrounding environment. Negativity and introspection affect interactions, with helplessness and hopelessness making such bouts a dangerous time. As one veteran put it, referring to the vulnerability caused by suicidal thoughts during those times, 'depression kills'. Another veteran shared his surprise that the images all revealed elements of his own thoughts, which seemed to offer some comfort in that he was not alone with his experiences. The images also showed the presence of better times when clouds are lightweight and tinged with multi-colours. They represented times of connection and achievement.

The following day, the group participated in the second workshop at The Lightbox. Knowing what to expect, the veterans seemed more confident and very motivated to attend. They chose to visit an exhibition of the work of Heath Robinson. Gallery staff gave an introduction to the work and they were available to guide and answer questions. The veterans made full use of their time at the gallery and visited the museum and a gallery with some of the permanent collection, as well as the café and shop. They expressed their interest in techniques and the pleasure of image-viewing. The workshop involved creating three-dimensional landscapes from a range of materials provided. Gallery staff were attentive and kept the conversation lively and upbeat. Again, the art therapists participated in the image-making, which is not the case in art therapy groups.

In later discussions about the programme, the veterans suggested that the gallery visits and workshops could be longer because they passed too quickly; a veteran suggested that taking a packed lunch would enable the group to spend the whole day there. Another veteran, who avoids public places, planned to take his wife there as he was so impressed, and one veteran was inspired to try a mixed-media technique in the activities room that afternoon.

There were two further art therapy groups after the second gallery workshop. The theme for the first one was a 'Change in the wind'. Clouds appeared in the work again but this time to represent movement. Symbols of warmth, light, optimism and achievement appeared. A door to the outside world is blown open in one image (Figure 12.2). This stimulated a discovery that sometimes two of the participants stand at their own front doors looking out without venturing out. Another image showed the positive influence of the gallery visits, with the wind of inspiration from The Lightbox blowing away the storm clouds that interfere with the ability to be creative (Figure 12.3).

The theme for the final group was 'Seasons'. One of the advantages of providing a series of closed art therapy groups was that the group developed a shared history. The facilitators and veterans were able to refer back to different stages, particular images, discussions and observations across the two weeks. The shared knowledge held in mind by the participants enabled deeper

Figure 12.2 Change in the Wind

Figure 12.3 The Lightbox

and richer discussions. Symbols and ideas echoed across the images. Through Seasons, the veterans created landscapes that contained all conditions, conveying a sense of managing change. They discussed the experience of four seasons in one day, i.e. unpredictable changes in mood. They spoke about weathering the storm, using symptom management strategies, in the knowledge that the bad feelings will pass. This touched upon notions of resilience, endurance, optimism and hope.

Discussion

The gallery visits and workshops offered a further dimension to the art therapy admission. Without them, it is likely that the veterans would still have bonded as a group. The trust built and the continuity of the sessions would still have enabled deeper expression, reflection and discovery. However, the gallery work introduced different factors that would not have occurred as part of usual inpatient treatment. These factors allowed participants to have experiences outside the confines of the treatment centre and to reflect on this during subsequent art therapy sessions.

The gallery provided a change of environment with associated challenges to face. Anxiety was high among some of the participants prior to the first visit to The Lightbox. Several had a poor night's sleep beforehand and one veteran nearly dropped out at the last minute. PTSD manifests as a heightened sense of threat. Veterans tend to expect the worst and sometimes can talk themselves out of trying new experiences. Social life can be non-existent and avoidance becomes the default position. Attending the workshops as part of a familiar and trusted group of veterans and staff helped to moderate anxiety. Preparation and discussion enabled questions to be answered and apprehensions to be explored beforehand. However, the workshops could not have progressed without the willingness of the veterans to try this new experience.

The cultural context and atmosphere of the gallery captured the veterans' interest. As its name suggests, The Lightbox offers a bright, spacious environment. In places, the windows are floor to ceiling and some of the windows have transparent bands of coloured film attached to them that create filtered stripes of colour on walls and floors. The veterans fed back their enjoyment of the environment. The use of light boxes, i.e. a form of light therapy, came into the discussion during the art therapy group that followed the first gallery visit. One of the veterans said that he owns a Seasonal Affective Disorder (SAD) light box to help him manage the darkness of the winter months. The group acknowledged this echo and the symbolic brightness that the gallery visit had provided. Indeed, one of the hoped-for objectives of the workshops was to facilitate the internalisation of a positive experience; an inner light box that might increase confidence and promote a desire to seek similar cultural environments.

The visits involved looking together at artwork created by professional artists as opposed to that of peers. The veterans were fascinated by artists' techniques. They asked questions, made observations and gained inspiration. When viewing each other's responses to art therapy group themes, connections are made through symbolic meaning and emotional resonance. In the case of the gallery exhibitions, it was particularly style, artistic competence and pure pleasure that captured the veterans' interest. One veteran fed back that he had felt 'nourished' by the gallery visits.

Gallery staff took a friendly, sociable and art-focused approach, encouraging enjoyment of the experience. The role of the two art therapists changed during the art-viewing and workshops, as the group facilitation was done by gallery staff. This put veterans and art therapists in a similar position as art viewers and art makers. Conversations between the art therapists and veterans were not necessarily associated with mental health issues but art-based topics. The situation provided an opportunity for a different type of interaction that was more upbeat and informal, although mindful of professional boundaries. Using art materials together offered a time to play and experiment with techniques.

This change in relationship has been seen in other studies on the subject of health interventions in museums and galleries. Describing an art gallery-based group involving mental health staff and clients, Colbert, Cooke, Camic and Springham (2013) remark on the significance of personhood in the experience. Rather than maintaining traditional roles of patient and professional, the sense of 'us and them' diminished as commonality prevailed. The gallery provided a safe space where a different kind of relationship could happen. This was seen as potentially beneficial to all parties in terms of increasing well-being, fostering social inclusion and reducing professional burn-out.

In the first art therapy group of the pilot, the veterans had expressed their desire to return to a pre-trauma state of mind where they could be playful and curious. During traumatic situations, those traumatised become overwhelmed by the raw reality of the experience. Basic assumptions about life were shattered and the world is now viewed differently. Over the course of the two-week art therapy programme, the veterans were able to demonstrate playfulness and curiosity. The gallery visits and workshops seemed to be an essential ingredient in this. They provided an enriching opportunity for veterans to connect with artistic interests and to extend parameters beyond familiar patterns of behaviour.

Exhibiting art therapy images in public places

At the Combat Stress treatment centres, every corridor, bedroom, therapy room, office and lounge displays paintings made by veterans in the activities rooms. Visitors, staff and veterans alike make admiring and appreciative comments. The artwork represents a mixture of abilities from simple forms to detailed, skillfully crafted work. Veterans can find inspiration from studying styles and techniques, or just benefit from the environment, whether consciously or subliminally.

In Chapter 1, reference was made to Hill and Adamson's association with the British Red Cross Picture Library in the 1940s, which provided reproductions of famous artwork to hospitals through a lending scheme. In a recorded interview, Hill described his time in hospital recovering from tuberculosis. He was bed-ridden without stimulation. That experience caused him to champion the use of pictures to assist recovery – 'a picture could change' when there was no window, and offer changing stimulation such as 'excitement' or 'serenity' (Darracott, 1975). The previous studies in this chapter and the use of paintings to adorn the walls of the Combat Stress treatment centres echo this recognition of the therapeutic value of viewing art.

However, art therapy images are made with different objectives from those of art activity, and one might argue that they are not for public viewing. Art therapy images are not intended for aesthetic evaluation. Revealing an image to others, whether within the context of therapy or in the public arena, involves the risk of criticism or rejection. It is not unusual for veterans to write in the corner of an art therapy image something like 'made by Jimmy, aged 5'. This underlines the struggle inherent in self-expression through a medium that might be unfamiliar and experienced as exposing deficiency.

Art therapy images do not adorn the corridors of Combat Stress. Occasionally veterans have asked for their work to be displayed in the art therapy room to help others, or in recognition that something of immense personal value had been created. This has been helpful for some veterans who have been able to connect with the meaning of the images on the wall, but has been too distressing for some others to see for the same reason.

Veterans are slow to seek help, and stigma connected with having mental health problems is a significant barrier. This puts veterans at risk of social exclusion and contributes towards the number of veterans who are homeless or in prison. A study of barriers to help-seeking within UK Armed Forces by Murphy and Busuttil (2014) highlights *internal stigma*, *external stigma* and *access factors* as being key obstacles. They refer to 'convincing evidence' that contact between people who have had mental health problems and the general public can help to reduce stigmatising beliefs (Murphy & Busuttil, 2014, p. 4; Corrigan & Penn, 1999). Consequently, at Combat Stress, the aims for art therapy are not only to treat PTSD but also to encourage veterans to seek help by increasing public awareness through the exhibition of art therapy imagery.

Sometimes Combat Stress is invited to submit veterans' work for exhibition, but the organisation also actively seeks opportunities to exhibit, particularly on occasions such as Remembrance Day, when veterans are the focus of public attention. When opportunities are presented, it is up to the veterans whether or not they choose to submit work. It is usually the case that veterans are keen for their work to be displayed with the aim of helping other veterans.

Three exhibition partnerships

The following section presents an outline of three exhibition partnerships: 'Wind Tunnel' which was held at Farnborough Airport on Armed Forces' Day, 2014; 'Road to Recovery' at Guildford Cathedral during Armed Forces' Week, 2015; and 'The Way Ahead', St Pancras Hospital Conference Centre, 2015.

The Wind Tunnel exhibition commemorated the beginning of the First World War. Curator Polly Hughes and her colleagues wanted a contemporary feel to the exhibition, and so approached established artists including Derek Eland and Anna Redwood, both of whom had been embedded war artists in Afghanistan. Whereas Anna painted life-size portraits, Derek explored the psychology of warfare. This stimulated Polly to approach Combat Stress about exhibiting some of the veterans' art therapy images. The exhibition juxtaposed the contemporary work with original voice recordings of soldiers and civilians during the First World War, sourced from the Imperial War Museum.

Wind Tunnel was held in a derelict hangar originally used for testing prototype aeroplanes. As a listed building, it was not permitted to hang anything on the walls, so paintings were displayed on white boards that were held in place by sandbags. Combat Stress veterans' poems were printed in large type and suspended from the ceiling on rolls of wallpaper. This enabled viewers to read them from some distance away. Work was selected by the curator for exhibition during a visit to Combat Stress. She was able to discuss the images and poems with the veterans and to gain a deeper understanding of personal meaning. Her overall observations of the exhibition process were that it was both heart-breaking and heart-warming. Postcards of veteran's work were included in the Army Benevolent Fund 'goodie bags' handed out at the end of the event. The postcards had an image on one side and information about Combat Stress on the reverse.

An objective of the Guildford Cathedral Road to Recovery exhibition was to highlight the work of Combat Stress to the Cathedral community and the large number of visitors during Armed Forces Week. The Cathedral's Director of Operations, Matthew O'Grady, felt that these visitors would naturally have an affinity with the armed forces but would not necessarily have any knowledge of Combat Stress. The artwork was exhibited on easels, initially in two locations (the Baptistery and the Regimental Chapel), and then later in the week the easels were moved into the nave aisles in order to give the exhibition greater visibility during the Armed Forces Day service itself. The exhibition offered a very different perspective on the risks taken by members of our armed forces, during a week when the thoughts of many were on this very subject.

The Way Ahead exhibition also aimed to mark the centenary of the First World War, and to present within a major inner London mental healthcare centre, an exhibition exploring the power of the arts in recovery from the experience of war. It was organised through The Arts Project by curator Peter Herbert, and was in support of introducing arts therapy for veterans at the London Veterans' Service, which is based at St Pancras Hospital, London. The public response was positive. Quotes from the visitors' book included: 'incredibly moving and thought provoking'; 'I just can't walk past this exhibition without looking'; 'at times I have been moved to tears'. Peter Herbert planned to hold a future exhibition for a particular contributing veteran seen as deserving more public attention, which will continue the valuable work opened up by the exhibition.

In summary, the three exhibitions of Combat Stress veterans' art and art therapy images aimed to raise awareness of the effects of psychological injuries associated with military service; to promote the use of creativity as part of recovery; and to challenge the stigma that prevents veterans seeking help. Veterans who submitted images were prepared to share their work, sometimes with pride, often with modesty, but always in the hope that it would help other veterans in some way.

Conclusion

The military ethos involves teamwork and co-operation towards the attainment of mutual goals. In parallel, art therapy objectives may also be enhanced by working in alliance with other organisations who share cultural objectives. Working in collaboration with galleries and museums opens up further creative opportunities for veterans that can assist social re-integration and promote positive self re-evaluation. It can also refresh art therapists' connections with their cultural roots and provide professional nourishment. Exhibiting images can make the work of art therapy more accessible to the wider public, and help to tackle the stigma associated with having mental health problems.

The role of partnerships is seen as core in achieving outcomes based on trust and interdisciplinary understanding. These illustrations present positive outcomes and point to the necessity of continued and more strategic partnerships ahead. The examples here have shown that improved mental health and challenges to stigma are shared-sector responsibilities, not solvable in isolation.

References

Camic, P. & Chatterjee, H. J. (2013). Museums and art galleries as partners for public health interventions. *Perspectives in Public Health*, *133*, 66–71.

Chatterjee, H. J. & Camic, P. (2015). The health and well-being potential of museums and art galleries. *Arts and Health*, *7*(3), 183–186.

Chatterjee, H. J. & Noble, G. (2013). *Museums, health and well-being*. Farnham: Ashgate.

Colbert, S. M., Cooke, A., Camic, P. M. & Springham, N. (2013). The art gallery as a resource for recovery for people who have experienced psychosis. *The Arts in Psychotherapy*, *40*, 250–256.

Corrigan, P. W. & Penn, D. L. (1999). Lessons from social psychology on discrediting psychiatric stigma. *American Psychology*, *54*, 765–776.

Darracott, J. C. (1975). Adrian Hill IWM interview. Reel 4. Retrieved from www.iwm.org.uk/collections/item/object/80000557.

Friere, P. (1998) *Pedagogy of freedom.* London: Rowman & Littlefield.

Kolb, D. A. (1984). *Experiential learning: Experience as the source of learning and development.* Upper Saddle River, NJ: Prentice Hall.

McArdle, L. (Director) (2011). Art for heroes: A *Culture Show* special [Television series episode]. In L. McArdle (Producer), *The Culture Show.* London: BBC.

McKeown, E., Weir, H., Berridge, E. J., Ellis, L. & Kyratsis, Y. (2015). Art engagement and mental health: Experiences of service users of a community- based arts programme at Tate Modern, London. *Public Health*, *130*, 29–35.

Murphy, D. & Busuttil, W. (2014). PTSD, stigma and barriers to help-seeking within the UK Armed Forces. Retrieved from http://jramc.bmj.com/.

Pringle, E. (2009). The Artist as educator: Examining relationships between art practice and pedagogy in the gallery context. Tate Papers, 11 (Spring). Retrieved from www.tate.org.uk/research/publications/tate-papers/11/artist-as-educator-examining-relationships-between-art-practice-and-pedagogy-in-gallery-context.

Shaer, D., Beaven, K., Springham, N., Pillinger, S., Cork, A., Brew, J., Forshaw, Y., Moody, P. & 'S', C. (2008). The role of art therapy in a pilot for art-based information prescriptions at Tate Britain. *International Journal of Art Therapy*, *13*, 25–33.

Tate (2016a). Art into life workshops at Tate Modern. Retrieved from www.tate.org.uk/visit/tate-modern/group-visits/art-into-life-workshops.

Tate (2016b). *Staircase-III.* Retrieved from www.tate.org.uk/art/artworks/suh-staircase-iii-t13344.

Wood, C. (2007). *Museums of the mind: Mental health, emotional well-being, and museums.* Bude: Culture Unlimited.

Chapter 13

Art in action

The Combat Art Project

Jon England, Tim Martin and Stuart Rosamond

> There has always been a link with art and the military, going back to the First World War and before that ... There are two aspects to this: there are long periods on operations when you have time on your hands – filling in dead time is important; secondly, this allows the mind to move into a different sphere ... one of the things that art does is to provide a counter to the horrors of war and, in many ways, it can be very therapeutic ... a release of stress can be very, very helpful.
>
> (Colonel Alan Hooper RM)

This and other quotations from serving and former personnel are transcribed from post-tour interviews conducted in autumn 2013. This chapter has been written by three artists who offer their perspectives on the formation of the Combat Art Project.

Introduction

The Combat Art Project developed a bespoke art kit (as illustrated in Figure 13.1) as a proactive support to emotional well-being for members of 40 Commando Royal Marines embarking on their final tour of Afghanistan. Through distribution of the kit its designers hoped to enable Royal Marines to participate in art activities that would allow them to record and reflect upon their final tour, fill their time with creative purpose, prevent boredom and help them deal with the inherent tension of being on operations. It was integral that the kit's design would enable it to be utilised both individually and collectively, initiating a shared endeavour and camaraderie as well as a private outlet to express the Royal Marines' deepest thoughts at difficult times in their lives.

It was hoped that the project would initiate skills such as slowing down, looking intently and considering emotions more calmly, as well as generating an archive of work for future contemplation. The desire was that the project would culminate in an exhibition of the Royal Marines' work, presenting a range of perspectives on the tour.

Figure 13.1 A Combat Art Project art kit

As a live project, the aims evolved and expanded to include consideration of matters such as how engaging in art on tour might form a bridge to accessing therapy in the future if required. A conversation was also initiated around how art might provide an alternative to alcohol as a coping mechanism post-deployment.

Context

Somerset-based 40 Commando Royal Marines were the first Royal Marine unit to serve in Afghanistan when they supported Special Forces in the hunt for Osama bin Laden in the Tora Bora mountain caves in 2001. They were subsequently deployed on Operations Herrick 7 and 12 and were the last Commando unit to leave after their Herrick 17 deployment on 9 April 2013.

The Combat Art Project was initiated by the widow of a Royal Marine officer, Anita St John Gray, who had seen at first hand the effects on young men returning from a combat zone. The project developed from Anita St John Gray's discussions with the Reverend Andrew Rawding, who saw it as a tool for pastoral care. In 2012 she approached artist/curator Tim Martin (then Visual Arts Coordinator at The Brewhouse, Taunton) about using art to support the well-being of Royal Marines. The loss of 14 Royal Marines on operation Herrick 12 in 2010 provided added context. As part of the extended

Royal Marines family, Anita's wealth of military contacts would help make the project possible.

MacManus *et al.* (2013) found that men aged 30 or under who had served in the armed forces were three times more likely than their civilian peers to have been convicted of violent offences. Further, although military populations may be predicated to violent behaviour, men who had seen combat in Iraq and Afghanistan were 53 per cent more likely to commit a violent offence than those in non-front-line roles. Personnel who had multiple experiences of combat had a 70–80 per cent greater risk of being convicted of acts of violence.

Although the exact number of veterans within the criminal justice system is uncertain, it is estimated that there are more than 20,000 veterans under correctional services control (Busuttil, 2012). Critically, the Forces in Mind Trust's Transition Mapping Study, 2013 estimated that unsuccessful military transition costs the UK £114 million per annum; veterans in prison account for £4.4 million; mental health costs for veterans are estimated at £26 million, with alcohol misuse costing £35 million; and homelessness £5.5 million. Large numbers of veterans struggle to make the transition back to civilian life and become trapped in the criminal justice system (Forces in Mind Trust, 2013).

Rationale

When it was learned that 40 Commando would be deployed for operation Herrick 17 in 2012/2013, it became clear to both Tim Martin and Anita St John Gray that the losses suffered among friends and comrades on 40 Commando's previous tour would have a significant impact on those asked to return to Afghanistan. It was also thought that an acute awareness of those losses would affect those embarking on their first tour of duty. Although Tim had no previous interest in things military, both could see that the situation demanded intervention, innovation and urgent change. Conversations started about how art can be useful to people at various times in their lives, as both preventative and reactive processes, and the potential of using art in support of the well-being of military personnel.

Logistics

The mechanics of supplying materials were discussed with Commanding Officer Colonel M. J. A. Jackson RM, DSO, former Commanding Officer Colonel Alan Hooper RM, who joined the team as military advisor and former Chaplain Andrew Rawding. It became clear that 40 Commando's role on Herrick 17 would be quite different from their previous tours and that wherever possible they would be handing over day-to-day operations to the Afghan security forces.

Art therefore could have a significant impact in preventing boredom, filling time with creative purpose and dealing with the inherent tension emanating from the number of 'green on blue' incidents (insider attacks when an Afghan policeman or soldier fires on a member of coalition forces) that had taken place. 'You don't have to be in a war zone to be affected by deployment, when you are away from home so many changes happen, so to have that therapeutic tool would be great for all services' (Reverend Paul Andrew Chaplain RN).

The Army Arts Society had previously supplied 20 larger communal operational art packs to Afghanistan in 2011. Although their aims of 'enabling [personnel] to record and reflect upon their time deployed' (Army Arts Society, 2016) aligned with those of the Combat Art Project, and the contents of their kits were similar, it was the firm desire of the Combat Art team that every member of the tour should have access to their own pocket-sized art kit. This would support the most personal forms of expression in snatched moments of privacy as well as a communal endeavour for those comfortable with working collectively and collaboratively.

Reverend Paul Andrew, Chaplain RN, became the regular point of contact for the team, and Somerset-based artist Jon England was invited to join the project. His involvement was partly inspired by his former collaboration with World War II prisoner of war artist Ted Milligan. When viewing the 'black bag' distributed to each deploying Royal Marine, it was deemed important that if the art kit was to be accepted as a natural extension of this larger deployment kit, it must be of high quality, functional and 'look the part'. No existing products were found to fit within the map-sized pocket of a combat trouser and carry the desired range of materials and so fundraising began and the manufacturing of a bespoke kit was pursued.

Through military suppliers, the team negotiated the use of camouflage-patterned fabric that was embroidered with the 40 Commando crest and branding specific to the Herrick 17 tour. This gave it a real sense of value, making it special and exclusive to these Royal Marines. The pouch was zipped and waterproof to withstand the rigours of life on deployment and contained high-quality materials including sketch pad/journal, watercolour paper, watercolour paints, brushes, viewfinder, pens and pencils. 'The kit was excellent for many reasons, partly because it was so portable, they could take it anywhere. The kit was well put together; the guys were even more inspired to use it' (Reverend Paul Andrew Chaplain RN).

Anita St John Gray, Tim Martin and Jon England visited the 40 Commando base at Norton Manor Camp to present the idea to second-in-command Major Karl Gray RM and various other ranks including the Company Commanders. They received mainly positive feedback and were shown a place full of artistic and creative responses to life in the military, from sculpted metal shell cases to a history of paintings and prose in many forms. These works emphasised the historic and continuing link between art and the military and increased the expectation that the kits may be accepted and welcomed.

Funding was secured to supply kits to 500 of the 600 plus Royal Marines who would deploy. The project was mainly funded by the Royal Marines Charity and without their support the project would not have happened. Brigadier Mark Noble RM convinced the Trustees of the value of the project and all effort was made to provide the funding speedily in order to get kits made in time for the Unit deployment.

It was acknowledged that many Royal Marines would have little or no experience of art-making outside of school art lessons and a great deal of work would need to be done to begin breaking down preconceptions about what art is or what it could be. It was anticipated that there could well be some resistance to something new, outside of the Royal Marines' comfort zones and counter to the predominance of physical activities within the conventional ethos of the military. 'I thought the kit was useful ... it is an interesting way of recording an event from the viewpoint of everybody, right from the Marines up to the Commanding Officer' (Major Karl Gray RM).

It was hoped that the Combat Art team could introduce the project and the kit to all the Royal Marines prior to deployment, either through workshops or a simple presentation. Unfortunately, the intensity of the pre-deployment exercises and the challenges of securing funding, and therefore the lack of lead-in time, meant that this would not be possible. These challenges also meant that only about half of the personnel set off for the tour with their kits in hand. Although the remaining kits were shipped shortly after, the logistics of distributing kits to Royal Marines in their forward operating bases and other locations meant that many did not receive their kits until a significant way into their tours or did not receive them at all.

As a response to the lack of personal contact, the Combat Art team decided to create a film and 'idea cards'. Initial difficulties in getting the film approved for distribution by the Ministry of Defence (MoD) meant that it would not be viewed en masse prior to deployment and so the idea cards became a very important mechanism for communication.

It was expected that one of the biggest challenges and most vital elements of the project would involve breaking down the aesthetic value judgements that Royal Marines might attach to their work. Knowing that these judgements could become barriers to engaging with the materials provided, it was intended that the idea cards would provide a catalyst for the broadest possible forms of expression and promote the sense that the process of looking and making was immensely valuable whatever their perception of the quality of the work produced.

The idea cards offered the Royal Marines different ways of responding to their time in Afghanistan both through use of materials from within the kit and through suggestions of how other resources likely to be to hand might be utilised to expand the scope of their creativity. The aim became to promote an awareness of the Royal Marines' surroundings beyond the militarised, to encourage them to look intently and to engage all senses. The cards promoted the recording of thoughts, feelings, experiences and observations and the creation of images, objects and words in response to daily or more infrequent events. Through the inclusion of postcard pads it was also hoped that forces personnel would be able to communicate their experiences to families and communities back home.

The use of the kit for the writing of diaries was also actively encouraged:

> The only time I have ever kept a diary … I've found it a release valve … it recorded the key things but also the way I felt … it became a release for my emotions … and when I go back into those diaries, maybe years later, that particular thing that I describe or the emotions that I felt comes flooding back to me … it seems to connect you back to what you experienced at the time.
>
> (Colonel Alan Hooper RM)

It was planned that the project team would have an ongoing dialogue through email but due to the disparate activities of the group and the intensity of activities undertaken by the Chaplain these communications were sporadic at best. The Combat Art team were always anxious that the distribution of the remaining kits would not be a priority among the logistics of deployment. Even though more materials (such as larger pads of paper) were requested and sent, the team were largely left to hope that the kits were being put to positive use; that the unique nature of the project and the exclusivity of the opportunity would encourage many individuals to engage with the kits; and that through individual and collective endeavour, much work would be generated.

At this point, Stuart Rosamond (retired head of Higher Education Fine Art, Plymouth University), who had in the past worked for the Inner London Education Authority (now defunct) as an art therapist, joined the team to help determine what might happen to any work that returned from Afghanistan.

Gathering the artwork

Although Royal Marines were made aware that there was the potential for their work to be put on public display, it was integral to the project that there was no obligation for the work to be shared, thus enabling the unhindered creation of very personal responses. The Combat Art team heard anecdotally of work being made but it was always unknown how self-conscious individuals might be about sharing it and so the logistics of collection became paramount. A request was made that the Company Sergeant Majors should gather the work but as this was never going to be an operational priority the team had to overcome many difficulties to do so.

Delight was expressed on two fronts, first when the work began to surface and second in response to the range and diversity of the work that came

Figure 13.2 Decorated Cup by Marine Conway

back. This included observational drawings, watercolours, paintings, finger painting, photography, film, signs, military range drawings, tattoo designs and objects such as decorated cups (an example being Figure 13.2 by Marine Conway), cartoons and caricatures.

The intensity and sensitivity of the drawings and watercolours was fantastic. They provided a multitude of perspectives on day-to-day activities – small postcard-sized works that drew you in and then confronted you with the realisation of the subject matter. For instance, the interplay between light, nature and the specific features of a building that are only revealed as a Legacy Firing Point (a point from which they had previously been engaged by the enemy) by the accompanying annotation.

Among many other works were a very delicate drawing of a working dog, many images that depicted the paraphernalia of the tour (guns, caps, vehicles, etc.) and a range of interesting perspectives such as views recorded from the back of a Chinook helicopter.

The greatest amount of work received came from members of 13 Troop under the command of Captain Morgan. Responding to the death of Corporal David O'Connor on 24 October 2012 (the sole fatality from 40 Commando on the tour) one of the artists, Robbie Neen, said in an interview for BBC news online,

Everyone was shocked. It was quiet up until that point, and when it did happen, everyone was speechless really. It was a sad, sad loss for 40. You pay your respects and then you have to get on with your job once you're out there.

(BBC, 2017)

Stuart Rosamond had seen first-hand how the bringing together of a group of individuals engaged in art activities could have strong therapeutic outcomes. The team were delighted therefore to see evidence of shared endeavour among the troops and between various ranks – for instance, in terms of the latter, a competition between Captain Morgan and his junior to paint a Land Rover silhouetted against a sunset; 'He said his was best because he is a Captain' (A. Lowry, postcard annotation; see Plate 13.1).

Military humour can be an outlet for underlying tension and this was strongly evidenced in the work returned. The intensity of the experience of deployment and the rigid hierarchies that are necessarily maintained provided a fertile ground for artists to let off steam through humour. In one instance, caricatures were left on the desk of one Company Sergeant Major (CSM) by an anonymous artist from his troop who evidently did not consider he paid as much attention to his physical fitness as he might.

Drawing on the ideas of both Sigmund Freud and Arthur Koestler, Brigadier J. Nazareth wrote in his book, *The Psychology of Military Humour* that, 'military humour has a particular appeal because it is created in an environment that offers the maximum opportunity for its exploitation' (Nazareth, 2008, Preface).

Both the tongue-in-cheek comment by the Corporal about his Captain and the works left for the CSM reflect that the work became a safe context for the gentle collapsing of hierarchies without affecting operational performance. Obviously, each artist must assess the situation and be sure not to overstep the mark but the fact that the CSM was adamant that the postcards be exhibited and returned to him indicates the right balance was reached and a valuable release of tension achieved.

The designing of tattoos provided a bridge between the regular forms of creativity that many Royal Marines already engaged with and furthered the use of the kits. Many tattoos were designed that reflected artists' pride in their identities as Royal Marines, and their shared experience of the tour, while others were created in memoriam of comrades previously lost. Similarly, being in a location where printed images were not viable, there was a functional requirement to have large-scale accurate topographical drawings annotated with the ranges of surrounding features, which manifested in several incidences as very sensitive line drawings. These drawings were a regular reference and used to monitor any changes in the surrounding landscape to detect possible threats, but were embellished beyond the ordinary.

Among the more unexpected creative activities happening alongside the use of the kit were those from Marine Eddie Conway. Delta Company was tasked with the handover of lead security responsibility to the Afghan Security Forces. As part of this process all existing patrol bases with UK names were renamed in Pashto, symbolising the shift in responsibility. Marine Conway was tasked with producing 10 new signs in Cyrillic text. Conscious of the sensitivities of their Afghan partners, this process had to be completed without writing any of the Arabic phrases such as 'God is Great' and the Muslim creed (written at the top and bottom of the emblem) in his own hand.

The only practical solution was to use a stencil. To enable this, Marine Conway 'borrowed' a sharp scalpel from the doctor and took advantage of the large amount of spray paint available. This paint was used to mark the location of improvised explosive devices (IEDs) by the point men of every patrol. In recognition of the skill with which he completed this task he was awarded the Royal Marines Commandant General's Commendation Coin.

This creative environment extended into the production of many signs from a range of found and recycled materials. These works both demonstrated a sense of belonging to a collective group and express the specific identities and symbolism of sections within the whole. Their generation also allowed the troops to claim 'ownership' of the spaces they would inhabit on a temporary basis. One Royal Marine photographed himself each day in a range of humorous guises and poses, his various states of dress and coiffure reflecting significant moments in the tour such as the Christmas celebrations.

It is known that lots more work was produced and the Combat Art team are both tantalised and reassured by this fact and by the strong expectation that more will surface later. It was hoped the team could initiate group workshops with the Royal Marines on their return from Afghanistan but unfortunately this follow up contact time was unable to happen as Royal Marines passed through Akrotiri for debrief and 'decompression' and then were either demobbed or immediately went on extended leave.

Exhibiting

The Royal Marines' work was first exhibited in Taunton, Somerset (the town of the Royal Marines' home base) in November 2013. The location provided both a geographical and emotional connection with the visitors and created a platform for dialogue, facilitating greater respect and understanding as well as nurturing an awareness of the continued stresses and sacrifices of lengthy periods away from home. The range of different experiences and sensitivities depicted provoked a reassessment of many people's preconceptions of Royal Marines. This strength of connection is illustrated by the often-emotional responses of audiences and the many positive comments received during the exhibition both verbally and through written feedback; 'Feelings, thoughts, creativity – incredible work evokes deep meaningful conversations and ... understanding of what you all must go through' (anonymous comment).

The very 'real' nature of the work, removed from the value judgements of the commercial art market, added to this feeling. Importantly there was no desire among military hierarchies to censor the work exhibited and Royal Marines had the opportunity to talk freely and in some cases critically about their experiences. The exhibition also gave the Royal Marines an opportunity to display a shared experience, to recap and talk among themselves and find worth in what they had produced. Furthermore, the exhibition provided an unparalleled visual perspective for their partners, children and other family members, providing a unique insight into the environment and activities experienced during their separation.

The works were subsequently exhibited at the Menier Gallery in London in spring 2015 with guests of honour including General Gordon Messenger, CB, DSO and Bar, OBE, RM (then Deputy Commander of NATO's Allied Land Command in Turkey, now Vice Chief of Defence Staff), who supported the project from the outset. The Combat Art kit and resulting work was also featured in the exhibition 'Moved by Conflict' at the M-Shed, Bristol.

Legacy

The legacy of the project to those involved will be in many ways unquantifiable, but project partner Jon England's collaboration with World War II prisoner of war Ted Milligan has given him a genuine conviction as to the long-term benefits of using creativity at the most intense periods of peoples' lives. Ted was on his first mission with the crew of a 49 Squadron Lancaster Bomber when they were shot down with the loss of three of his crewmates. Ted was taken prisoner and transported to Stalag Luft 7 at Bankau, modern day Bâkow, Poland.

Ted produced extensive diaries in his wartime log supplied by the International Red Cross, charting his journey from his 'arrival in France' (through a humorous cartoon of him hanging in a tree by his parachute) through to the horrendous long marches they were forced to undertake as the advancing Russian forces threatened to overrun the camp in the freezing January of 1945. With advice, materials and encouragement from fellow inmate and prominent post-war abstract artist Adrian Heath, Ted produced portraits of many of his fellow inmates as well as recording the surrounding landscape, helping to form a camp newspaper and creating a production line of Christmas cards for prisoners of the various nationalities. Remarkably he was also able to complete the first part of his Bachelor of Arts degree in Architecture. He transformed a highly traumatic event and the ongoing uncertainty that followed into a positive circumstance that would pave the way to becoming a successful post-war architectural illustrator.

When Jon met Ted, he was in his late eighties and in failing health but, through the new drawings he made based on his memory of the marches and the subsequent exhibitions they put together, he gained a new lease of life. Jon saw the enormous value that Ted gained from being positively employed during the time of his hardship and how that archive of work allowed him to reconnect honestly with and reflect upon that most intense and formative period of his life in a way that had not been possible at the time (Holbrook, 2017).

By its very nature, military conflict is incumbent on combatants not overly reflecting upon the task they are asked to fulfil, as such reflection may inhibit their ability to do their job. It is not conducive to the role for personnel to see themselves as vulnerable or to reveal these vulnerabilities to others. It is therefore understandable that emotions may become buried leading to issues of stress, anxiety, depression and trauma-related illness. Colin, a veteran supported by the charity Gardening Leave stated 'The Army takes you in, breaks you, moulds you into what they want, but they don't retune you to fit back into civilian life' (McVeigh, 2014).

The 'military mindset' requires that violence is an accepted mechanism for resolving conflict in certain circumstances. Moreover, when anger and frustration may build over many years in the aftermath of service, it can be no surprise that there is a high percentage of violent offences among veterans in the criminal justice system. Similarly, when alcohol is a culturally accepted form of 'decompression' it is no wonder that veterans turn to it for release when they fail to deal with the fall-out from their experiences. Heather Budge-Reid, chief executive of the charity Gardening Leave suggested that about 80 per cent of the veterans turning to them for help have or have had a problem with alcohol (McVeigh, 2014).

The Combat Art Project did not offer 'art therapy'. In fact, it was fundamental that the word 'therapy' was not used when promoting the kit to the corps. What it did offer was the opportunity to perform a task that was challenging, fully engaging and universally accessible, and for some an opportunity to express their deepest thoughts at the most difficult time of their lives. By introducing art as an alternative coping mechanism during the intensity of deployment, and highlighting it as a mechanism that could be returned to later, it is hoped that the project has created an ongoing legacy, which will be beneficial when the difficulties of readjustment to civilian life are encountered.

The use of the kits offers a release that is calm and quiet; reflective by its very nature and often involves fine motor control. This alternative mechanism may work for some in a way that other outlets do not. Although it remains to be seen whether the project will fulfil its aim of breaking down barriers to engaging with art therapy if required, the work previously made may provide a point of departure for these activities, allowing what may be traumatic and emotional experiences to be viewed from a safe perspective.

Conclusion

The World Health Organization's definition of health (unchanged since 1948) is, 'a state of complete physical, mental and social well-being and not merely the absence of disease or infirmity' (World Health Organization, 2014, p. 1). In line with this definition, use of the kits provided a tool for the pro-active support of the health of service personnel; provided an opportunity to create a real-time archive of visual and emotional experience for future contemplation; and introduced an activity that has the potential to be carried forward and used by individuals in supporting their well-being in the future.

Positive feedback from participants who the Combat Art team could contact (gathered both informally and through interviews) is supportive of their claims as to its value and is contributing to the growing body of evidence about the benefits of art and creativity in support of mental health. The kit allowed them not only to document and reflect on their final tour of Afghanistan but also to use it as a vehicle for personal expression, initiating the creation of open, honest and contemplative responses.

> I do honestly believe it has therapeutic value ... Combat Art was a really good tool for the lads to express their emotions through drawing, a great opportunity to get down on paper what their thoughts and feelings were at the time during the seven months we were there.
>
> (LA (Phot) Rhys O'Leary)

The range of work made, the participants' wishes to keep it long after their service, their desire to share it with a wider public and the strength of the public's engagement with it, is representative of the positive impact of this scheme and the growing support for this and other similar initiatives. Two participants in the project have also gone on to art school on leaving the corps.

Art Kits is a not-for-profit company limited by guarantee and like so many other organisations, faces difficulties in acquiring ongoing funding. As conflicts in Iraq and Afghanistan fade from media consciousness, many veterans are just starting to confront their legacies. And with British Forces actively engaged in operational duties across the globe, this work will remain as vital and timely as ever. It is now necessary to build on the foundations of this pilot scheme, the strength of the concept and the many positive outcomes already witnessed. It is the team's hope that this evidence will facilitate wider distribution of the kits (including into the Criminal Justice System) allied to programmes of activity such as introduction and debriefing workshops and follow-up sessions to harness their full potential. The project's long-term benefits are not yet known, but it is hoped that it will be possible to re-engage with participants well into the future to evaluate this. It may also be interesting to more rigorously assess feedback received to date through qualitative means, and when and if sufficient data becomes available, assess the efficacy of future interventions through statistical analyses. It is the team's belief though that for creativity to be useful to individual personnel it is important that art becomes a regular and accepted form of expression. Ultimately the team's aim is that the kits will become standard issue; a bridge to making art therapy available to all forces personnel and allied to a national programme of art therapy for forces veterans.

References

Army Arts Society (2016). Retrieved from www.armyartssociety.org.uk (superseded by www.afas.org.uk/).

BBC (2017). Afghanistan memories from 40 Commando Royal Marines. Retrieved from www.bbc.co.uk/news/uk-england-somerset-22342490.

Busuttil, W. (2012). Military veterans' mental health: The long-term post-trauma support needs. In R. Hughes, A. Kinder & C. L. Cooper (eds), *International handbook of workplace trauma support* (pp. 458–474). Oxford: Wiley-Blackwell.

Forces in Mind Trust (2013). *The Transition Mapping Study: Understanding the transition process for Service personnel returning to civilian life.* Retrieved from www.fimtrust.org/wp-content/uploads/2015/01/20130810-TMS-Report.pdf.

Holbrook, E. (2017). POWWOW – Ted Milligan and Jon England. Retrieved from www.youtube.com/watch?v=5rjP_iEfqRk.

MacManus, D., Dean, K., Jones, M., Rona, R. J., Greenberg, N., Hull, L., Fahy, T., Wessely, S. & Fear, N. T. (2013). Violent offending by UK military personnel deployed to Iraq and Afghanistan: A data linkage cohort study. *The Lancet, 381*, 907–917.

McVeigh, T. (2014). The garden of peace: Helping veterans heal the mental scars of war. Retrieved from www.theguardian.com/society/2014/nov/30/garden-of-peace-heals-mental-scars-of-war-gardening-leave-observer-guardian-christmas-charity-appeal.

Nazareth, J. (1988). *The psychology of military humour.* Atlanta, GA: Lancer.

World Health Organization (2014). *Constitution.* Retrieved from www.who.int/about/mission/en/.

Chapter 14

Reclaiming life through art

David Murtagh and Janice Lobban

Introduction

This book began by revisiting the roots of art therapy in the context of military rehabilitation. Former First World War official war artist and one of the founders of the profession of art therapy Adrian Hill promoted the benefits of art-making and art-viewing for assisting recovery from physical and psychological ill health. He and his contemporaries recognised how art can tap into the source of difficulties and promote healing. In this final chapter we further consider the healing properties of art. Without placing an emphasis on art therapy alone, we employ the concept of post-traumatic growth to explore how creativity through art can help to reclaim life after trauma.

After presenting contemporary theory regarding post-traumatic growth and resilience, observations of the role of art in recovery are offered by two veterans from personal experience, using their own words. This is followed by a discussion of their observations using Joseph's THRIVE model for working with post-traumatic growth (Joseph, 2012a, 2012b) to examine the processes involved.

Post-traumatic growth and obstacles to overcome

The term 'recovery' is often used in health settings. Recovery, in a physical sense, has been defined as 'getting back to normal' ('Getting back to normal after an operation', n.d.). In mental health it might be understood as 'the belief that it is possible to regain a meaningful life, despite serious mental illness' (Mental Health Foundation, 2016). Moreover, the mental health recovery model, as proposed by Jacob, looks beyond basic 'survival and existence' (2015, p. 118) to developing fresh aspirations and life goals. However, the terms 'beyond' and 'back to normal' are incongruous. Recovery for many people will mean getting back to original functioning unless this is explored differently. For those veterans who do not want to go back to premorbid normal functioning after trauma having re-evaluated life through experiences and treatment, something different might be sought. Redefining normality in this case might offer a 'blank canvas' and a challenge to rise to involving post-traumatic growth.

The concept of post-traumatic growth emerged in the mid-1990s (Tedeschi & Calhoun, 1996; Joseph, 2012a) as interest grew in the possibility of positive change after experiencing suffering. According to Joseph, post-traumatic growth concerns 'how adversity can be a springboard to higher levels of psychological wellbeing' (2012a, p. 816). Joseph identifies three areas of growth that people report consistently following trauma: (i) the enhancement of relationships, such as valuing friendships and increased compassion; (ii) changed views of themselves, such as increased acceptance of frailties and acquired wisdom; (iii) alterations in outlook, such as re-evaluating priorities and appreciating each day at a time (Joseph, 2012a). The following text examines how this concept might be applied to traumatised veterans with acknowledgement of factors that might influence progress.

Developmental theories help to inform how people change over time and obstacles that might be encountered, for example, stages of psychosocial development, as proposed by Erikson (1959). He identified a series of stages through which we all pass during life, with each stage building upon the success of the previous one. He considered that problems during developmental stages, or stages not successfully completed, might impact on the individual in the future. According to Erikson, the late teenage years and early twenties are the time when a person develops his/her identity. At an age when young people normally experiment with clothes, peer groups and music, and develop an identity through discovery, trial and error, many veterans already would have enlisted into military service. The UK Armed Forces Annual Personnel Report (Ministry of Defence, 2014) states that 26.6 per cent of serving personnel are under the age of 25, and Louise, Hunter and Zlotowitz (2016) inform that 22 per cent of UK Army recruits are under 18. Thus, at a crucial age when people usually experiment with taste and identity, this group is issued with a military identity, along with its related structure and culture. For some of those young recruits, readjusting back into civilian life after leaving the armed forces might present challenges. The influence of pre-service vulnerabilities might also be a factor in psychosocial and identity development in some cases, such as having experienced childhood abuse, bullying, poor education or few opportunities to demonstrate creativity (Ahmed, 2007).

Despite that, Meichenbaum (2012) explains how individuals can not only survive exposure to traumatic events but can go on to thrive. Spirituality and identity factors are seen as crucial to the recovery process and can stimulate post-traumatic growth and thriving. Meichenbaum (2012) observes that many world religions accept that suffering is inevitable in life but we can learn and grow from our suffering. Spiritual perspectives might help to construct and evaluate meaning, see a bigger picture, foster acceptance and find direction.

During trauma treatment, a veteran might review his/her sense of identity as part of the recovery process. Art therapy and occupational therapy provide opportunities for experimentation; for example, to become involved in messy play that perhaps childhood circumstances did not permit. Veterans can explore and develop creative skills that might not have been encouraged or nurtured during school years, perhaps because of academic pressure or difficult circumstances. Under-achieving at school is sometimes a reason why people join the Forces, maybe seeking better job prospects or trade training. The development of new skills and abilities, along with an associated review of personal identity can lead to re-evaluation of one's place in society. Therapists can grasp this opportunity, facilitate veteran recognition and acceptance of growth, and move towards the application of the new-found skills, thereby enabling post-traumatic growth to thrive.

Joseph (2012a, 2012b) offers a model called THRIVE to guide practice. The process involves:

- *Taking stock*: improving post-traumatic stress management strategies.
- *Harvesting hope*: acquiring hope, for example, through the inspiration of others who have faced similar challenges.
- *Re-authoring*: creating a narrative to explore new views, for example, through expressive writing and artwork.
- *Identifying change*: acknowledging post-traumatic growth and monitoring changes.
- *Valuing change*: growing recognition of fresh priorities.
- *Expressing change in action*: purposefully applying post-traumatic growth into daily life, such as by planning specific activities.

However, there can be obstacles to recovery. For instance, there is a risk that a person with PTSD might start to identify him/herself by the diagnosis. This might lead to becoming immersed within Parson's model of the sick role (1951), which proposes certain expectations and obligations. In some circumstances, this might lead to family and friends adopting a caring role rather than a role as, for example, a partner, lover or friend. If the social group respond in this way then it is possible that the individual will take on the actions and behaviours of someone in a sick role. The sick role may then serve many purposes, such as providing an excuse to avoid activities and events, while others take up the duties of the person who is unwell. This can lead to secondary gains from being ill (Kwan & Friel, 2002) and impact on motivation.

Joseph (2012a, 2012b) uses the metaphor of making a mosaic from a shattered vase to describe the post-traumatic growth process. The metaphor is also relevant for contrasting the process of adopting a sick role with that of embracing post-traumatic growth. Consider approaches towards an ornament that has been dropped. The ornament has broken and shattered. It can be repaired with glue and tape but it will always appear broken and imperfect. Those who see it will recognise it as damaged and fragile and will treat it as such, being careful handling it or leaving it unused. It will remain imperfect and might just gather dust, perhaps out of sight. Alternatively, the broken pieces of the ornament could be used to make something new and beautiful, such as a mosaic, that others will get pleasure from. Although still the same compound, it has now taken on a different form with a new function.

Resilience

Resilience is another key concept relevant to the effects of experiencing trauma. Definitions of resilience vary and indeed Southwick and associates (2014) acknowledge that there is no one accepted definition. However, many sources explain psychological resilience in similar terms. The American Psychological Association defines it as 'the process of adapting well in the face of adversity, trauma, tragedy, threats or even significant sources of threats' (2016). Meredith *et al.* define it as 'an ability to recover from or adjust easily to misfortune or change' (2011, p. 2). Resilience comes from the Latin *resiliens/resilire*, which means to rebound, bounce back or recoil; and *salire* to jump/leap (Oxford English Dictionary, 2016).

Resilience, or lack of it, has been identified as the reason why some people get PTSD when exposed to trauma when others do not; or why over time, some will or will not make a full recovery back to a pre-trauma state of being, or at least appear to not be affected. Indeed it must be noted that the majority of people exposed to trauma will recover naturally over time. Meichenbaum identifies six areas for building resilience in military trauma victims and their families. He describes these as 'fitness' areas, namely physical, interpersonal, emotional, thinking (cognitive), behavioural and spiritual fitness, suggesting that each area needs consideration to maintain a healthy balance (Meichenbaum, 2012).

Many authors (Ahmed, 2007; Lukey & Tepe 2008; Maddi, 2013; Meredith *et al.*, 2011) agree that contributing elements to resilience include biological, attachment and control factors. This might involve a high internal locus of control, with acceptance that one is not able to control everything; or behavioural control whereby emotional reactions are monitored and evaluated, assisting self-regulation and self-management. Key aspects to building and maintaining resilience include resourcefulness, compassion, empathy, capacity for bonding and trust. Self-esteem and interpersonal abilities such as social skills, problem-solving skills and impulse control are recognised as advantageous for resilience building, as is the ability to ask for help, creativity, optimism and a sense of humour (Ahmed, 2007; Meredith *et al.*, 2011). This list of factors highlights many areas that art therapy and occupational therapy can target to help develop and maintain resilience.

Furthermore, Gonzales (2012) consulted people involved in traumatic events, looking at how they had 'survived survival'. He observes that those engaged in creative activities following a traumatic event were able to self-soothe and move on from pain, thus enabling the healing process to occur and access to a sense of joy. One person described how forming a creative idea stimulated a blissful state whereby traumas were forgotten in the excitement. Gonzales explains that this process offers 'salvation' in the wake of trauma and that it is from the 'madness' within (2012, p. 141), meaning the excitement and creativity, that one can remain sane. It is a madness that 'takes over emotions and redirects them away from our agony and towards something meaningful, useful, purposeful, and even blissful' (p. 141). In this way art-making is an effective response to trauma and assists resilience-building.

Applying a metaphor first used by Moran (1945) when describing courage, resilience might be viewed as having a bank account set up from an early age. There will be a certain amount of resilience in the account from the start. Over time, through life experiences and through nurture, the bank account can be added to, for instance by parents or families showing love and support; and schools allowing access to the full curriculum of possibilities, exploring and celebrating strengths and skills. On the other hand, some may have to dip into the bank account to get through difficult times, perhaps as a result of abuse or bullying. When one dips into one's account of resilience on a regular basis it depletes reserves, causing a vulnerability that makes it more likely to develop PTSD when subjected to trauma.

As well as personal resilience, environmental and community factors also play an essential role in healthy functioning, recovery and growth. Meredith *et al.* (2011) found that there are four resiliency factors identified at the community level: belongingness, connectedness, cohesion and collective efficacy, but only two with good evidence, these being belongingness and connectedness. Belongingness refers to social integration and group membership, such as participation in spiritual or faith-based practice, or membership of schools/ colleges. Meredith *et al.* report that studies have assessed this as 'strong community spirit' (2011, p. 28) and it is associated with low rates of PTSD. An example might be the strong sense of community during the London Blitz of the Second World War, and how community spirit and togetherness kept people resilient. Camaraderie is strong in the military and is a formidable source of support before, during and after conflict. Consequently, its absence can become an issue when leaving the armed forces. Connectedness refers to the quality and number of contacts with people and places, including aspects such as commitment, structure, roles, responsibility and communication (Meredith *et al.*, 2011). It is important for veterans to re-establish community links in order to review identity, explore strengths and discover new possibilities.

Resilience and post-traumatic growth are key concepts applicable to many aspects of life on our planet. The natural world, with its abundance of wildlife, has survived catastrophic events and adapted to the changes. Some of the biggest and strongest creatures, such as the dinosaurs, did not survive but others did, adjusting and evolving to fit a new environment, and thriving. A popular quotation paraphrasing Charles Darwin and his theory of evolution sums up the essence of resilience and post-traumatic growth – 'It is not the strongest of the species that survives, nor the most intelligent that survives. It is the one that is most adaptable to change.'

Art and recovery: veterans' stories

The following section has been written by two veterans about the role that art has played in the management of their symptoms and recovery from PTSD. It is followed by a discussion of their observations in terms of post-traumatic growth.

Spike

I first attended Combat Stress in 2004 having served in the Royal Navy during the Falklands War in 1982 and during the civil war in Lebanon in 1983–1984, in support of British Forces. I was very ill when I first walked through the gates of Combat Stress, Tyrwhitt House. I spent a great deal of my spare time at home in an alcoholic stupor trying to forget the things that I had seen, smelt and felt. Having been shown around the treatment centre, I was drawn to the activities room where I was introduced to Kay, a bright, lively lady who led the activities. We had a chat and I explained my liking for binge drinking, to which she replied 'Well, we can't have that. Have you ever thought about art?' I hadn't. I considered myself lucky to get a 'D' for art at school. We sat and chatted as she helped me draw my first picture as an adult, a self-portrait of van Gogh. The time flew by and I felt at ease with her, and when I had finished it looked just like van Gogh!

The next time I attended Combat Stress, I couldn't wait to get back to the activities room but I was in for a shock. Kay put a canvas in front of me with some oil paints, and in a very gentle way told me that we were going to have a go at oil painting. 'I can't' I said, but I could and I did. When I had finished, it looked like a stag that I had found on a calendar in Kay's store of pictures. I took it home and proudly presented it to my wife. She was very impressed, at least I think she was. I suffer from very low self-esteem and am never sure of the compliments I receive. I decided that I would paint whenever I attended Combat Stress, which tended to be twice a year for two-week admissions.

I used to watch other artists there and wonder if I could ever paint a picture as well as they could. There were some very skilful artists. I would sit with them and learn, always striving to do better. I began to buy art equipment and paint at home. Drinking became a burden. How could I paint if I was drunk or hung-over? Art became my saviour, not alcohol. I began to get better in leaps and bounds. I was asked to put a painting into an exhibition. 'Who me?' I said, 'don't be silly, I'm not good enough'. It gave me enormous pleasure to see my painting on a wall alongside those by people I considered professional artists. It spurred me on to achieve more and more, and never to go back to drinking.

When I paint, I put my all into it. I can put unhappy memories and intrusive thoughts away and concentrate on painting. I can spend hours with a brush in my hand losing myself in art. It relaxes and calms me, and now I can take compliments. At last I believe in something that I do, that I am good enough (Plate 14.1). I have been asked many times now to display my work. I won a prize and sold two paintings at the Mall Galleries in London. Not bad for someone who can't paint. I now display on a regular basis and have sold work on numerous occasions. It's nice when people believe in you, but even better when you believe in yourself.

Ron

From the army to art school

I left the army in February 1968 and enrolled in art school in September that year. I spent four years there and a further year in teacher training. I was teaching art in a large secondary school by the end of 1973, which was an immense jump for me.

I had moved from a military environment that was ordered with its own unique culture, into a creative environment. The military vocabulary is limited and sparse. It is not given to creative or emotive expression. So I had to acquire a new means of communication. Education is full of words such as 'cognitive' and 'intuitive'. I never heard those words used in the six years I spent in an infantry platoon.

I had a student grant and my days were filled with interesting art activity. I was in an environment where students were trying hard to be creative and to find a unique style. I thought everything to be wonderful. I now compare my experience in those student days to a voyage that had set me ashore on the 'New World'. It was to be a joyful exploration of a new and uncharted land that I set out to chart and explore for myself.

The army was my university

I learned an enormous amount in the army. I was a trained rock climber, canoeist, Morse code operator, navigator and had many other skills that I enjoyed learning. I was an avid and bright pupil when acquiring military skills. I was the top student on the non-commissioned officer (NCO) cadre I took and considered to be a bright young NCO. I tackled tasks with enthusiasm and never gave up. Unlike some others who have served, I for my part loved the army and the regiment I served in. I felt I could do anything and had huge reserves of motivation and concentration.

Art-making and the difficult years

Art-making was what I fell back on during the difficult years of my PTSD. I had found the process of producing artwork both fascinating and rewarding.

I had a more than average knowledge of techniques, styles and the work of other artists. I had developed solid skills that became intuitive. All of this knowledge was acquired by me of my own volition – I sought out the knowledge and skills, they were not imposed. Even during the worst effects of PTSD, my artwork stayed with me (even though I became disconnected from other aspects of life).

Putting back what is being drained and lost

The process of painting and drawing never succumbed to being weakened or abandoned. I never contemplated stopping my art activity. It put back anything that PTSD tried to purloin. The activity was very much a retreat process. Time spent painting or drawing was free from distraction – it was a safe place. Time would stop. Sometimes I could spend hours immersed in a piece of work – adding to it, editing, looking intensely, only focused on what was in front of me. This input was stronger than what might have been drained away.

What followed was the satisfaction that what I had achieved was worthwhile. I had an unwritten code that I would draw or paint every day without any time limits. It could be doodling for 10 minutes or painting for 2 hours. If I had a piece that was resolved and going well, I would save it up for later, and look forward to sitting down in the evening and enjoy doing it.

Spiritual antibiotic

I have looked up the term 'spiritual antibiotic' and I was surprised to find it used by evangelists. I thought I had coined the phrase myself. I meant the phrase to convey a medicine taken each day to avoid spiritual decay, a medicine taken to keep an inner light burning and slowly fuelled. The making of art is a spiritual antibiotic. It feeds the inner being with higher things. Making art is homage to the wonder of our existence. Coming into the world is an astonishing riddle of chance. Making art is an acknowledgement of the wonder and riddle of being. Hence we must constantly medicate our better selves to preserve this wonder.

Creativity is a slow release process

For me, making art is an ongoing process. Nothing happens in a flash with art-making. It is a slow and calculated process. The slow release is embedded in the work. It is released when the viewer contemplates the work with the same attention that the artist gave to its creation. It is an investment. Making art requires patience and care. These two qualities are symbols of slow release. Slow release is also growing – and growing needs nurturing. Art-making is nurturing the best in us. Plants and life forms grow and spread un-noticed. Slow release is the hidden growth measured by the appeal of the final piece of art.

The activity is more important than the end result

Planning for me is an important part of making art. Thinking and planning can be done anywhere, anytime; done in the mind or simply doodling in a small notebook. Ideas are the source of artwork. The idea taken from a tiny flash of insight to an end result is an important activity. More important than the end result is the journey, which starts with an idea. This process is an activity – part and parcel of the whole process. Planning and execution are like bricklaying – an activity. The laying of the bricks is very therapeutic. The planning activity should be a joy and relished. The wall is finished but the bricklaying was a pleasure.

The encouragement of others

An important part of art-making is to cherish the encouragement that others give us. Kay in occupational therapy, Jan in art therapy, my wife, my daughter and many others have encouraged me to carry on painting. This encouragement is the vital component in art-making. I make art for others to see and enjoy. It is very fulfilling when feedback is positive – again encouragement is also a form of spiritual antibiotic. We are often in debt to others and unaware of the positives they see in us. PTSD tries to block out the goodness of other people who are around and with us.

Quiet and calm work

In my work I have always tried to convey a sense of calm and quiet. I take my subject matter from the world I see around me rather than from the world of inner feelings, emotions or drama (Plate 14.2). I am looking outward both with optical vision and inner vision. I aim for a quiet visual melody to stream from the work to the viewer. The work should charm without being superficial. I shun drama related to PTSD. My painting is about stillness, new perceptions of design and colour arrangement. Quiet forms as near to melody as I can achieve.

Discussion

Both veterans were invited to share their thoughts on the role that art has played in their recovery from PTSD. The following text uses Joseph's THRIVE model involving six 'signposts' for working with post-traumatic growth (2012a, 2012b) to chart their journeys. The first signpost of the model involves 'taking stock'. When Spike first encountered art-making at Combat Stress he was still reliant on alcohol as a way of trying to suppress PTSD symptoms but he had willingness to try new experiences. He discovered and built new skills and found that in a relaxed atmosphere he could become creatively absorbed.

Time would fly by and he would not be troubled by intrusive thoughts. In Ron's case, he realised that he was able to fall back on art when his PTSD symptoms were at their worst because art had remained a constant in his life. When he became disconnected from the world around him, art remained an anchor and an effective symptom management tool.

'Harvesting hope' is the next factor in the THRIVE model (Joseph, 2012a, 2012b). Spike described the discovered pleasure of art-making and how he would look around to other veteran artists for inspiration. He strived to learn from others and to see his work hung alongside theirs. He aspired to improve his abilities and used the help and guidance available. Ron could rely on art as it put back what PTSD took away and never abandoned him. Skills became intuitive. The process provided a focus that he knew would sustain him through the challenges of PTSD. It provided an inner light that kept burning. Both veterans looked forward to art-making with the knowledge of its restorative qualities.

Joseph refers to 're-authoring' as another component of post-traumatic growth (2012a, 2012b), with the discovery of new perspectives through creativity. Ron outlines the creative journey and the delight inherent in planning and nurturing the art form. New ideas and insights grow. Art is ever-changing and enriching. Through art-making Spike learned and accepted that he is good enough and that he can achieve. He was able to chart his progress and to challenge earlier negative self-appraisals. The skills learned were transferable to everyday life. Initially only painting while at Combat Stress, Spike took his work home to show his wife and received encouragement and validation. Subsequently, he incorporated painting into home life.

Identifying and recognising change through post-traumatic growth is seen as crucial. Art was considered a saviour for Spike. For Ron art offered a spiritual antibiotic that had slow-release qualities. These comments suggest being able to tap into something that transcends the ordinary. As well as offering direction, art can provide meaning and purpose. As an alternative form of medication, the conclusion is that art-making needs to be taken regularly.

'Valuing change' through awareness of different priorities is further aspect of the THRIVE framework (Joseph, 2012a, 2012b). Spike acknowledged that over-use of alcohol interfered with his ability to engage in art-making and so he made the choice to concentrate on the latter. This provided an alternative form of coping that did not rely on avoidance. For Ron, art-making requires planning and daily investment which in return provides satisfaction and achievement. The whole process is relished.

'Expressing change in action' (Joseph, 2012a, 2012b) is seen through Spike's investment in art materials, creative engagement and development of a renewed sense of identity as an artist. Self-esteem increased and he was able to take compliments. Crucially, he regained self-belief. He never went back to drinking because he had moved on. Ron makes art for others to see and enjoy. In this way it is a shared experience and a bridge of communication with others that overcomes disconnection.

Conclusion

Trauma can have a profound effect that shatters previously held assumptions about life. However, in recent years there has been growing recognition that trauma can also provide a stimulus for positive change; for example, in outlook, priorities and relationships (Joseph, 2012a), with attention given to post-traumatic growth and resilience factors. This chapter has explored how art might be used to optimise recovery from trauma by fostering post-traumatic growth and resilience-building. The restorative qualities of art-making have been eloquently expressed through the lived experiences of Spike and Ron. The healing ingredients inherent in art-making are seen as an investment that helps to rebuild reserves of resiliency and serve to replace what has been drained away by PTSD. The artwork created is a contribution for others to share and enjoy, with embedded properties that can only be released through viewer engagement. Art appreciation itself provides further opportunities for growth and healing. The veterans' personal accounts underline how it is possible to reclaim life after trauma through art.

References

Ahmed, A. S. (2007). Post-Traumatic Stress Disorder, resilience and vulnerability. *Advances in Psychiatric Treatment*, *13*(5), 369–375.

American Psychological Association. (2016). *The road to resilience.* Retrieved from www.apa.org/helpcenter/road-resilience.aspx.

Erikson, E. H. (1959). *Identity and the life cycle.* New York, NY: International Universities Press.

Getting back to normal after an operation (n.d.). Retrieved from www.nhs.uk/Conditions/surgery/Pages/getting-back-to-normal.aspx.

Gonzales, L. (2012). *Surviving survival: The art and science of resilience.* New York, NY: W. W. Norton & Company.

Jacob, K. S. (2015). Recovery model of mental illness: A complementary approach to psychiatric care. *Indian Journal of Psychological Medicine*, *37*(2), 117–119.

Joseph, S. (2012a). What doesn't kill us … Retrieved from https://thepsychologist.bps.org.uk/volume-25/edition-11/what-doesnt-kill-us.

Joseph, S. (2012b). *What doesn't kill us: A guide to overcoming adversity and moving forward.* London: Piatkus Little Brown.

Kwan, O. & Friel, J. (2002). Clinical relevance of the sick role and secondary gain in the treatment of disability syndromes. *Medical Hypotheses*, *59*(2), 129–134.

Louise, R., Hunter, C. & Zlotowitz, S. (2016). *The recruitment of children by the UK Armed Forces: A critique from health professionals.* London: Medact.

Lukey, B. J. & Tepe, V. (eds). (2008). *Biobehavioural resilience to stress.* Boca Raton, FL: CRC Press.

Maddi, S. R. (2013). *Hardiness: Turning stressful circumstances into resilient growth.* New York, NY: Springer.

Meichenbaum, D. (2012). *Roadmap to resilience: A guide for military, trauma victims and their families.* Miami, FL: Institute Press.

Mental Health Foundation (2016). *Recovery.* Retrieved from www.mentalhealth.org.uk/a-to-z/r/recovery.

Meredith., L. S., Sherbourne C. D., Gaillot, S. J., Hansell, L., Ritschard, H. V., Parker, A. M. & Wrenn, G. (2011). Promoting psychological resilience in the U.S. military. Retrieved from www.rand.org/content/dam/rand/pubs/monographs/2011/RAND_MG996.pdf.

Ministry of Defence (2014). *UK Armed Forces annual personnel report.* Retrieved from www.gov.uk/government/uploads/system/uploads/attachment_data/file/312539/uk_af_annual_personnel_report_2014.pdf.

Moran, (Lord) (1945). *The anatomy of courage: The classic WWI study of the psychological effects of war.* London: Constable & Robinson.

Oxford English Dictionary (2016). Retrieved from www.oed.com.

Parsons, T. (1951). *The social system.* London: Routledge.

Southwick, S. M., Bonanno, G. A., Masten, A. S., Panter-Brick, C. & Yehuda, R. (2014). Resilience definitions, theory and challenges: Interdisciplinary perspectives. *European Journal of Psychotraumatology*, 5, 1–14.

Tedeschi, R. G. & Calhoun, L. G. (1996). The Post-Traumatic Growth Inventory: Measuring the positive legacy of trauma. *Journal of Traumatic Stress*, 9, 455–471.

Index